"AN IMPORTANT BOOK. Reasoned, dead-accurate and fascinating, this book is a must-read for Canadians interested in our society." – Diane Francis, *The Financial Post*

"Dubro has unscrambled the facts from the myths in the history of the Asian underworld, and, at the same time, through good reporting, made it more FASCINATING than ever." – Howard Engel, author of the Benny Cooperman mysteries

"An informative document, the first of its kind to have a broad historical scope." – Neal Hall, author of *The Deaths of Cindy James*

"WELL-RESEARCHED . . . A must-read for any serious scholar of crime or anybody involved in criminal justice." – *Hamilton Spectator*

"An EVEN-HANDED AND INSIGHTFUL look at a very touchy subject." – *Eye Magazine*

"Dubro's intention is to expunge the miasma of ignorance that obscures the subject of Asian crime today . . . His sensitivity towards, and empathy with, the Asian community [is] convincingly heartfelt, but he is no wilting forgiver of crime and criminals." – Michael Coren, *Books in Canada*

"FASCINATING . . . scathing about how Canada came to let the gangsters in." – John Gold, *South China Morning Post* (Hong Kong)

"GRIPPING TALES OF MAYHEM, GAMBLING AND PROSTITUTION . . . Dubro is undoubtedly Canada's most knowledgeable writer on organized crime." – Philip Mathias, *The Financial Post*

"What **Dragons of Crime** offers is a historical context that neither sensationalizes nor downplays criminal activity." – *The Toronto Star*

ALSO BY JAMES DUBRO

Mob Rule: Inside the Canadian Mafia

Mob Mistress

With Robin Rowland

*Undercover: Cases of the RCMP's
Most Secret Operative*

*King of the Mob: Rocco Perri and the
Women Who Ran His Rackets*

JAMES DUBRO

Dragons of Crime
Asian Mobs in Canada

An M&S Paperback from
McClelland & Stewart Inc.
The Canadian Publishers

An M&S Paperback from McClelland & Stewart Inc.

Copyright © 1992 by James Dubro

First printing October 1993
Cloth edition printed 1992

Published by arrangement with Reed Books Canada

All rights reserved. The use of any part of this publication, reproduced, transmitted in any form or by any means, electronic, mechanical, photocopying, recording, or otherwise, or stored in a retrieval system, without the prior written consent of the publisher – or, in case of photocopying or other reprographic copying, a licence from Canadian Reprography Collective – is an infringement of the copyright law.

Canadian Cataloguing in Publication Data

Dubro, James, 1946 –
Dragons of crime: Asian mobs in Canada

Includes bibliographical references and index.

ISBN 0-7710-2903-9

1. Triads (Gangs) – Canada.   2. Organized crime –
Canada.   3. Asians – Canada.   I. Title.

HV6453.C33T75 1993   364.1'06'08995071   C93-094577-8

Cover photograph: Norm Betts/
Canada Wide Feature Service Ltd.

Printed and bound in Canada by Webcom Ltd.

McClelland & Stewart Inc.
The Canadian Publishers
481 University Avenue
Toronto, Ontario
M5G 2E9

1 2 3 4 5   97 96 95 94 93

To Martyn Burke, Diane Francis, Peter Herrndorf,
Bill Macadam, Richard Nielsen, and Jan Whitford,
for their support of this project, and to all innocent
victims of organized crime, especially those in the
Oriental communities across North America.

If Chinese restaurants are one feature of Chinatowns, Chinese secret societies are another. Secret societies have always been endemic to overseas Chinese. . . . All over the world these gangs survive on fear and corruption, are engaged in the same kind of business, are likely to have figurative language in common, and very possibly share contacts in Hong Kong.

— Social historian Lynn Pan from her 1990 book, *Sons of the Yellow Emperor.*

CONTENTS

THE DRAGONS:

A Glossary of Principal Characters and Terms

BIG CIRCLE BOYS (a.k.a. Dai Huen Jai) — name for gangs of mainland Chinese criminals operating in North America and worldwide since the late 1980s.

BORN TO KILL (BTK) — violent New York City/New Jersey Vietnamese gang with ties to Toronto and Montreal Vietnamese gangs.

CASTRO, RICHARD — former Kung Lok triad treasurer; murdered in the centre of Chinatown in Toronto in July 1981.

CHAN, EDDIE (Chan Tse Chiu) — former Hong Kong policeman who became the head of the On Leong tong in New York.

CHEE KUNG TONG (CKT) — tong founded in the nineteenth century with branches in Vancouver, Montreal, San Francisco, and other North American cities.

DAI LO ("elder brother") — a respected and senior Chinese gang leader.

DRAGON HEAD — the senior officer in a triad.

THE FIVE DRAGONS — five of the corrupt former Hong Kong policemen who sought refuge in Canada.

FLYING DRAGONS — New York City Chinese youth gang associated with the Hip Sing tong.

14 K — a powerful Hong Kong-based triad active internationally; primarily in the heroin business.

FU, DAVE (Fu Lo-Jen) — former tong leader who worked undercover for the RCMP and the DEA.

GHOST SHADOWS — New York City-based Chinese gang associated with the On Leong tong and allied to the Kung Lok triad.

HIP SING TONG — one of the largest of the criminally active tongs in the United States; associated with the Flying Dragons youth gang.

HUNG MUN (a.k.a. the Hung League or the Heaven and Earth Society) — established in the seventeenth century as a political group, this association is acknowledged as the first triad society in China.

INDEPENDENT COMMISSION AGAINST CORRUPTION (ICAC) — Hong Kong's powerful, civilian-led, anti-corruption agency.

KUNG LOK SOCIETY ("the house of mutual happiness") — the major triad operating in Canada, mostly in Ontario. Founded by Lau Wing Kui.

LAU WING KUI (a.k.a. Keung) — triad leader who came to Canada and founded the Kung Lok triad. Lau is commonly known as Lau Wing Kui (pronounced "koy" as in "toy"), but Lau Wing Keung is his legal name.

LOMO — protection payments to the triads, often put in a red envelope and called "lucky money."

LOTUS FAMILY — Vancouver-based Chinese gang; associated with the Jung Ching gang.

LOUIE, NICKIE (Louie Yin Poy) — former head of the Ghost Shadows gang in New York City.

LUI LOK — former Royal Hong Kong Police staff sergeant and leader of the five dragons.

MO, DANNY (Mo Shui Chuen) — longtime leader of the Kung Lok triad.

SHU MOY (a.k.a. Shue) — British Columbia organized crime boss in the 1920s and 1930s; known as King of the Gamblers.

ON LEONG TONG — the largest tong in the United States;

headquartered in New York City; associated with the Ghost Shadows gang.

RED EAGLES (Hung Ying) — a major Vancouver-based Chinese gang.

SUN YEE ON — largest triad society in Hong Kong and involved internationally.

TONGS — Chinese benevolent associations in Canada and the United States that have often been infiltrated or taken over by organized crime.

TRAN, ASAU — longtime leader of a major Vietnamese gang in Toronto; murdered in the middle of Chinatown in Toronto in August 1991.

TRIADS — Chinese secret societies formed originally for political goals, but now primarily criminal organizations in Hong Kong and around the world; the Chinese version of the Mafia.

TRUNG CHI TRUONG — Boston-area Vietnamese gang leader who started Vietnamese gangs in Toronto and Montreal.

TUNG ON TONG — New York City area tong with Sun Yee On triad affiliations.

VIET CHING — the main Vietnamese gang in Vancouver.

WAH CHING — San Francisco-based triad; associated with the Kung Lok triad.

WO HOP TO — Hong Kong and California-based triad.

YUE, BIG JOHN (Yue Kwok Nam) — former Kung Lok triad leader in Toronto.

PREFACE

There has been an explosion of news articles in the media in the last couple of years about the sudden rise of Asian gang activity in Canada and the United States. But the story is not a new one. There has been organized crime in the various Chinatowns across North America for more than a hundred years. Moreover, a lot of the press coverage both today and over the past 130 years has been full of hyperbole, insensitivities and inaccuracies. Today we see front-page headlines in Canadian, American, and Hong Kong newspapers about students in the high schools of Toronto living in "terror" of Mafia-like Asian gangs known as triads. Even a respectable national news magazine like *Maclean's* emblazoned its March 25, 1991, cover with "Terror in the Streets: Young Asian Gangs Are Spreading Fear, Violence — and Death — in Canadian Cities" and "Imprisoned Prostitutes." The accompanying posed picture showed a young Asian gun-toting male actor made to look like the real thing.

There was also a September 1990 *Vancouver* magazine cover story that preposterously claimed that the triads "are about fifty times more powerful" than the American Mafia and that their total membership was more than a quarter of a million compared to the only fifty thousand in the Mafia. *Maclean's* and other major media outlets have quoted similarly dubious and inflated figures in their coverage of the triads. The truth is less dramatic. Although growing rapidly, the triads and Asian gangs have far *less* power and fewer members in Canada and the United States than the Mafia, whose decline has been much exaggerated in the media. Major international unions, big construction companies, and whole industries are still controlled by major Mafia families in the United States. No tong, Asian gang, or triad yet has this kind of power and control in North America.*

Journalists reporting on Asian crime should be a bit more sensitive to the feelings of the legitimate members of the community. Wild exaggerations of the extent of criminal activity should be avoided. Also, police intelligence — often unsubstantiated information gleaned from confidential sources, informers, wiretaps, and other law enforcement agencies — should never be reported as fact, unless, of course, it is confirmed by several independent sources other than the police. Today one sees reported as fact in otherwise reputable publications and books unsubstantiated rumours from United States Justice Department intelligence reports that several billionaire investors in Canada and the United States are triad members. These statements give the triads a lot more mystique and power than they really have. There can also be disastrous consequences for the reporter, the target, and even the police in

---

* The massive law enforcement effort against the mob in the 1980s and early 1990s under the stringent provisions of the anti-racketeering RICO Act in the United States and the anti-Mafia laws in Italy have had their impact on the Mafia in both countries. There is considerable disorder at the top echelons of Mafia families, particularly in New York City, Boston, Philadelphia, and elsewhere as a result of long jail terms given out to top bosses, most notably John Gotti in New York last spring. But the effect has not been to dismantle the Mafia, but rather to create new leadership possibilities for younger members and a lower profile for older bosses. Over the last fifty years in the United States particularly, there have been periodic campaigns against the mob in which a high-profiled individual, such as Thomas Dewey in the thirties, Senator Estes Kefauver in the fifties, Robert Kennedy and Senator John McClellan in the sixties, and Rudi Giuliani in the 1980s have waged highly publicized wars against the mob. Although battered, the Mafia in the United States has always come back, because eventually the pressure diminishes, that is, until another politician comes along to make an issue out of it again. In short, although the Mafia in the States is certainly suffering and in decline, it is far from finished, in spite of all the public relations campaigns that say the opposite.

publishing law enforcement intelligence information as if it were fact. As any honest cop will hasten to confirm, police intelligence is frequently wrong.

This journalistic hype is not new. The sensational press coverage of the opium dens, gambling houses, white slave trade, and the tong wars in the first two decades of the twentieth century led to a racist reaction across Canada and the United States. The "yellow peril" notion, which suggested that Oriental hordes were coming to our shores to undermine our "civilized" way of life, was openly promoted in newspaper and magazine articles. Canadian immigration policy itself was shaped by racist misunderstandings. In the late nineteenth century, when Chinese workers were needed to help build the railroad, a discriminatory head tax was charged for all Chinese immigrants. But by 1923 racism against Orientals was at such a fever pitch across the country that Chinese were completely excluded by law from immigrating to Canada. This racist law was repealed only just after World War II.

The reaction inside the Chinese community in Canada to this overt racism has often been to turn a blind eye to the organized crime activity in the Chinatowns. Ethnic historians have written weighty tomes on the history of persecution and racism against Orientals in Canada, but an account of the organized criminal activity, if mentioned at all, is relegated to obscure footnotes at the back of the books. Until fairly recently, the Chinese Canadian National Council also had a tendency to ignore criminal activity while strenuously attacking reporters and their newspapers for reporting on Oriental, Chinese, or Vietnamese gangster activity. However, with the 1991 murders of Asau Tran and nine others in just eight months in Toronto's main Chinatown, the council has admitted that there is organized crime in the Oriental community, just as there is in many other ethnic communities in Canada.

Chinese scholars around the world, such as American political scientist Dr. Peter Kwong, are now much more open about the history and reality of organized criminals in their midst: "To suggest that the extent of crime in Chinatown is exaggerated is absurd. . . . When thirteen- and fourteen-year-old boys carry guns and shoot each other in daylight on crowded streets with hundreds of witnesses, none of whom will testify in court, the problem is serious indeed." Moreover, Dr. Kwong, in his 1989 book, *The New Chinatowns* (in a chapter entitled "Tongs, Gangs and Godfathers"), lists a number of specific criminal activities of the tongs and triads in New York City, including the operation and protection of a number of illegal gambling houses, protection and extortion rackets, the fencing of stolen goods, and drug trafficking.

Kwong is not the only Chinese scholar in recent years to explore the Chinese criminal underworld. "If Chinese restaurants are one feature of Chinatowns, Chinese secret societies are another." That is how Lynn Pan, a Chinese social scientist and journalist who was born in Shanghai and now lives in England, candidly began her chapter on triads in her detailed 1990 study of the story of the Chinese overseas, *Sons of the Yellow Emperor*. Dealing with a subject that has generally been avoided by other ethnic historians, Ms. Pan was brutally frank:

Secret societies have always been endemic to overseas Chinese communities, and although their nature has changed, a mysterious Chinatown murder or a gang war may still remind one of the days when secret brotherhoods fought each other in the tin mines of Malaya. All over the world these gangs survive on fear and corruption, are engaged in the same kind of business, are likely to have figurative language in common, and very possibly share contacts in Hong Kong. Liaison may be tenuous between city and city, or even gang and gang, but set almost any two secret society men side by side, whatever their affiliations, from East or West, speaking Cantonese or Teochiu, and they would not altogether feel strangers to each other. To outsiders, this makes them seem like members of a huge worldwide conspiracy, and yet they may not be linked at all in their operations; may, indeed, be split by deadly rivalry.

Another American-Chinese academic who has recently explored the criminal subculture in a scholarly way is Ko-Lin Chin in his 1990 book, *Chinese Subculture and Criminality: Non-Traditional Crime Groups in America*, a sociological study of Chinese criminal activity in the United States.

In anguishing over the publication of an article on triads, the editor of *Asiam*, a U.S. magazine for Asian Americans, wrote in 1989 that while printing the piece "had the potential for adding fuel to the erroneous perception of the Chinese community as crime-ridden, on the other hand the Triads are an important feature of the Pacific Rim scene from both the law enforcement and economic standpoints. An awareness of their activities is necessary to enable us to keep from falling victim to them and to understanding the economic forces that may affect such practical concerns for Americans as real estate prices and a sane drug policy for the United States."

Even taking the painfully honest assessments of Dr. Kwong, Ms. Pan, Dr. Ko-Lin Chin, and the *Asiam* editor into account, it is important to state that there is no special danger from Chinese, Vietnamese, or any other Asian immigrants. These immigrants are no more crime-prone than others. There are organized crime groups operating in these and in many other immigrant and indigenous groups in Canada and the United States. No one group has a monopoly on organized crime. Yet for generations many have played upon our fear of admitting criminals to keep all immigrants, particularly Chinese, from coming to North America.

The story of the triads and the other Chinese and Vietnamese gangs in Canada and the United States is a complex one, with a cast of exotic characters living here and in faraway places, including Asia, Europe, and Central America. I have spent many years researching the material for this book in Canada, the United States, Europe, and Hong Kong. I have interviewed many current and former triad members, including high-level triad officers in Canada, as well as many associates and victims of the triads and gangs, and, of course, law enforcement specialists in Asian crime throughout North America and in Hong

Kong. My research began in 1974 while I was helping to produce the award-winning "Connections" television series on organized crime for the CBC. As research director and associate producer of "Connections," I spent years following and uncovering the activities and movements of the corrupt former Hong Kong policemen known as the five dragons and their fronts and associates in Vancouver and Toronto. Later, as an investigative journalist for "The Fifth Estate," I spent two years researching the chilling story that aired on November 10, 1983, on the brutal extortion activities of the Kung Lok triad in Ontario and its association with other triads and gangs throughout North America. Finally, with the help of a Canada Council grant, I travelled across North America and to Hong Kong from 1988 to 1991 in search of human and archival sources on Asian organized crime activities in North America, past and present. Even after all of this in-depth research activity, it is with trepidation and humility that I approach this book-length study on a subject that has eluded many other researchers.

I hope to present in this book an account of the leadership and activities of the various gangs that operate in the Chinatowns across North America; to detail the highlights of the history of how this organized gang activity started in Canada and the United States from the mid-nineteenth century through to the Roaring Twenties; and finally, to focus on a few major criminals and organizations to show how and with whom they operate in both the criminal and legitimate worlds. I will also examine the new elements in the complex mosaic that is organized crime in Canada's Chinatowns.

What I cannot hope to do in this book alone is to present a full account of the origins and activities of the gangs over the years as well as a complete picture of the many Chinese and Vietnamese organized crime groups involved in drug trafficking, gambling, alien smuggling, extortion, murder and other criminal activities from coast to coast. That is simply too vast a subject, covering too wide a territory for one book. The lost history of the Chinese criminal organizations operating across Canada alone, if done as a full scholarly account, would be a hefty tome. But what I have recovered of the history of Chinese organized crime activity, especially in Vancouver and Toronto, richly illustrates a number of themes, such as the troubling, recurrent problem from the 1920s until today of criminals doubling as police informers or police agents while carrying on with their organized crime activities, leading to the appearance (and sometimes the reality) of police corruption.

I hope that this book will help put the events of the modern period into an historical context which is all too frequently absent in reporting (and policing) on this sensitive subject, and that my analysis of the range of criminal activities in which the gangs are involved will lead to more effective ways of dealing with the growing menace to society from these dragons of crime.

TRIADS, TONGS, AND ASIAN GANGS

The recent hyped coverage in the media of Asian gang activity has created a confusion in the public's mind about the names of the different groups involved in organized crime in the Chinese community. The terms "triads," "tongs," and "Asian gangs" have all too frequently been used interchangeably in television, radio and newspaper coverage. Yet they are all quite different.

The tongs did not exist in China. They were established as social clubs by Chinese who immigrated to North America in the nineteenth century. "Tongs are," former tong leader Eddie Gong wrote in his 1930 book *Tong War*, "as American as chop suey," a dish created in the United States. In their origins, they were not *intrinsically* criminal organizations, but rather protective, benevolent associations that provided legal services, a credit union, and other advice and social services to their members. They were not unlike Masonic lodges.

The tongs were structured like secret societies. Professor Peter Kwong has written, "Tongs were started in the United States by individual members of small and weak clans who did not want to be pushed around by the powerful and prestigious [families of] Lees and Tams, or by the Toishanese [immigrants from the area around Canton]. Since members of a tong were not related, they pledged allegiance to one another as 'brothers in blood oath.' Their bonds were further strengthened through mystical, religious rituals, a secret language, and signs. "

By the late nineteenth century, however, tongs had taken control of gambling houses, prostitution establishments and opium dens, as well as collecting taxes on other illicit activities in Chinatowns, such as the slave trade. Individual tongs, such as the On Leong tong under Tom Lee and the Hip Sing tong in New York under Mock Duck, fought to the death to protect their turf in New York City. Up until the early 1930s, according to Henry Anslinger, one of the chief drug-trafficking law enforcement officials in the United States from the 1920s to the 1950s, the tongs — which he described as something like an "Oriental Mafia, except that they existed openly" — had "a virtual monopoly on the opium trade in America."

In the modern period in the United States and Canada, all too frequently the leadership of a tong, such as the On Leong and the Hip Sing in New York City and other tongs on the U.S. west coast, has been taken over by organized criminals and triad leaders. The longtime leadership of the On Leong in New York City in the 1970s and 1980s by Eddie Chan, the triad-connected ex-Hong Kong policeman, is a good recent example of organized crime taking over a tong. Chan used the Ghost Shadows youth gang to protect On Leong gambling houses, while the rival Hip Sing tong used another Chinese youth gang, the Flying Dragons. According to the U.S. Justice Department, the Tung On tong has recently emerged in New York City and is fronting for the Hong Kong-based Sun Yee On triad.

In Canada the Chee Kung tong (CKT), which had chapters in Vancouver and Montreal, was founded in the nineteenth century by Hung Mun members who maintained certain triad traditions and political goals, though the CKT was essentially a social organization. For a period in the 1950s and 1960s, however, criminal elements controlled the leadership of the CKT in Montreal.

Just like the tongs, the triads were not originally criminal organizations, but secret societies with patriotic political goals. The term "triad" (for "three") is an English designation referring to the triangle that was the sacred emblem of the Hung Mun or the Heaven and Earth Association, the first triad society, according to some accounts. The three sides of the triangle, now used by most triad societies as an important symbol, refer to the three essential elements of the Chinese universe living in harmony: Heaven, Earth, and Man. The number three (in all its variations) is of special significance to triad members. For example, extortion rates — even in Toronto — are often arrived at by using three as a base for calculations.

Secret societies have a long tradition in China because of the enormous power of the imperial system. Emperors, like the popes of the Catholic Church, were considered infallible. According to Chinese tradition, the emperors were obliged to be super human beings, totally virtuous, honest, benevolent, and above personal reproach, as they were morality incarnate. Like Jesus Christ in Christianity, the emperor was the Son of Heaven on earth. An emperor who was unable to live up to these ideals was said to "forfeit the mandate of Heaven," according to historian Barbara Ward, "and it was the duty of the people to resist and even depose him."* Thus, the first secret societies were formed as organized opposition to the emperor.

The first known secret society in China surfaced in the first century. The last (Western) Han emperor, Ai, was deposed in 9 A.D. by Wang Mang after Ai tried to name his male lover, Dong Xian, as his successor. The Red Eyebrows band, named after the makeup they wore in battle, fought to restore the Han dynasty. The usurper, Wang Mang, was assassinated and a new (Eastern) Han dynasty was established in 25 A.D.; after their victory, the Red Eyebrows became brigands — mere bandits who roamed the country.

In the fifth century, the White Lotus Society, or the White Lily Society, was begun by a persecuted sect of pious Buddhists who were also involved in a dynastic dispute, this time engineering the overthrow of the newly installed Mongol Yuan dynasty. Their patriotic aim was achieved with the installation of the first Ming emperor, a Buddhist monk by the name of Chu

---

* "Chinese Secret Societies," by Barbara E. Ward, in *Secret Societies*, edited by Norman MacKenzie.

Yuan-Chang, who later took the name Hung Wu. (The Chinese character "hung" is the same as used in "Hung Mun," the original name of the triad movement.) Some historians and triad researchers claim that the White Lotus Society was the first triad.*

But according to Chinese legend, the triads really got going in the late seventeenth century, near the end of the reign of the last Ming emperor, Sung Ching. It was a time when the country was threatened from within by corrupt officials and a hedonistic emperor, and from without, by aggressive Manchu and Mongul neighbours. A few dozen honest officials in the government heroically formed a secret society in order to recruit patriotic citizens in the fight against corruption. They were led by Kam Shun. There followed a successful peasant revolt led by Li Chi Shing, alias Li Chong. The emperor was forced to commit suicide, and Li then declared himself emperor. But a Ming general allied with the Manchu invaders soon forced him from power. In the ensuing turbulence, Peking (Beijing) was taken. The Manchus eventually seized power and set up the Ch'ing dynasty in 1644.

Soon Kam Shun and his followers started a rebellion against the new Ch'ing dynasty, and many of Kam's colleagues were killed. Kam himself took refuge in Shaolin, a Buddhist monas-

---

* The dynastic name of "Ming" was provided directly by the White Lotus Society, whose members revered two messianic Buddhist figures, Big and Little Ming Wang, who according to legend had been sent to restore peace to the world. Other early secret societies in Chinese history include the Yellow Turbans, a late second-century group that fought for a Taoist leader named Chang Chu and led a rebellion that subdued most of Northern China and helped to fragment the empire. For a thorough, reliable account of the Chinese historical background, based on years of research and in-depth interviews with triad members, see Inspector W.P. Morgan's book, *Triad Societies in Hong Kong*, published and distributed by the government of Hong Kong. Published originally in 1960, it has been reprinted as recently as 1989. The colourful photos of triad leaders in their ceremonial outfits, though, are actors in costumes, not the real thing. Several English books and many articles on triads reproduce these pictures as if they were the real thing.

tery in Fukien province, a part of southeastern China that had successfully resisted the Manchu invasion. During the reign of the Emperor K'ang Hsi, an invasion by the Monguls was allegedly repulsed by the same monks. In 1674, 128 of the 133 monks who had earlier sworn a blood oath in support of the Ming restoration were, according to triad legend, captured or brutally murdered by K'ang Hsi's army, and their monastery was destroyed. The remaining five monks, known by the triad societies as the Five Ancestors, founded the Heaven and Earth Society, the Hung Mun (also known as the Hung League). It was also called the Triad Society, as the Hung Mun's symbol was a triangle that represented the three essential elements of the Chinese universe in harmony with each other: Heaven, Earth, and Man. The Hung Mun remained active throughout the Ch'ing dynasty, fomenting rebellions, along with the White Lotus Society, which organized uprisings against the Ch'ing dynasty, most notably in 1774 and 1794.

Until the first years of the twentieth century, triad leaders continued to launch rebellions against the Ch'ing dynasty, which alienated many of the people with its repressive system of controls. Triad leader, Luo Dao-Gang allied himself in 1848 with Hung Hsiu-Ch'uan, a Hakka farmer from the Canton area and founder of the Society of God Worshippers. Together they led an army in the unsuccessful Taiping Rebellion, and later they managed to lay seige to Canton and start a revolt in Shanghai. Although still a secret society, the triads had a good deal of support among the Chinese masses and made steady inroads against the Ch'ing dynasty troops throughout the century. A popular aphorism in China was that although it was "the armies that protected the emperor," it was "the secret societies that protected the people."

"Taiping" literally means universal peace and social harmony, a concept that appears in triad rituals. The Boxer Rebellion of the late nineteenth century, although not a triad-led movement, did claim a descent from the earlier White Lotus Society, which mysteriously disappeared as an important force in the mid-nineteenth century. Triad scholars such as William

Stanton, author of the 1900 book, *The Triad Society, or Heaven and Earth Association*, have theorized that its functions were absorbed or transferred to the Heaven and Earth Society, the Hung League.

Only in the twentieth century did the triads emerge as predominantly criminal secret societies. This was accompanied by the emergence of newer triads in Hong Kong, China, Taiwan, North America, and elsewhere.

A number of secret rituals and ceremonies have evolved through the hundreds of years the secret societies have existed. Many of the older triads today maintain many of the colourful rituals. They include the elaborate initiation ceremonies that can take up to eight hours to complete and that involve secret hand clasps, ritual dances, "the passing of the mountain of knives" (during which the initiate bows under a number of swords), the decapitation of a live chicken whose blood is mixed in a bowl with that of the initiate (pricked usually from his finger) and drunk (with a good bit of wine added to the mixture) by all in attendance, and the burning of the yellow paper as a show of loyalty. Later the burning of the yellow paper became a ritualistic way for members from different triads or gangs to signal agreement and an auspicious beginning for a new project. When the contents of the bowl are consumed, it is often ritualistically broken to show the fate of those who might betray the brotherhood.

The initiate then swears the "thirty-six oaths," a formulaic way of expressing loyalty to the triad over everything else, including loved ones and family. The thirty-six oaths date back to the seventeenth century. The first oath is that "after having passed through the Hung gates," the initiate "must treat the parents and relatives of sworn brothers" as their own kin. "I shall suffer death by five thunderbolts if I do not keep this oath." Other oaths include working for the benefit of other brothers and their families, such as number four: "I shall always acknowledge my Hung brothers when they identify themselves. If I ignore them, I will be killed by myriads of swords." Many of the oaths repeat the message "Be loyal or be killed."

The final oath is the standard one for all Hung societies: "After entering the Hung gates, I shall be loyal and faithful and shall endeavour to overthrow Ch'ing and restore Ming.... Our common aim is to avenge our Five Ancestors." It is, however, curiously out of date, since the Ch'ing dynasty has long since been removed, and today there is no longer any effort to restore the Ming dynasty. But these rituals continue because of their mystical significance in triad circles.

The titles of the officers of the triad, whose organization even today is strictly hierarchical, are highly ritualistic and influenced by numerology. The Dragon Head (Shan Chu or Chu Chi, also known by the number 489) is the leader or head of the society. In some triads that also operate openly as clubs he is known informally as the president; in other, less structured triad lodges he is the Dai Lo or Elder Brother. The White Paper Fan (Bak Tse Sin or Pak Tse Sin) acts as a financial adviser (or *consigliere* in Mafia terms) and is known by the number 415. The Red Poles (Hung Kwan), or 426, function as society enforcers and are knowledgeable in kung-fu. Other officers include the Straw Sandal (Cho Hai or 432) who is responsible for communications; the Fu Shan Chu or 438, who is the dragon head's number two; and the Incense Master (Heung Chu and generally a 438-ranked official though under the Fu Shan Chu), who is in charge of all the society's rituals. Finally there is the ordinary triad member, or soldier, known as Sey Kow Jai, or 49. All the numbers used for titles have mystical significance for the triad membership. For example, the three digits of 489 or dragon head, add up to twenty-one, the characters of which approximate the characters for "Hung." The number 21 is also 3 (meaning Heaven, Earth, and Man) multiplied by the lucky number 7. In other words 489 represents the whole life cycle of the society.*

The triads also make extensive use of sign language and secret signals to communicate. A certain way of holding or placing

---

* The explanation for 21 comes from triad mythology as explained by Martin Booth in *The Triads*, as well as in earlier accounts.

chopsticks or the number of fingers used to grasp a glass can be of great significance. A complicated system of hand signals can be interpreted only by other triad members. Certain Chinese phrases represent a kind of triad code (for example, the Chinese words for "bite clouds" stood for "smoke opium" and "black dog" meant a gun).* Today drug deals are often done, much to the chagrin of police authorities worldwide, through non-verbal sign language. This language also foils audio surveillance and wiretap teams.

Today in Hong Kong there are approximately thirty active triad societies with a membership estimated at approximately seventy thousand. The Royal Hong Kong Police Force (RHKP) estimates there are between 70,000 and 120,000 triad society members, but this includes many part-time or inactive members. A more realistic figure for total membership in Hong Kong is approximately fifty thousand — not the quarter of a million or more that many sensational journalistic accounts have recently claimed. The largest triad society is the Sun Yee On, which has an estimated membership of twenty thousand. The dragon head of this triad was successfully prosecuted for triad membership in the late 1980s under Hong Kong's anti-triad statutes, which make it illegal to be a member of a triad. One of the smaller triads, the Luen Kung Lok, is said to have only two hundred members. Hong Kong is still the major centre for triad society activity in almost every aspect of daily life. According to a recent Royal Hong Kong Police report, they remain "a major threat to law and order" because of their influence and numbers.

In Toronto and Vancouver as well as in Montreal, Calgary, and other Canadian cities, there are several active triad organizations. Among the triads are the Kung Lok Society (meaning

---

* A list of the code phrases and their meanings was published in the *RCMP Gazette*, Vol. 49, No. 9, 1987, in an article by Constable R.B. Hamilton of the RCMP National Crime Intelligence Service. The complete list has appeared in other publications and books over the past decade, and as a result, it is doubtful that any of the codes is valid any longer.

literally "the house of mutual happiness"), which was started by a Hong Kong triad member and has an active membership of over a hundred (though police have stated in official reports for the past decade that there are 450 members); the 14 K, a branch of the famous Hong Kong-based triad started after World War II with a small but elite membership in Canada; the Wah Ching, a branch of the main San Francisco triad with close ties to a society in Hong Kong; the Gum Wah; the Lotus Society; the Sun Yee On; and others. These triads are active in gambling, extortion, prostitution, alien smuggling, credit card fraud, murder, and other organized crime activities. In 1991 the Police Chiefs of Canada compiled a report with the help of the Criminal Intelligence Service of Canada — run by the RCMP in Ottawa, this law enforcement group includes representatives of most police intelligence units in the country. "The Organized Crime Report" concluded that "ethnic crime groups" (a new euphemism the policemen use for Chinese triads and Vietnamese gangs) are growing in numbers and are particularly violent.*

George Best, a seasoned triad investigator for years for Canadian Immigration intelligence, told me that no matter what name they go by, the members of the triads are basically hardened, professional criminals who "use the mystique of the triads to glorify themselves. Even with their rituals and initiation ceremonies, the triads are basically image."

The Asian youth gangs, whose names frequently change or are often unknown to investigators, include both Chinese and Vietnamese as well as other groups and are composed mostly

---

* Curiously, no other ethnic group is singled out for this unique designation, though the Mafia is primarily made up of Italians of Sicilian or Calabrian descent and the posses are made up mainly of blacks from Jamaica. Also, inexplicably, the 1991 annual chiefs' report changed the official number of members of the Kung Lok in Canada from 450 (this was always too high a count for hard-core members) to a mere fifty. Nothing is said of what happened to the other four hundred alleged Kung Lok members who had been listed in every annual organized crime report since the mid-1980s.

of male youths from as young as thirteen to their late twenties. As one high-level tong official said to me, "Chinese youth gangs are really just like any other juvenile delinquents. They group together as long as they have a little money to spend. But if a tong or triad moves in, they have a direction. Then they are not going to extort people for a little money, they are going to try to manipulate the whole city." A good example of the latter case is the Ghost Shadows youth gang in New York City. Organized in the 1970s under the leadership of the charismatic Nickie Louie (Yin Poy Louie) merely as a group of Chinese youths involved in crime, but they evolved into a semi-sophisticated and deadly enforcement and protection arm of the On Leong tong. Nickie Louie became a legendary figure in New York's Chinatown, fighting it out in the streets of New York City with the Hip Sing's youth gang, the Flying Dragons. Nickie Louis is thought to be like the cat with nine lives. He has survived several shootings over the years, including one in which he was shot point-blank at least three times.

In Vancouver there are many youth gangs, some Chinese and some Vietnamese. Leaders are often referred to as the Dai Lo (elder brother). One of the Vietnamese gangs, the Viet Ching, has many members who are well into their thirties, and it really is closer to a triad than a youth gang, both in structure and organization. (There is also a very active and violent Latino youth gang, Los Diabolos, which in often involved in turf-battle conflicts with the Chinese and Vietnamese youth gangs and which has more than four hundred members, including many Chinese, according to recent police intelligence reports.)

In Toronto there are several violent Vietnamese gangs. Many of the members of the Vietnamese gangs in Canada met originally in refugee camps in Hong Kong or elsewhere where they forged their criminal ties. Most have come from war-torn Vietnam and have had a horrific childhood both in Vietnam and refugee camps. Compared to members of the sophisticated and ritualized Chinese triads, they are much more prone to violence, and many murder as an initial response to a real or imagined threat. Some of the Vietnamese gangs in Toronto, such as the one run by the late Asau Tran, assassinated by his rivals last year in the busy streets of Toronto's Chinatown, and the one led by Trung Chi Truong, a transplanted Massachusetts resident with imperial ambitions in Canada, began as youth gangs and later became organized crime gangs.

A Chinese youth gang in Toronto in the seventies called the Ghost Shadows (after the New York gang) under the leadership of Nickie Louie's brother, Eddie, had some ties with several triad organizations in Toronto, New York City, and Hong Kong. Certain journalists erroneously and variously claim that Eddie Louie is the Sun Yee On triad leader, the 14 K triad leader, and the Ghost Shadows gang leader in Canada. In fact Eddie Louie has left the triad and gang activity behind and is now a legitimate restaurateur and businessman. The Toronto Version of the Ghost Shadows, which he helped organize, has not existed for some time, though Eddie Louie continued to organize some gambling in Toronto until the mid-1980s.*

Finally, in Toronto, there is the Kung Lok triad, which started as a youth gang run by a triad leader and evolved into a full-fledged triad. The Kung Lok has used members of Vietnamese gangs as enforcers and in business endeavours, and it has been the most criminally active and successful triad to operate in Canada to date. The story of the Kung Lok's founding, growth, criminal activities, and international connections is

---

* If there is one thing I have learned over the past eighteen years of researching and investigating organized crime, it is that it is absolutely essential to check out police intelligence information independently and thoroughly because it is often wrong. Yves Lavigne in his unevenly researched book, *Good Guy/Bad Guy* reports without reservation that Eddie Louie is the 14 K leader in Toronto. In 1990 an otherwise well-researched and well-written English book, *Sons of the Yellow Emperor: The Story of the Overseas Chinese* by social scientist Lynn Pan erroneously stated that Eddie Louie was the Sun Yee On triad representative in Toronto and that his restaurant, the E-On, had been named after the triad. The truth is less sinister. "E-on" literally means "peaceful mind." These are just two recent examples in which various police intelligence information has become garbled in transmission or is simply repeated as fact.

the subject of many of the chapters to follow.

Even among experienced law enforcement personnel, there is often confusion in the terminology, especially between the terms "triad," "tong," and Asian "youth gang." This is especially true in the United States where police only started using the term "triad" in the mid-1980s. Before that everything was either a tong or a gang. A senior Canadian Immigration intelligence official explained the confusion this way:

> We all agree that members of tongs can be members of a triad or at least triad-connected. But I've heard the Americans refer to street gangs as triads. In my opinion, a street gang is not a triad, but simply a gang of young people — in other words, a youth gang. They may take on pretensions of being a triad, but they really aren't. In many cases, they are used by the real triads or by the tongs. They may even have initiation ceremonies. But in most cases, it was just a case of trying to act like a triad. A youth gang member becomes a "serious" criminal when he gets older and more experienced. That's not to say he can't be a serious criminal when he is younger, for example, Nickie Louie. [Toronto Kung Lok founder] Lau Wing Kui, at his age and position in life when he came to Toronto, obviously couldn't be just a youth gang leader. But that didn't prevent him from using youth gangs for his own purposes.

There are also groupings other than tongs, triads, and Asian youth gangs involved in organized crime in the Chinatowns across North America. Among these are ex-mainland Chinese gangsters who belong to a loosely organized network of gangs across North America generally known as Dai Huen Jai, or the Big Circle Boys. On the whole, these gang members, ranging in age from the late twenties to the early forties, come from the area around the southern provincial capital, Canton, which in China is known as "the big city" and is designated on maps by a large circle. These gangs are made up mostly of ex-members of the Chinese military or, though there are fewer of these, former members of the élite Red Guard. Many Big Circle Boys are professional criminals wanted in mainland China. They are secretly brought into Canada and the United States, usually by way of Hong Kong, by illegal-alien-smuggling networks, and then claim refugee status. (It is truly amazing how many of the gangsters in this group say they were in Tiananmen Square in June 1989, so that they will be granted political refugee status here.) Their organizational structure is triad-like, though they are not triads.

The media in North America frequently make the mistake of referring to the Dai Huen Jai gangs as if they were one big gang. They are not. There are many Big Circle Boys gangs in North America, and often several in a large city like New York City or Toronto. Moreover, these gangs often co-operate with similar gangs in other cities. (For example, a Toronto Big Circle Gang will operate an alien-smuggling network with a New York City-based Big Circle gang and, simultaneously, be importing heroin in partnership with a Hong Kong-based Big Circle gang.) The major Big Circle gang in Vancouver was started in 1987 and has about fifty members. In Toronto there are even more members — about one hundred hard core — and about ten separate gangs. They are feared in many North American Chinatowns because of their military and criminal backgrounds, and they are known to be particularly violent. They certainly provide stiff competition to some of the triads and Vietnamese gangs operating in the major cities.

More recently there have been signs in Canada of other mainland Chinese gangs from Fukien province, next to Canton. In one recent case, a Fukienese gang with bases in New York City and China co-operated in a major alien-smuggling operation in Canada with a Big Circle Boys gang centred in Toronto. (Gangs of mixed ethnic backgrounds, as well as independent youth gangs, operate in several Chinatowns.)

There are also groups of criminals, like the so-called five dragons, led by corrupt former Hong Kong policemen who emigrated from the British colony to North America in the mid-1970s. They brought with them millions of dollars obtained from bribes and, in some cases, through the drug trade. They have ties to other criminal groups, including various triads.

In examining the tongs, triads, and gangs in the Chinatowns of North America, it is important to realize that no neat, monolithic, hierarchical organization controls all criminal activity. Even in Hong Kong, there are literally scores of rival triads and gang groupings: the many gangs and the various crime bosses may or may not interrelate. In North America one can be a member of a triad without belonging to a tong or a youth gang; one can be a youth gang member and have no triad or tong affiliation; or one can be a member of a tong, triad, and youth gang at the same time. Often membership in a particularly active youth gang leads to initiation into one of the triads operating in North America. And, all too frequently, senior tong officials are secretly (and in some cases openly) members of a triad with direct ties to Hong Kong.

Chinese organized crime in Canada has a long and colourful history. In 1928 a Chinese gangster in Vancouver, Shu Moy, known locally as the King of the Gamblers, was the focus of a special inquiry involving the corruption of that city's police chief and mayor. As early as 1918, records in the archives from the Ontario attorney general's office detail the busting of major illegal gaming houses in Toronto run by Chinese gang bosses, some with troubling ties to the police. Throughout the 1920s and 1930s, scores of opium-smuggling syndicates operating between Hong Kong and China and Vancouver, Toronto, Montreal, New York City, San Francisco and the Maritimes, were broken up by the police. The principal figures in most of these drug-smuggling rings, which used the luxury passenger liners of the day for transporting the drugs, were Chinese. Many of the hundreds of individuals who were caught in Canada and convicted were deported to their country of origin after their jail terms.

Although organized crime and criminal activity is not new to North American Chinatowns, in the last decade two new elements have entered the organized crime scene in the major

Chinatowns. First, there has been the emergence of a number of Vietnamese gangs in Vancouver, Toronto, Montreal, and elsewhere in Canada and in the United States. Second, the Big Circle Boys gangs and other mainland Chinese gangs have been transplanted to North America from mainland China and Hong Kong. Both these developments have led to a dramatic increase in criminal activity and a great deal more violence in Chinatowns across Canada and the United States.

PART ONE

Of Tongs, Dragons, and Kings

Chapter One

THE BRITISH LEGACY
Hong Kong and the Opium Traffic

And close your eyes with holy dread,
For he on honey-dew hath fed,
And drunk the milk of Paradise.

— from Samuel Coleridge's 1797 poem, "Kubla Khan"

The story of the triads and their massive involvement in international organized crime began in the last century. Hong Kong was founded in the middle of the nineteenth century as a free trade port by British opium traders. This was at a time when opium use was legal in England and North America. The Chinese had specifically outlawed opium use and trafficking in the nineteenth century. Still, the British insisted on importing it into China from their huge opium poppy fields in India, which were run by the East India Company. This enabled imperial Britain to balance the payments due to China for popular Chinese exports, most notably tea, silk, and spices. Rather than deplete precious British gold and silver reserves or even British and Indian-made cotton products for these Chinese imports to England, British traders developed and ruthlessly exploited a lively market for opium-smoking in China. By 1839 more than forty thousand chests full of opium (worth more than four million British pounds sterling) were exported annually from India to China, driving out all legitimate imports.

19

This system allowed huge quantities of Chinese tea, spices, and silk to come into England without any drain on the British treasury.

The Chinese emperor, Tao-Kuang, was adamant that opium not be imported into China. In the early 1830s, he appointed Lin Tse-hsu as the new imperial commissioner with special powers and a mandate to end the British-run opium trade. "How, alas, can I die and go to the shades of my imperial fathers and ancestors, until these dire evils are removed?" the exasperated emperor asked Lin.

In early 1839 Commissioner Lin wrote to Queen Victoria that all the opium in China was to be destroyed and threatened that ships entering China with opium shipments would be set ablaze. Lin, headquartered in thriving Canton, the southeastern Chinese city that was a popular mercantile capital for British and foreign traders, including the opium traffickers, had thousands of Chinese opium traffickers and users imprisoned, and by 1839 had even started the mass execution of Chinese dealers. In March 1839 Lin ordered the confiscation of all opium in the possession of foreign merchants in Canton; in July, a Chinese peasant named Lin Wei Hi was murdered in Kowloon, the peninsula across from Hong Kong Island, during a skirmish with British merchants whose ships had taken refuge on Hong Kong Island after Lin's actions in nearby Canton. Lin demanded that the British hand over the murderer and destroy all shipments of opium newly arrived in Hong Kong and ordered the Chinese in Hong Kong to cut off supplies to foreign merchants. A mismatched battle took place between the Royal navy frigate *Volage* and a fleet of Chinese junks. Badly out-gunned, the Chinese fleet of junks was destroyed. The Opium Wars had begun.

By 1842 the first Opium War was over. The Chinese government was forced by the victorious British to agree to the Treaty of Nanking, which allowed five treaty ports for the British on China's seaboard, and the establishment of the tiny, barren, rocky Island of Hong Kong as a free trade port under British control. It was only thirty-two square miles and located on

China's southeast coast in the South China Sea.*

The prime minister of the time, Sir Robert Peel, defended the opium trade in an emergency debate in the House of Commons in 1843, explaining that if the British-run East India Company did not provide the opium, then the Chinese demand for opium would simply be filled by others. Prohibiting the export of opium, "a most safe, most profitable, and most healthy employment," would only hurt England. Lord Palmerston, Peel's foreign secretary and later prime minister himself, also actively and openly supported the interests of the East India Company and the British opium traders.

But many leading British theologians and politicians, led by Anthony Ashley Cooper, the seventh Earl of Shaftesbury, a noted social reformer of his day, opposed Britain's central and growing role in the opium trade as immoral and reprehensible. He urged that the cultivation of opium in India be prohibited and that the opium monopoly be broken up:

> What would be said if any other nation were to treat us as we treat the Chinese? What would be said in this country, and what amount of just indignation there would be in this House, if we were told that French buccaneers were ravaging our coasts, defying our laws, and murdering our fellow subjects! Should we venture to act thus towards any other

---

* Across the harbour, on the mainland, were (1) the neighbouring and now bustling three-and-a-half-square-mile patch that makes up the Kowloon Peninsula, which was added in 1861 after another war, and (2) the comparatively spacious New Territories, comprising more than 350 square miles, which were "leased" from China for ninety-nine years in 1898. Still, the entire colony of Hong Kong even today is just a little over four hundred square miles, with most of its inhabitants living on crowded but very small Hong Kong Island and Kowloon. James Clavell's blockbuster best-seller, *Taipan*, published in 1966, is a compelling and insightful fictional treatment of the epic story of Hong Kong's founding by two of the most prominent British opium traders, Scotsmen William Jardine and James Matheson. For a more literary treatment of the same theme, read Timothy Mo's 1986 novel, *An Insular Possession*. There are many non-fiction accounts of the role of the opium trade in the early days of Hong Kong. See the Bibliography for a list of some of them.

state that was bold enough, and strong enough to make reprisals upon us? Certainly not. And in admitting this we admit that our conduct towards the Chinese is governed by our pride and our power, and not by our estimate of justice .... Sir, the condition of this empire does demand a most deep and solemn consideration; within and without we are hollow and insecure ... with one arm resting on the East, and the other on the West, we are in too many instances trampling under foot every moral and religious obligation .... It is the duty of every man who cares for the faith of Christianity, and the duty for everyone who cares for the honour of his country, to combine in protesting, in memorializing, in giving no rest to the authorities of this country until such time as they shall have wiped out this foul reproach from the forehead of the British empire ....

But Lord Shaftesbury's eloquence was not to prevail, and the British continued the opium trade in China from India and Hong Kong until the late 1920s.*

Ironically, opium use was quite popular in England itself. One has only to read Samuel Coleridge's accounts of his opium habit in his letters and poems such as his rhapsodic, opium-inspired "Kubla Khan; Or a Vision in a Dream: A Fragment,"** or Thomas de Quincey's 1822 autobiographical masterpiece, *Con-*

---

* Dr. J. Wesley Bready, a Canadian scholar writing about Shaftesbury's role in opposing the opium trade as late as 1926, wrote, "The opium trade to this day remains the vilest stain on the British flag. As late as 1924, our Indian government was deriving some £4,000,000 annual revenue from this death-dealing trade." *Lord Shaftesbury And Social-Industrial Progress.* Bready devotes a whole chapter to Britain's leading role in the opium trade. As Bishop Brent, representing the United States at the League of Nations' Conference on Opium in Geneva, declared in 1923, "Under no conditions must Western nations be allowed any longer to pervert the Lord's Prayer by saying to Orientals, 'Give them this day their daily *opium.'"

** Coleridge himself wrote that "Kubla Khan" was composed "in a sort of reverie brought on by two grains of Opium taken to check a dysentery." In fact, Coleridge, like de Quincey, became addicted to opium and may have taken the drug to help him to write poetry.

fessions of an English Opium-Eater, to see how far reaching opium taking was in fashionable England in the early nineteenth century. De Quincey refers to opium as his "celestial drug," which, though a narcotic, excited and stimulated his whole body. De Quincey quickly became an all-too-willing addict after his first use of the drug as a painkiller:

> O just, subtle, and mighty, all-conquering opium . . . . What an apocalypse of the world within me! That my pains had vanished was now a trifle in my eyes; this negative effect was swallowed up in the immensity of those positive effects which had opened before me, in the abyss of divine enjoyment thus suddenly revealed. Here was a panacea . . . for all human woes; here was the secret of happiness, about which philosophers had disputed for so many ages, at once discovered; happiness might be bought for a penny, and carried in the waistcoat pocket; portable ecstasies might be had corked up in a pint bottle; and peace of mind could be sent down by the mail.*

But in spite of the attraction to the drug by some of England's leading literary lights, and despite the fact that the drug was in wide use in the first half of the nineteenth century as a remedy for a number of illnesses, opium and morphine use was not a major problem in England in the nineteenth century. The

---

* De Quincey was not the only literary opium-eater in England. Other nineteenth-century literary examples of opiate use include Charles Dickens's description of opium smoking in *The Mystery of Edwin Drood*, some of the recreational drug activity in the Sherlock Holmes stories by Sir Arthur Conan Doyle, and Oscar Wilde's *The Picture of Dorian Gray*. The celebrated Victorian novelist Wilkie Collins was also addicted to opium, and hallucinations induced by the drug pervade his work. Another literary English opium taker of the time was Branwell Brontë, the only brother of the famous Brontë sisters, Charlotte, Anne, and Emily; he started taking opium as a substitute for alcohol after reading De Quincey's *Confessions* in 1839. Branwell Brontë died as a result of his dissipation at the age of thirty-one in 1848 just a year after the publication of his sister's celebrated novel, *Jane Eyre*. De Quincey eventually cured himself of opium addiction.

masses never became addicted to the drug in the way people became attached to alcohol (though many used laudanum, an opium preparation, which contained alcohol, distilled water, and opium). The government discouraged use of the drug in England, later making its importation illegal. But, hypocritically, the British government allowed and even encouraged English merchants abroad to cultivate and export the drug from British territories, primarily India where the opium poppies were plentiful, to other markets — mostly to China. British opium traders then helped to addict a significant number of Chinese citizens by providing massive quantities of the drug at very low costs.

It was through Hong Kong that most of the British opium made its way into China. British opium traders brought ships full of the drug to the Crown colony for sale there and to the rest of China. Later in the nineteenth century, with the massive emigration of Chinese overseas and with the help of the triad syndicates, opium was distributed internationally via Hong Kong. Though they did significantly help the British in the nineteenth century with the importation and distribution of opium in China and Hong Kong, the triads became a major *international* criminal problem only in the early twentieth century when several of them began major international opium-and-heroin smuggling rings. It is only in this century that we see the birth of new triads in China, Hong Kong, Taiwan, and elsewhere solely organized around and devoted to organized criminal activity such as drug trafficking, alien smuggling, and extortion.

The triads flourished throughout the nineteenth century in Hong Kong, which according to Lynn Pan has always been the capital of "the Chinese criminal diaspora." Official government and police records of 1842, the first year of British rule in Hong Kong, report that there were at least four triad lodges in Hong Kong at its founding and that "Secret Societies . . . were reported as established in Hong Kong and possessing much influence." At that time triads were primarily secret societies with political and quasi-religious functions. Still, the new

British-governed colony of Hong Kong in 1845 immediately took steps to outlaw triad membership as "incompatible with the Maintenance of good Order" because they increased "the Facilities for the Commission of Crime and for the Escape of Offenders." It became a crime in Hong Kong even to pretend to be a member of a triad society, and participation in triad ceremonies could result in a three-year jail term. The anti-triads statutes, or the "Societies Ordinance" as they are called today, still stand and are, very selectively, enforced today in Hong Kong.

It was in the last quarter of the nineteenth century that a definite connection was established between triads and criminal activity. In 1886 three Chinese men who had informed on triad members were found stabbed to death, and a Chinese member of the appointed Hong Kong Legislative Council was threatened with death by the triads. A committee of three Chinese justices of the peace reported to the government that there were approximately fifteen thousand triad members in the Crown colony involved in many crimes, including extortion, bribery, assault, and unlicensed opium trafficking. There were even police and government civil servants in the triads, according to the study, and many of the guilds and associations that helped the local Chinese people were in the control of the triads. A government crackdown resulted in a temporary curbing of their activities in the late 1880s.

At the turn of the century, the triads, in keeping with their original political goals, supported Dr. Sun Yat-sen's successful 1911 revolution, which finally overthrew the hated Manchu Ch'ing dynasty, establishing the first republican government in China. There is strong evidence that Dr. Sun Yat-sen himself was a red pole (enforcer) in the Green Gang, or the Three Harmonies Society (San Ho-Hui), a triad society. It is even alleged by some historians that in a secret meeting in Shanghai in 1894, Dr. Sun Yat-sen met with Charlie Soong (also known as Charlie Jones Soong from his American days), the founder of the so-called Soong Dynasty (a powerful family in China throughout the twentieth century) and himself a triad member, and other triad leaders who pledged their support to him in exchange for Sun's sacred vow to rid China of the Ch'ing regime.* Other scholars state that at a secret meeting in Hong Kong in 1890, Sun Yat-sen and his followers formed a new triad, the Chung Wo Tong Triad Society, as "an external base for a political struggle to overcome the Manchu dynasty."** Shortly after his victory in February 1912, Sun Yat-sen made a pilgrimage to the tombs of the Ming emperors and publicly declared that the Ch'ing dynasty had finally been overthrown.†

Despite the success of the revolution, there was a lot of in-fighting within Dr. Sun Yat-sen's circle, and the newly elected president resigned just four months after being elected. In 1921 Dr. Sun re-emerged as the dominant force in southern China, where he was made the president of a self-proclaimed republic, but after his death in 1925, China broke down into warring factions, with both the Communists and the Kuomintang party (KMT), led by Sun's former aide, Chiang Kai-shek, claiming to be Dr. Sun's true heirs.

In the 1920s and 1930s, General Chiang Kai-shek, a former Green Gang triad soldier, with the support of the triads and warlords, fought the Communists for control of the country, ruthlessly using the might of his triad supporters in the populous, thriving port of Shanghai, which was his headquarters. One of his major triad partners was longtime friend and criminal colleague, Tu Yueh Sheng, known as "Big Eared" Tu, the dragon

---

* For a detailed analysis of Sun Yat-sen's alleged triad affiliations and his connection to the famous Soong family, which included Dr. Sun and Chiang Kai-shek among others, see Sterling Seagrave's fascinating 1985 study, *The Soong Dynasty*. See also Barbara Ward's essay, "Chinese Secret Societies" in *Secret Societies*, edited by Norman MacKenzie. Many other modern books on the triads and on Hong Kong history listed in the bibliography emphatically state that Dr. Sun was a triad member. There is little doubt that Chiang Kai-shek was a triad officer too.

** Richard Deacon is a pseudonym for a London journalist/scholar who wrote several books on the British Secret Service. This information is from his fascinating 1974 book, *The Chinese Secret Service*.

† Dr. Sun Yat-sen's statues are today found world-wide, even in the heart of cosmopolitan Toronto in Riverdale Park.

head of the Green Gang triad who ran the criminal underworld of Shanghai and became known as the Opium King. During the late thirties, when the Japanese invaded China, Chiang briefly had a Chinese nationalistic alliance with Mao against the Japanese occupation, but he later betrayed Mao and secretly allied himself with the Japanese against Mao, to wipe out the communists once and for all. When the Communist forces, under the leadership of Mao Tse-tung, finally triumphed after the civil war in the late forties, Chiang and his followers were forced out of mainland China. Many of the triad leaders who remained in China were executed.

Of those triad officers and members who fled, most, like Big Eared Tu, went to Hong Kong; others turned up in Singapore, Malaya, England, North America, and even Australia, where new triads were established. A great many of the triad bosses escaped to the island of Taiwan with General Chiang Kai-shek, who in 1949 set up a Chinese government in exile there. Just as Chiang Kai-shek's political party, the KMT, had earlier relied heavily on triad financial and physical support to stay in power in China, so Chiang continued to use the triads in Taiwan, where a new triad, the Chu Lien Pang, or the United Bamboo, later emerged. Today the United Bamboo has branches in Hong Kong, Europe, New York City, and California.

During World War II, after the brutal Japanese invasion and occupation of Hong Kong (during which two thousand Allies, mostly young, inexperienced Canadians, were either killed or imprisoned under savage conditions while trying to defend the Crown colony), the triads made an accommodation with the new Japanese overlords, much as Chiang and his triad colleagues had done during the occupation of China. Some triads even provided an unofficial espionage arm for the Japanese, who essentially let the triads carry on their normal business, unlike Mussolini in Italy, who brutally put down the Mafia when he seized power, or Mao Tse-tung, for that matter, who was anything but gentle towards the triads.

After the war the triads in Hong Kong proliferated. In the early fifties, they precipitated a serious crisis in Hong Kong by organizing violent student riots during which many citizens were killed or seriously injured. The Royal Hong Kong Police (RHKP) and the government of Hong Kong were pressured to put a lid on the triads. But in the mid-sixties, there was once again a series of deadly disturbances in the colony, the so-called Star Ferry riots. This time the rioting was primarily organized as a political tactic by the Communists and the left-wing opposition, though the triads certainly took advantage of the confusion. As a result the Royal Hong Kong Police set up a new special squad on triads, known as the Triad Society Bureau. A public outcry led to a major police crackdown and the imposition of new legislation that allowed police to hold people without charges. More than ten thousand triad officials and members were arrested and more than four hundred of the top triad officers were deported, most to Taiwan, according to police records.

One of the major triads in Hong Kong is the 14 K Triad Society, which was established by nationalists from China who fled to Hong Kong after World War II. The 14 K, so named because its predecessor organization was headquartered at number 14 Po Wah Road in Canton, now has control of one of the major heroin-trafficking routes into Europe and North America. In 1968 the Tak Group of the 14 K Triad Society was formed; in 1972 a formerly non-triad painter's guild, the Kwong Hung Society, became a triad; and in 1973 there was a mass initiation ceremony of new members to the Wo Shing Wo Society in Macao. By 1974 the Royal Hong Kong Police felt that there were definite signs of a triad renaissance in Hong Kong.

These were some of the highlights of a mid-eighties "confidential" Royal Hong Kong Police Force report on the triads entitled *Triads and Their Involvement in Organized Crime in Hong Kong*, which summarized triad events in Hong Kong in the 1970s. The force had undertaken a review of the triad problem in 1976 that stated there had not been any reduction in triad numbers nor any "significant disruption of Triad activities" over the past years. One of the problems the police said they were having in combating the triads was the "indefinite composition" of the triads. It was decided that emphasis had to be placed on investigating the criminal activities of the triads. Some in the RHKP in the late 1970s thought that triads had simply "degenerated into loose-knit gangs of criminals which usurp the names of Triad Societies of years past." But by 1983 this was considered too rosy a view, as "the triad problem has become more serious in the last five years."

One of the problems noted in the RHKP report of 1983 was that "the Force had no established criminal intelligence system," and that RHKP involvement itself with triads at many levels was far more serious than had been realized previously, leading to what was gently called "the input of misleading information" into the triad files by RHKP officers. The collusion of certain top police officials with the triads and the drug syndicates was one of the most serious dilemmas facing Hong Kongers. Indeed, in the frank words of the RHKP report itself, the "main cause of the triad revival" in the late 1970s and early 1980s was "syndicated Police corruption." Many of these triad-corrupted policemen, including the notorious five dragons, eventually came to Canada in the 1970s to invest some of their criminal proceeds.

Because the triad problem had been understated from the mid-1970s until 1983, the force was caught unprepared in 1983 when a power struggle erupted between the powerful Sun Yee On triad and the Wo Shing Wo triad in the red light district of Yau Ma Tei. In the revelatory conclusion of the thorough Royal Hong Kong Police report, the triad problem was neither minimized nor exaggerated. It said that there were thirty-three known triad societies operating in the colony, ranging from groups with memberships as small as one hundred to larger societies such as the Sun Yee On, which was thought to have from ten thousand to twenty thousand members. Total triad membership was estimated to be between 70,000 and 120,000, though this figure included many inactive members who were no longer involved in criminal activities. The triads had central committees of elected office bearers. Once in office, a person "with money, a strong personality and a power base" could turn a triad society into "a very effective fighting unit."

No one triad society was found to have a monopoly on any single criminal activity. In fact, it was up to individual members and officials how they made their money. However, several triad societies were found to have a "dominance" over one or more specific areas in Hong Kong. For example, in the red light district of Wanchai, the Wo Hop To Triad Society was the most active triad in the extortion and protection rackets.

The RHKP report concluded that the triad societies were far from defunct — "but very much alive" — and the triad societies were "a *major* threat to law and order." They were involved in many aspects of everyday life in Hong Kong, from extortion of street vendors to control of whole industries, including certain sectors of the construction and real estate industries. As well, they dominated auto theft gangs, drug-trafficking groups, counterfeit money operations, and fraudulent credit card rings.

Alleged senior members of the Sun Yee On triad who were prosecuted in the mid-1980s under the anti-triad laws included politicians and other members of the establishment in Hong Kong. Although they were convicted in 1988, the convictions were later overturned in an appeal. Since the late 1980s, there have not been any more attempts to use the anti-triad statutes to get at the leadership of the triads.

Various government-run campaigns in Hong Kong against the triads and corruption have contained but not stopped triad activity. These campaigns have included everything from the special Royal Hong Kong Police's Triad Society Bureau (TSB), which closely monitors the triad leadership and enforcement of the anti-triad laws; to the Independent Commission Against Corruption (known locally as the ICAC), established in 1974, which targets bribery and corruption of the civil service and police to the civilian-run Triad Renunciation Tribunal, which sponsors graphic anti-triad advertising on television, in newspapers, and on billboards throughout Hong Kong on the dangers of joining a triad and how to get out of one if you are already a member. Many triads threaten members with death if they attempt to leave the society. There is even a government form that hundreds have signed over the past few years that grants the signatory (after an independent confirmation of the facts by the Triad Renunciation Tribunal) immunity and officially takes him out of the triad by ensuring the bureaucratic paperwork that he will not be prosecuted for his former triad life. Today in Hong Kong there is legislation pending, similar to the powerful American Racketeer-Influenced and Corrupt Organizations Act (RICO), which has recently been responsible in the United States for putting hundreds of Mafia leaders, including John Gotti, out of business and in jail for life. The new Hong Kong legislation would allow the government to seize the assets of convicted triad members and give them much longer prison terms after proving in court a lengthy pattern of organized criminal activity.

There have also been mass marches in Hong Kong against the triads. In mid-January 1992, for example, a number of Hong Kong-based film stars, including popular soft-porn star Amy Yip, marched for a crackdown against triad violence. In Hong Kong entertainers are often targets of triad extortions, though some famous Cantonese actors have bit parts in the real world as triad members — ceremonial officers, and in at least one case, a triad dragon head. The triads also have control and influence over certain Hong Kong-based film production studios that churn out hundreds of Cantonese gangster pictures, the kind that often portray triad leaders as glamorous role models in the same way that Hollywood has often romanticized Mafia leaders.

The reality is anything but glamorous. Recently, in April 1992, a prominent Hong Kong film producer, Choi Chi Ming, of Fully International Film Distribution, was shot to death as he emerged from an elevator in his office building in Hong Kong. Royal Hong Kong Police said that he was murdered by one of the triads because he had been laundering drug profits, and Choi had allegedly skimmed off some of the illicit money for himself. According to a senior police officer, Choi personally had also been in the heroin trade with the triads in Holland. In the murky, cut-throat world of the triads in Hong Kong, nothing is ever as it appears to be.

Chapter Two

THE TONG WARS
The Hatchetmen of New York and San Francisco

The bloody tong wars in several major U.S. cities from 1875 to the late 1920s brought to the public's attention the organized crime activities rampant in many of the major Chinatowns across North America. By the 1920s the Chinese gangs in Canada and the United States were already involved in crimes that would later become their staples — illegal gambling, prostitution, alien smuggling, extortion rackets, drug trafficking, violent assaults, corruption of public officials, and infiltration of legitimate Chinese community organizations. Serious tong rivalries also resulted in a number of murders that were luridly splashed across the front pages of North American newspapers. The pulp magazines also exploited the tong wars in many overwrought fictional stories with titles such as "It's Raining Corpses in Chinatown" and "Dragon Lord of the Underworld."*

---

* For an analysis of the popular "yellow peril" stories of the period, see Don Hutchison's well-researched essay, "Yellow Shadows," which introduces his entertaining sampling of some of the classic pulp magazine pieces of this theme in his book, *It's Raining Corpses in Chinatown*. Sax Rohmer's Fu Manchu thrillers are the most celebrated novels on this theme. The many Fu Manchu films of the twenties and thirties made Rohmer's sinister fictional characters, as well as his detective, Charlie Chan, very well known around the world.

As described earlier, the tongs were originally benevolent associations established to help Chinese immigrants become part of a network and ease the way into their life in the United States. Starting in the middle of the nineteenth century, Chinese immigrants, mostly from southern China in the area around Canton — Toishan, Sun We, Yan Ping, and Hoi Ping, known collectively as the Four Districts — came to the west coast of North America to work as cheap labour first in the gold fields and later on the railroads. Their numbers grew from just two in 1848 to more than thirty thousand by 1870 and more than one hundred thousand by the first decade of the twentieth century. In order to make their life less monotonous, organizers in the new Chinese communities, led mostly by the new tongs, provided gambling clubs and activities, opium dens, and women for the predominantly single men working out west. There was also a lively (and legal) slave trade in healthy young Oriental women and girls. From 1870 until the end of the first decade of the twentieth century, there were "22.5 whores to every 100 inhabitants in Chinatown" according to Lynn Pan, who noted that "females were precious commodities, bitterly fought over by rival gangs."

The selling of women was pervasive in the Chinese community in North America at the time. Women were sold at open markets in San Francisco, where many highly organized Chinese houses of prostitution were also operating. After gambling houses, prostitution was the most lucrative activity in the city's Chinatown. There were hundreds of "cribs" in the poorer section of Chinatown where girls, usually dressed in sexy black silk, were packed into tiny one-storey shacks, some as small as twelve by fourteen feet. Chinatown also offered prostitutes in many "parlour houses," elegantly furnished places where up to thirty Oriental girls were available in more comfortable surroundings. The girls and young women, who ranged in age from as young as two to their early twenties, were brought in in bulk by ship. "The backbone of prostitution in San Francisco was a system of slavery under which girls were owned and bartered as if they were cattle," stated an elegantly written 1930s' account of vice in Chinatown in the period.* The girls and young women were brought in at an average cost of under $100, but were sold in San Francisco for as much as $1,000 each. At first the importation of young women was legal, but after the United States tightened its immigration laws in the late nine-teenth century, the women had to be smuggled into the United States by crate, often via Canadian ports. It is conservatively estimated that by the turn of the century there were more than two thousand prostitutes in San Francisco alone. The tongs got a percentage from the importation of the females, but most of them were brought in by individual slave traders via China steamers.

The first tong war in North America was over a woman. It started in 1875 in San Francisco. Low Sing, a member of the Suey Sing tong, was found groaning in the middle of an inter-section in Chinatown by San Francisco police. His skull had been split by a hatchet, which lay nearby. The *boo how doy* or "highbinders," a term that came from the police street name for Irish hoodlums, were the enforcers and professional hit men of the tongs who used ceremonial but deadly hatchets in their executions, thus becoming known as the hatchetmen. There had been no witnesses to the attack on Low Sing. He told his colleagues that Ming Long of the Kwong Dock tong (which meant, ironically, "a broadening of the humane side of man") had tried to kill him because of a young woman. Ming Long had been an enforcer for Chinese gambling and prostitution orga-nizers in the railway camps and gold mines where Chinese were working. Low Sing had fallen in love with Kim Ho, the "Golden Peach," and had been trying to buy her freedom. Ming Long became his rival for her affections.

After hearing of Low Sing's attack, the Suey Sing tong leaders challenged Ming Long and his tong to a battle on a major

---

*   Herbert Asbury's *The Barbary Coast: An Informal History of the San Francisco Underworld*. Asbury goes on to state that "four Chinamen in the middle of the eighteen seventies owned 800 girls, ranging in age from two to sixteen years."

intersection in San Francisco's Chinatown. It was a question of the tong's honour. According to tong leader Eddie Gong, who wrote the first reasonably complete history of the tong wars in 1930, the challenge, which was signed and sealed by the Suey Sing tong leadership, read:

The Kwong Dock Tong is hereby sincerely and earnestly requested to send its best fighting men to Waverly Place at midnight tomorrow to meet our boo how doy. If this challenge is ignored, the Kwong Dock tong must admit defeat and make compensation and apologize for the assault upon Low Sing. However, we sincerely hope that the Kwong Dock tong will accept this challenge.*

The Kwong Dock tong replied within the hour with a posted message of their own, and the hatchetmen for both tongs were soon in the streets to begin the war. Hundreds of observers watched from windows and placed bets on which side would win. There were at least twenty-five tong hatchetmen on each side. Eddie Gong stated that the police were not called because many of them were on the take anyway, and because "in those days the Chinese minded their own business. No appeals were made to the police." Eddie Gong and Bruce Grant vividly describe the scene in *Tong War*:

---

* Eng Ying Gong's (Eddie Gong) excellent book with New York City journalist Bruce Grant, *TONG WAR!: The First Complete History of the Tongs in America; details of the tong wars and their causes; lives of famous hatchetmen and gunmen; and inside information as to the inner workings of the Tongs, their aims and achievements*, covers the history in great detail as does Asbury's accounts of the underworld history in New York City and San Francisco. Gong was a Hip Sing tong leader for twenty years and owned a restaurant at the Bloody Angle at Doyers and Pell Streets. Gong's brother was the longtime head of the rival On Leong tong, the largest tong in the United States. In his own two books that recount the drama of the tong wars in San Francisco and New York (*The Barbary Coast* and *The Gangs of New York*), crime journalist and historian Herbert Asbury borrowed some details from Gong's book.

Silently, sometimes singly and sometimes in pairs or threes, the hatchetmen began to arrive at Waverly Place. On one side of the street were the boo how doy of the Suey Sing Tong and on the other the boo how doy of the Kwong Dock Tong. The highbinders, who were the best fighters of both tongs, had wound their queues about their heads, wore black, slouch hats well down over their eyes, walked with their hands folded indolently across their abdomens and with their knives, daggers, clubs and hatchets stuck in their six-foot long silken belts beneath their large blouses.

Herbert Asbury, who in 1933 wrote about the San Francisco tong war in two chapters of his "informal" look at the San Francisco underworld, *The Barbary Coast*, finished the story:

. . . Promptly at midnight the leaders of both sides began screaming insults. After a moment or two of this sort of preparation, they gave the signal, and with a flash of knives and hatchets, the boo how doy rushed forward and clashed in the centre of the street. For at least fifteen minutes the hatchetmen fought with great ferocity, and the tide of the battle surged back and forth while the spectators leaned over the balcony railings and the window-sills and cheered or groaned, accordingly as they had placed their bets . . . .

Gong and Grant's account makes the crowd of onlookers look a little less bloodthirsty than Asbury's, as they added that "many persons watching the sanguinary conflict from the windows and balconies withdrew from the sight and smell of so much blood." Finally the police arrived. By then nine men had been seriously wounded — six Kwong Docks and three Suey Sings; three of the Kwong Docks and one of the Suey Sings later died of their wounds. According to Gong, "The police gathered the wounded without making a single arrest. Five minutes later Chinatown was as quiet as a factory at noon hour. The police never learned what the trouble was about." Nobody had seen anything, the police were told. Amazingly, Low Sing recovered and later married and lived happily ever after with the Golden Peach. According to Gong and Grant, Ming Long, the hatchetman who had attempted to murder Low Sing, was forced to flee to China "where by the code, vengeance is never carried." The Suey Sing tong had won the war and it grew in prestige in Chinatown.

Many other tong wars ensued over the next fifty years, but none in San Francisco was as intense or spectacular as the first. At one point there were as many as twelve active tongs in the west. Some of them fought violent tong wars, while others operated quietly as free mason associations. The Hip Sing tong, the second to be organized in San Francisco, began with only fifty members but later became the only tong with branches from coast to coast, including one in New York City. It remains a major power in that city's Chinatown even in the 1990s.

One of the most colourful hatchetmen in San Francisco was the poet Hong Ah Kay, whom everyone referred to as Ah because of his gentleness and scholarly manner. According to Asbury, Ah Kay was a killer of great renown who ranked "with the best of the gunmen produced by the white man's gangland." In one tong battle, Ah Kay "split the skulls of seven foes with seven blows," for which he was honoured by his tong. However, the law took a dimmer view of his dubious achievement, and he was later hanged. There were also characters such as Yee Toy, known as "The Girl" because of his delicate features that belied the efficient practice of his trade, who groomed his victims after he killed them; and Sing Dock, known as "the Scientific Killer" because of his meticulous planning of the details of every murder.

The best known and most successful of all of San Francisco's tong leaders was Fung Jing Toy, known by everyone as "Little Pete." A notorious gangster, he had a long and prosperous reign of more than ten years as the head of the Sum Yop tong, or the Three District Men's Association, as well as other tongs. Eddie Gong, who had grown up with the legend of Little Pete and who had once met with the tong leader's assassin, devoted two chapters alone to his story in *Tong War*. Little Pete, who was only five years old when he came to San Francisco from his native Canton, quickly rose as a major power in Chinatown. By his early twenties, he was running gambling houses and opium dens and had a piece of the slave trade. By his twenty-fifth birthday, Little Pete was the undisputed leader of the Sum Yop, said to be responsible for more than fifty murders in Chinatown. His first major rivalry was with the Four District Men. Through connections with the police on his payroll, he was able to have all his rivals' gambling houses closed. After one of his hatchetmen was arrested for murder in 1887, Little Pete attempted to bribe the district attorney as well as members of the jury. Convicted of attempted bribery and sent to San Quentin for five years, Little Pete became stronger than ever when he emerged from jail and entered into an alliance with a local political boss, Christopher Buckley, whom Little Pete called the Blind White Devil. With Buckley's support, Little Pete became the king of Chinatown vice and collected money from every brothel, opium den, and gambling house in Chinatown no matter which tong they were associated with. If they didn't pay him, Little Pete had the clubs closed by the police. They would then re-open under Little Pete's control. Seeking to expand his power base outside Chinatown, Little Pete also got involved in the race tracks of San Francisco, bribing jockeys and even having horses whom he was betting against killed, if necessary, to keep them from winning. He was guarded by two fierce dogs and his own *boo how doy*, as well as by hired white detectives who acted as enforcers and bodyguards.

Little Pete was untouchable. People in Chinatown lived in fear of him. Finally, perhaps inevitably, all twelve of the tongs in Chinatown, including his own Sum Yop, united to bring him down. A secret tong trial was held and found Pete guilty. A huge bounty was put on his head, and tong killers roamed Chinatown trying to find and murder him. But Little Pete was well guarded.

Little Pete was in his barbershop, just as was Albert Anastasia of Murder Inc. many years later, when he was finally assassinated, shot to death by two hit men brought in from Portland,

Oregon, especially for the murder by the leader of the Suey Sing tong. The hit men managed to escape after the killing, eventually returning to China. Four other men who had been near the barbershop at the time were charged with the assassination but were later acquitted.

Little Pete's funeral was one of the biggest and most spectacular San Francisco had ever seen. The cortège was more than a mile long, and firecrackers, three Chinese bands, and scores of black-gowned priests as well as many wagons laden with meats, rice, and tea accompanied the hearse. A gang of white hoodlums who had been involved in racist anti-Chinese activity attacked the mourners at the cemetery and stole the food.

As a result of the murder, hatchetmen of the Sum Yop tong still loyal to Little Pete began a massacre of other Sum Yop members. The bloodshed was stopped only by the personal intervention of the last emperor of China, who arranged to have most of the relatives of the Sum Yops in China imprisoned until the killing in San Francisco ended. A peace treaty was soon signed in San Francisco between the two warring tongs. Although there were other smaller tong wars later, things quieted down in San Francisco's Chinatown after the big 1906 earthquake.

Things were far from quiet across the continent in New York City, which by 1900 had its own tong war. The Chinese population had grown since 1858 when Ah Ken, an immigrant from Canton, arrived and set up his cigar store on Mott Street. By 1868 he was joined by another Chinese immigrant, Wah Kee, who ran a thriving fruit and vegetable business on nearby Pell Street. Upstairs, Kee also ran a very profitable gambling and opium den. The police were paid off, and soon there were many other thriving gambling and opium dens in the area. By 1872 there were seven hundred Chinese living in Chinatown. When the railroads were mostly completed, Chinese migration began to move from the west to the east. "If the pioneer spirit in the Chinese sent them across the seas," observed Eddie Gong, "it was a greater spirit of adventure that made them plough on Eastward." By "the east," most Chinese meant the immigrant capital, the burgeoning metropolis of New York City. By the Gay Nineties, in just three short, crowded, tenement-filled streets in the heart of a bustling Chinatown, right next to crowded Little Italy, there were more than two hundred gambling clubs and opium dens. But the actual Chinese population until the post-war period was never more than ten to fifteen thousand, and there were only two tongs in New York City, the On Leong and the Hip Sing. New York City was no San Francisco.

Traditionally (and to some extent this is still the case) the Hip Sing controlled Pell Street, the On Leong tong ran Mott Street, and both tongs shared the action on the smaller Doyers Street. At the corner of the tiny but neutral Doyers Street and Pell Street is the so-called Bloody Angle, where some of the most horrific fights took place. The On Leong tong was the larger and more influential, but the Hip Sing, with its roots in the west and across the country, always had ambitions to take over from the On Leong in New York.

The tong wars in New York, fought mostly over control of the gambling houses and opium dens, began in 1899. In the heart of New York City's small but lively Chinatown at the turn of the century, while Irving Berlin played the piano and sang at the Chatam Club at 6 Doyers Street and around the corner at the Pelham Club, downstairs from an opium den at 12 Pell Street, hatchetmen from the city's two tongs fought it out to the death in the street outside.

There were many Chinese games of chance played in the numerous gambling houses in the area, but the two most popular were *pai gow*, a Chinese form of dominoes, and *fan tan*, an ancient Chinese game that uses porcelain buttons placed in an inverted silver cup and moved around. After the bets are placed, the cup is lifted and the buttons are counted off in groups of four until there are only one to four buttons left. Bets are then made as to how many buttons will be left at the end of the count.

Along Doyers, Pell, and Mott streets, there were also many opium-smoking divans, usually located in dark, dank base-ments, where customers smoked opium from pipes while lying on a cot or mattress. New York's Chinatown was wide open, as the police were paid off handsomely — each opium and gambling dive paid at least $20 a week to the cops; some paid the police $25 for each *fan tan* and *pai gow* table. Less money was paid directly to the two tongs and a percentage of the profits went to the Gamblers' Union, which was also controlled by the tongs.

Tom Lee, the long-serving head of the powerful On Leong tong, was the unofficial "Mayor of Chinatown" and the boss of most of the gambling in Chinatown. He was so wealthy and powerful and so revered in the community that Tom Foley, the sheriff of New York County, actually made him a deputy sheriff. A tall, bearded, dignified man, Lee strutted around Chinatown, always with heavily armed bodyguards at each side, in his magnificent suit of chain mail with his sheriff's badge proudly on his chest.

Lee's rule went essentially unchallenged until the arrival in 1900 of Mock Duck (a.k.a. Mark Dock), known also in the local tabloids as the Chinese Kid Dropper, a fierce hatchetman who always carried two guns and a hatchet and had as his goal to overthrow Tom Lee and the On Leongs. He was a powerful and fearless man; alone one day, according to Asbury in *The Gangs of New York*, he was attacked and stabbed on both shoulders by two hatchetmen, but nonetheless "leapt up, the blades of the knives buried in both sinew and muscle, [and] grabbed these men and knocked their heads together, stunning them." A few weeks later, "he was as fit as ever . . . . Few men were shot at as much as Mock Duck." Asbury wrote in 1928 that he was also "a notable gambler in a race of gamblers" who would bet on anything — "he was known to have waged his entire wealth on whether the number of seeds in an orange he picked at random from a fruit cart was odd or even."

Mock Duck also gambled on getting control of the small Hip Sing tong from its feeble leader. He accomplished this within a year and increased the membership of the weaker New York tong. He also allied the Hip Sing to the Four Brothers Society, a powerful family guild made up of four New York City-based Chinese families who were bound together by oaths their ancestors had taken hundreds of years earlier. Mock Duck immediately demanded that Tom Lee give the Hip Sing tong a half interest in the gambling in Chinatown. Lee laughed. Several weeks later two of Lee's men died in a fire that mysteriously levelled an On Leong boarding house on Pell Street. Lee ordered the death of a Hip Sing member. Mock Duck immediately declared war on the On Leong — a deadly war that was to last several years. Mock Duck and his new ally, the Four Brothers, tried desperately to arrange the assassination of Tom Lee, even bringing in the best hatchetmen from San Francisco, including Sing Dock (the "Scientific" assassin) and Yee Toy ("The Girl"). But though Mock Duck's killers came close (once they shot at him in his bed but only hit his alarm clock!), they didn't succeed.

In desperation, Mock Duck became a police informer. He went to Frank Moss, an assistant attorney and former police commissioner who supported Dr. Parkhurst's (reform) Society by collecting information and evidence on illegal activities in Chinatown. Parkhurst was a Methodist minister who waged campaigns against what he called "the evils in Chinatown." Mock Duck gave Moss the exact locations of the On Leong brothels, gambling houses, and opium dens and told him how and when they were operating. Armed with Mock Duck's exact information, Moss pressured the police to act, but as fast as the police closed Lee's establishments, Mock Duck re-opened them under Hip Sing management. Tom Lee protested in vain to the authorities.

There were also bloody gunfights in the streets of Chinatown between On Leong and Hip Sing warriors. During one battle, an innocent bystander was killed by stray bullets, but most of the actual combatants came away with only bruises, protected as they were by bullet-proof vests. Then, in November 1904, Mock Duck himself was shot in the hip while walking down Pell Street. When he got out of the hospital three weeks later, he was out for blood. The streets were littered with On Leong hatchetmen. As the battles got more intense and men began dying on both sides, New York State judge Warren Foster was brought in as an arbitrator. Finally, in 1906 Foster invited the leaders of the Hip Sing and the On Leong to his home, where they signed a formal peace treaty. This document formalized the arrangement by which the On Leong controlled Mott Street, the Hip Sing, Pell Street; Doyers Street was to remain neutral territory. There were celebrations in the streets over the new peace.

But peace was short-lived; within a week a Hip Sing hatchet-man was killed by an On Leong gunman and the war was on again. Six months later yet another treaty was signed, this time under the auspices of the Chinese government as well as Judge Foster. Even this peace lasted only three years.

The next tong war, which started in 1909, began over the murder of a teenage girl. Bow Kum, known as Little Sweet Flower, was a sixteen-year-old Cantonese slave girl who had been bought by Low Hee Tong, a leader of the Hip Sing tong's ally, the Four Brothers. But after four years of living with the girl, the authorities asked Low Hee Tong to produce a marriage licence during a raid on his house. When he couldn't do so, Little Sweet Flower was seized and placed in a mission, where an On Leong tong member named Tchin Len found and later married her. When Low Hee Tong demanded at least the money he had paid for the girl, Len refused. Low Hee Tong petitioned the leadership of the Hip Sing and the Four Brothers for assistance. Len and the On Leong leadership ignored their requests for repayment. Finally, in August 1909, the red flag of the highbinder was raised at the Hip Sing tong houses on Pell Street, and war was also declared on the corner billboards in bold red lettering. Several days later Hip Sing hatchetmen raided Tchin Len's home and murdered Little Sweet Flower, cutting off her fingers and stabbing her a number of times in the heart. The tong war then entered a new and deadly stage, with random bombings of many houses in Chinatown, during which a large number of people were killed and wounded.

A few months after the murder of Little Sweet Flower, a

bloody new round of the tong war was precipitated by the performances of a well-known comedian connected to the On Leongs. Ah Hoon performed regularly at the Chinese Theater next to the Bloody Angle on Doyers Street, and as part of his regular routine, the popular Ah Hoon made jokes about the Hip Sings and the Four Brothers. They, however, were not amused and decided that Ah Hoon had to be killed. As a courtesy, the Hip Sing hit men informed Ah Hoon that his performance on December 30, 1909, would be his last. He was even told the exact time of his execution. It was an odd sight that evening, as Ah Hoon went through his monologue, now sanitized of jokes about the Hip Sings, with three uniformed New York City policemen summoned by a friend of the terrified comedian and led by Chief Inspector John Coughlin, sitting on the stage next to the comic. The theatre was very crowded, as Asbury told the story, "for word of the impending tragedy had spread throughout Chinatown." It was standing room only for what was billed as Ah Hoon's last performance. But nothing happened to Ah Hoon at the appointed hour. "Fearing the police," Asbury explained, "the Hip Sing went back on their sworn word and did not kill Ah Hoon."

But the reprieve didn't last long. After the show Ah Hoon was taken back to his apartment in Chatham Square guarded by heavily armed On Leong hatchetmen. His apartment, which had just one window, faced a blank wall, but guards were posted outside his locked door as well as on the street. During the night, a Hip Sing gunman was lowered down the narrow space between the buildings in a boatswain's chair and shot Ah Hoon through the window. When his downstairs neighbour, Hoochy-Coochy Mary, came for him in the morning, he was dead, shot through the heart.

The murder of the hugely popular comedian "caused the flashing of hatchets and blazing of revolvers all through the Chinese quarters," according to Asbury. He wrote,

The climax of the war came on New Year's Night. [The Chinese Theater] was filled with spectators, for this was the great Chinese celebration of the Year, and a report had been industriously circulated that the warring tongs had arranged a truce. The performance went on verve and fire, but suddenly someone threw a bunch of lighted fire-crackers into the air over a row of orchestra seats. They snapped and popped, and the crowd milled about in a panic. But pistols snapped and popped also during the excitement and when the audience left the building five On Leong men did not move: they had been killed quickly and efficiently under the cover of the exploding fireworks.*

Though Mock Duck was eventually arrested for the crime, there was no evidence against him, and charges were later dropped. He never did go to jail for the many murders he had arranged or committed himself, but he was finally sent to Sing Sing for six months in 1912 for operating a gambling racket. When Mock Duck emerged, the carnage in New York continued. Tom Lee pleaded for an end to the bloodshed as he feared a clean-up campaign by the authorities. Finally the captain of the police precinct near Chinatown, William Hodgins, with the backing of the Chinese merchants and residents, organized another peace conference. But the Hip Sing resisted and the fighting continued until 1910 when the Chinese ambassador in Washington appointed the Committee of Forty, made up of Chinese merchants, students, and residents, to arbitrate the dispute. This uneasy peace held together until 1912 when a new tong, the Kim Lan Wui Saw, challenged both the Hip Sing and the On Leong. A new treaty was arranged by the Chinese government and the New York City police and was signed on May 22, 1913, by all sides — including all the tongs and the Chinese Merchants Association.

Miraculously, the peace in Chinatown lasted for more than ten years. Then a short but bloody tong war began in 1924 when several expelled On Leong members joined the Hip Sing, taking with them a great deal of On Leong cash. Most of the fighting

---

* Herbert Asbury, *The Gangs of New York*.

in this war was not in Chinatown, but in Brooklyn and the Bronx, where several Chinese restaurant owners and laundry owners were killed. Several other tong wars broke out in the mid- to late twenties in San Francisco, Chicago, Boston, Portland, Oregon, and Seattle, as well as in Le Grande, Washington, a town on the Oregon Trail with only one hundred Chinese, where the Hip Sings fought the Hop Sings for one side of a street.

When asked by reporters in 1930 who had won the tong wars, Eddie Gong was succinct: "No one won. Both sides lost," though he also maintained that the On Leong lost more money (about $1 million). As a tong member himself, Gong pointed out that the main victims of the tongs — more than seventy people slaughtered in the streets of New York — were mostly members of rival tongs and only rarely had "neutrals" or Americans been killed. When asked who was in the right in the battle for New York City between the On Leongs and the Hip Sings, Gong was philosophical:

> Both tongs have the same joss god [the traditional Chinese source for good luck] on their altar, and each side prayed to this same god to aid it in destroying the other . . . . The God himself must have been confronted with a puzzling problem. Which side should he favour? Both sides revered him equally, and burnt as much incense to him. He must have been a harassed divinity.*

What did it all mean? Gong concluded that "human nature is odd among the Chinese, as well as [it is with] any other race." Gong added a final reflection to his 1930 history of the tong wars. "The tong stands forth as the strongest organization to promote the welfare of the Chinese in America. The only drawback is the tong war with its dread toll of lives. But I feel, as every other Chinese feels, that these wars are to become a thing of the past, and that the pages of tong history will no longer record such bloody deeds as those of Hong Ah Kay, Sing

---

* Gong and Grant, *op. cit*, p. 266.

Dock, Big Queue Wai, Yee Toy and scores of other highbinders, and hatchetmen, and gunmen." Curiously, while explaining how the Chinese Benevolent Society helped to keep the peace in Chinatown, Gong never mentioned the triads, which were already operating in North America, and especially in Hong Kong and elsewhere, at the time.

Today the tongs are still very active, especially in New York and San Francisco, but the triads and the newer Chinese and Vietnamese gangs have more than taken their place in violent and gruesome murders. But while tongs are no longer as bloody as they were earlier in the century, many still have criminal elements in their midst. In the 1970s and 1980s, killings in Chinatowns in Seattle, New York, and Boston were reminders of the old-style tong warfare. In his debriefing by Hong Kong police in 1983, Lau Wing Kui, the founder and one-time dragon head of the Toronto triad, the Kung Lok, told investigators that a Seattle massacre, where eleven people were killed in a shooting at a gambling house, was partially the result of an internal tong feud.

Chapter Three

GOLD MOUNTAIN
The Chinese in British Columbia

Chinese immigrants first came to Canada in large numbers in 1858, when gold fever hit the Fraser River area of British Columbia. By then many Chinese in the United States had become wealthy overnight by striking gold in California. Indeed, America had become known in China by the mid-nineteenth century as "gold mountain" (*gum shan*). But race riots against the Chinese working in California helped persuade a few thousand of their number to venture north to work in the gold mines in apparently peaceful Canada. But even here there was a backlash against Chinese immigrants, including several failed attempts in the 1860s to impose a discriminatory head tax on each Chinese immigrant.*

---

* Books that detail the early history of the Chinese in Canada include the extremely well-researched *From China to Canada: A History of the Chinese Communities in Canada*," by Harry Con, Ronald Con, Graham Johnson, Edgar Wickberg, and William Willmott; "*Chinatowns: Towns Within Cities in Canada* by David Chuenyan Lai; *The Chinese in Canada* by sociologist Peter S. Li; *In the Sea of Sterile Mountains: The Chinese in British Columbia* by journalist James Morton; and *Gold Mountain* by historian Anthony B. Chan. Also, there is Paul Yee's beautifully illustrated 1988 book, *Saltwater City: An Illustrated History of the Chinese in Canada*, which covers the history until the end of the nineteenth century. There certainly has been no shortage of books in the past few years on racism in British Columbia against the Chinese. One of the most scholarly is *White Man's Province: British Columbia Politicians and the Chinese and Japanese Immigrants, 1858–1914* by Patricia Roy.

As early as 1860, newspapers began to report on Chinese criminal activity in Canada. An editorial in the staid Victoria *Daily Colonist* on January 10, 1860, entitled "Chinese Gambling" discussed a decision by a police magistrate to throw out charges against a number of Chinese, including one Ah Pow, for playing *fan tan*, the traditional Chinese game of chance. The accused, it was pointed out, were released on a technicality, namely that *fan tan* (described in the article as "tantan") was not specifically listed in the Canadian legal code as unlawful. But the paper's editorial maintained that all gambling was unlawful and certainly the Supreme Court, if appealed to, would overturn the dismissal.

By 1861 many newspaper articles about Chinese were less neutral in tone. A story in the *Daily Colonist* about a Chinese gambling-house raid entitled "A Nest of Gambling" described police arresting dozens of "Chinamen" who were "rushing, shouting and tearing about the premises." A number of stories appeared throughout the next few years on the proliferation of Chinese gambling establishments operating in British Columbia. Soon the *Vancouver Daily World* had full-page exposés about "the horrible state of things in Chinatown" where "young girls [are] sold body and soul." "Chinatown," the paper thundered, was "infected with moral and physical leprosy, and upon Britain's free soil — the helpless are shackled." There was, indeed, a growing slave trade in Chinese girls at the time, and the story graphically detailed the horrors of the trade. But the article didn't stop there:

> The fact remains that in Christian Canada's banner city of
> Vancouver there are women of the worst kind and in a state

There are, in addition, numerous documents available under the Access to Information Act. Among many other documents, I found a hitherto classified account of the history of the Chinese in Canada prepared for the Immigration Department brass in Ottawa by longtime Vancouver Immigration Intelligence officer, Doug Sam. I interviewed Mr. Sam several times before his death in 1990 about the history and character of Chinese criminal activity in Canada.

of moral degradation alongside which the history of Babylon appears like a saintly record. Having opened up the matter, *The World* does not propose to allow the affairs to be a nine days' wonder, and there end. The evil must be rooted out and the moral atmosphere disinfected. *The World* first thought of delving into the nefarious traffic, but it has been deterred for several reasons . . . . The Chinese gamblers and women proprietors are past-masters in the art of duplicity and of cheating the devil. They can lie without a smile on their faces, and swear to it without winking.

Chinese labourers continued to arrive in great numbers even after the gold fever passed. In 1871, when British Columbia officially entered into Confederation, Sir John A. Macdonald's long promised completion of the Canadian Pacific Railway (CPR) was underway. Many hundreds of additional Chinese came in as labourers. In 1873 the Anti-Chinese League was established in Victoria. By 1879 there were more than six thousand Chinese in British Columbia, and the federal government set up the Select Committee on Chinese Labour and Immigration to allay the fears of many in British Columbia about the effects of Chinese immigration on jobs that might have otherwise gone to white citizens. Many of the witnesses before the Select Committee opposed Chinese immigration, and the final report of the committee recommended that Chinese labour should not be used on Canadian (Dominion) government public works projects and that large-scale Chinese immigration should be discouraged. But the government of Sir John A. Macdonald did not accept the recommendations as it did not want to interfere with the railway contractors.

At the peak of the Chinese influx, from 1881 to 1884, more than fifteen thousand Chinese from California and Hong Kong immigrated to British Columbia. A new backlash began immediately, with riots at railroad construction sites. Despite the fact that the Chinese workers, or coolies as they were called (from the Chinese for "bitter strength," *ku li*), were originally brought in by the CPR and other companies as disposable and very cheap labour, many British Columbians felt that they threatened their own jobs. The federal government commissioned the first of what was to be many commissions on alleged immigration abuses in 1884. It discovered, among other things, that many Oriental children were living in appalling conditions, often in sheds.

In 1881 a Chinese worker was killed during a riot against Orientals at a CPR construction site. As a deterrent to more massive Chinese immigration, the British Columbia government imposed a $15 gold licence fee for Chinese miners in 1884 and in 1886, a $10 head tax on all Chinese entering the province. This slowed immigration temporarily, for although four thousand Chinese entered the province in the first seven months of 1885, only an average of seven hundred a year came from 1886 until 1889. But there was still considerable racism against the Chinese, and in Vancouver in 1887 there were anti-Chinese riots in which several Chinese were seriously injured. The 1891 census revealed that Orientals now made up ten percent of the population of British Columbia — nine thousand of a total population of more than ninety thousand — and by 1895 there were more riots against the Orientals, one organized by a gang of hooligans after a boat docked with some Chinese immigrants. A considerable number of Chinese businesses were burned.

In 1896 the head tax was raised to $50 and just four years later to $100. The 1901 census determined that the Chinese population was sixteen thousand and growing fast. The government set up its third Royal Commission on alleged immigration fraud. There was more and more social unrest as an increasing number of British Columbians campaigned against the Chinese. Finally, in 1904, the government raised the head tax to a staggering $500 — at least $25,000 in today's money — which proved an effective block to immigration. Although 5,000 Chinese had come in the first half of 1903, only 120 Chinese entered Canada over the next three years.

In 1907, Chinese immigration began to take off again when local agents and merchants began to lend money to the new immigrants so they could afford to pay the hefty head tax. A racist group calling itself Asiatic Exclusion League demonstrated against the immigration and in favour of a "white Canada." There were a number of violent riots, the worst being the burning and looting of Vancouver's Chinatown in September 1907 by thousands of anti-Oriental hooligans and other racists.

The Opium Act was drafted as a direct result of this incident, one of the worst riots ever against Chinese in British Columbia, for which the newly founded Asiatic Exclusion League in Vancouver took some of the credit. The deputy minister of labour (and later prime minister), Mackenzie King, was brought in as a special commissioner to assess the damage and arrange compensation. Several opium dens and processing factories had been destroyed during the riots. In the process of examining the evidence, King discovered that there was a perfectly legal and lucrative opium trade in Canada. King himself even bought some opium, to prove how easy it was to obtain. (Perhaps "this was the first official undercover buy," quipped a modern Mountie, Staff Sergeant "Smokey" Stovern.) King learned that there were at least eight opium factories in Vancouver and that they earned more than $600,000 a year. Moreover, the city government was receiving $170,000 a year in licensing fees from opium dealers and manufacturers.

In his report King recommended compensation of $26,990 to the victims in Vancouver's Chinatown, but he also advised that the government immediately outlaw opium. The following year, the government passed the Opium Act of 1908, making it illegal to import, traffic in, or use opium and criminalizing the hitherto legally licensed opium dens. In 1911, when he was in the Cabinet of Sir Wilfrid Laurier as minister of labour, Mackenzie King introduced the Opium and Narcotic Drug Act, which stiffened the penalties for illegal drug use in the Opium Act, and throughout the teens, the original Act was modified many times. In 1912 The Hague International Opium Convention, which included most Western nations, called for stricter control of the opiate trade and a licensing system for medicinal use. In 1914 the United States adopted strict federal drug legislation, making opiate trafficking a major offence. But in 1918 U.S. authorities publicly complained about the amount of opium finding its way into the United States via Canada. In 1920, after a Royal Commission in Canada into organized Chinese drug smuggling, the Canadian Opium and Narcotics Drug Act was tightened up even more. Throughout the twenties there were numerous revisions of the Act, resulting in the criminalization of other drugs such as heroin (an opium derivative), cocaine, and, in the final revision in 1929 (which lasted until the 1960s), marijuana and hash. In the early days of the Opium and Narcotic Drug Act, the law was not very rigorously enforced, and violations were not considered very serious. A keeper of an opium den in Vancouver generally received only a $100 fine. Still, the levels of opium importation "dropped dramatically in the ensuing years from 88,000 pounds in 1908 to 3,576 pounds in 1910, and in the fiscal year 1926–27 the amount imported was only 1,020 pounds," according to an RCMP study.

From 1903 to 1911, Chinese immigration remained at approximately fifteen hundred per year, but in 1910 to 1911, almost five thousand new immigrants arrived, and the federal government ordered yet another investigation into immigration fraud. Under the chairmanship of Mr. Justice Dennis Murphy of Vancouver, this was the fourth such Royal Commission into Chinese immigration fraud, but it also investigated organized loansharking. The Murphy report cleared immigration officials but named a number of Chinese agents and others who were then charged with criminal fraud. It was shown that some Chinese merchants were systematically avoiding the head tax for people they were bringing in as "merchants" for a fee to them of $100. Murphy's report was released in July 1911, just before the federal election that defeated Sir Wilfrid Laurier's Liberal government. It showed how the port of Union Bay (the second largest British Columbia point of entry by Orientals to Canada after Vancouver) was "practically a free port for the entrance of Chinese and for the smuggling of opium." Murphy determined that the only thing that limited the amount of opium in the country was demand for the product.

Chinese secret societies were active in Canada from the earliest days. It was in the small northeastern British Columbia gold mining town of Bakerville that the first Chinese secret society is known to have been established in Canada. The Hong Shun Tang, organized in 1863, was a branch of a California-based secret society that was associated with the Hung Mun or Hong societies of China (set up in the seventeenth century to overthrow the Manchu dynasty and restore the Mings). The original secret society building was destroyed by a fire that levelled Bakerville in 1868, but a new building built that year still stands. One of the plaques on the building has the characters "Hong Shun Tang" and another has "Yixing Gongsuo," yet another designation for Hung Mun societies at the time.

The Vancouver Chinese Freemasons, associated with the Hung Mun secret society and akin to an American tong, has been in British Columbia since 1888. They were very active in helping Dr. Sun Yat-sen finance his revolution to overthrow the Ch'ing dynasty and found the Chinese republic. During a visit to Vancouver in the early 1900s, Dr. Sun Yat-sen was given a hero's welcome by the Freemasons, and in 1907 the Freemasons published a newspaper, *The Chinese Times*, to support his revolutionary goals. Even today the Freemasons survive with an active membership of more than three thousand people. But the Freemasons was never a criminal society, but a political one.

A more active secret society in Canada, associated in political activity with the Freemasons, was the Chee Kung tong (a.k.a. the Zhigongtang, Chi Kung tong but best known as the CKT), established in 1876 in Quesnel Mouth, British Columbia. The CKT was begun by Hung Mun members in the United States in the 1850s. In documents brought to light in 1960 by a group of Canadian scholars, the regulations and goals of the society are outlined: "The purpose in forming the Cheekungtong is to maintain a friendly relationship amongst our countrymen and to accumulate wealth through proper business methods for the benefit of all members."* The documents go on to list rules and regulations that describe the political and social functions of the CKT — settling disputes, collecting debts, providing housing, and even determining the proper behaviour of its members in gambling and whorehouses. Unlike some of the American-based tongs such as the On Leong and Hip Sing, which for many decades were almost solely organized crime organizations, the Chee Kung tong was a legitimate organization that, from time to time, was infiltrated and used by unscrupulous professional criminals. It is important to note, however, that according to a 1990 academic study of the tongs and the criminal underworld by Ko-Lin Chin, an American sociologist, the original CKT had "triad values" and political goals — they wanted to help overthrow the Ch'ing dynasty and restore the Ming. However, like the members of the triads, CKT members, even as late as the mid-1940s, when the main American headquarters was moved from San Francisco to Vancouver, "still burned yellow papers and took oaths at initiation ceremonies."** In Montreal, criminal elements seized the leadership of the CKT under the presidency of gambling boss Jack Wong from the 1950s through the 1960s.

The tongs' presence in Canada was far less violent than in the United States. The Hip Sings from Seattle, Washington, under Tom Dig sent Hock Hung to Victoria, British Columbia, in the early teens to start yet another branch of that expansionist tong. But the British Columbian branch had a brief life. It was closed almost as soon as it opened, allegedly because of Canadian regulations.

In May 1925, in Port Moody, British Columbia, just outside Vancouver, a dramatic series of killings occurred that seized the headlines for a week. The superintendent of provincial police,

---

* *From China to Canada: A History of the Chinese Communities in Canada* by Harry Con, Ron Con, Graham Johnson, Edgar Wickberg and William Willmott.

** See Ko-Lin Chin, *Chinese Subculture and Criminality: Non-Traditional Crime Groups in America*, pp. 54–55.

in his annual report, called it "an internal tong feud," when several men, including Lum But (also known as Fred Lambert) and Ng Hong, two prominent members of Vancouver's Chinatown, were murdered and two other men were seriously wounded. Actually it was not a tong war as reported in press and police reports, but a dispute between Vancouver factions of the Shon Yee Society (a British Columbia-based benevolent association) over the apportioning of money in a hospital fund; the bloodbath was an isolated event, not an ongoing war. Two men, Shui Sing and Shen Say Yung, were charged with murder in the shootings, and another of the gunmen, Mak Dip, killed himself. Although no convictions were obtained despite "considerable investigation work by the local police" and the attorney general's office, according to the provincial police report, there was no further bloodshed in this particular feud.

The Port Moody killings happened smack in the middle of the sensational trial of Wong Foon Sing, a Chinese houseboy, for the 1924 murder of Janet Smith, a British nursemaid who worked for a wealthy Vancouver businessman. It was a time of hysterical overreaction. On July 26, 1924, Janet Smith was found shot to death in the laundry room of the mansion in Shaughnessy Heights in Vancouver where she worked as a nursemaid to the daughter of businessman Frederick L. Baker. The Smith killing is one of the most sensational and intriguing events in Vancouver's criminal history. Smith had been ironing at the time of her death, and a revolver was found under her ironing board. An inquest found that she had died accidentally. Although some suspected suicide, the Baker houseboy, Wong Foon Sing, who had been the only person known to be in the house at the time of the death, was charged with murder after a second inquest disproved the accidental death verdict of the earlier inquest. There was no real evidence against Wong, and the charges appear to have stemmed from outright racism. One British tabloid, *The People*, said that Janet Smith had been the "victim of one of the terrible secret societies that have sprung up in Canada and the United States," namely tong associations and triads. "Chinamen," the author went on, "exercised a terrible influence over her." Wong, who was kidnapped and tortured by local police before he was officially charged in 1925, was eventually acquitted.* There was gossip in the newspapers of Wong himself being part of a Chinese criminal network, but this accusation was never substantiated. It is altogether unlikely that Wong was a member of a triad or any criminal group. No one was ever convicted in connection with Smith's death.

On the very day of the Port Moody killings, the *Vancouver Sun*'s lead editorial was about the Janet Smith murder case then playing itself out in court. The editorial attacked "Trial By

---

* Wong was allowed to take the so-called "chicken oath," swearing to tell the truth after cutting off the head of a live hen in court with a knife. This ritualistic decapitation was a variant of the fire oath for Chinese in court in Canada, whereby the defendant took the stand and set on fire his paper oath swearing to tell the truth on pain of dishonouring the memory of his ancestors. (Today, triads and Asian gangs use a variation of this oath, in a ceremony called "burning the yellow paper," during which a new alliance or criminal deal is confirmed through the ritualistic setting on fire of papers detailing the transaction.)

An excellent account of the trial and the subsequent events is Edward Starkins's 1984 book, *Who Killed Janet Smith?*, which concluded that Smith was definitely murdered and that the death was made to look like a suicide by the conspirators, who may have included, in the cover-up phase, local police and the coroner. Local gossip in Vancouver from 1924 until even today has the demented son of the then Lieutenant-Governor of British Columbia, John Nichol, having committed the murder after sexually assaulting Smith during a drunken binge. A letter from the Attorney General at the time, A. M. Manson, surfaced in the 1970s, stating that a member of the Lieutenant-Governor's family would have been disgraced if the real murderer were revealed. But Starkins dismisses the Nichol stories as a red herring devised to cover up "the real reasons for Janet Smith's death," the result of a carefully orchestrated plot. Starkins reveals that Smith's boss, the wealthy Shaughnessy Heights businessman Frederick Baker, had secretly been a major drug dealer, and that rivals were attempting to kill him or send him a message. Baker claimed that his involvement was in the legal importation of heroin, cocaine, and morphine bought from licensed dealers in Germany and France. There is evidence that Starkins found that Baker, while in England in the early twenties, was involved in a major Japan/Hong Kong-based cocaine and morphine smuggling ring. Starkins's book concludes that the Smith death will forever remain a mystery.

Prejudice," pleading that the defendant, Wong Foon Sing, get a fair trial, and not be found guilty simply because he was Chinese. — "It is the difference between civilization and savagery," the editorial concluded.

With all the violence in the Oriental community, the *Vancouver Sun* editorialized three days later, on May 23, 1925, that what Canada needed was policemen from Hong Kong to train our police:

> All this fighting among the Chinese of British Columbia will never be completely stopped until specially trained policemen are brought in to stop it. Hong Kong is one of the most efficiently policed cities in the world. There is less disorder among the 611,000 Chinese residents of Hong Kong than there is among the 12,000 Chinese residents of Vancouver . . . . And the secret of this wonderful policing is due to the specialized training of the English police sergeants who actively direct the work. Living among the Chinese for years, they understand Chinese psychology and the Chinese language . . . . What British Columbia wants is one of these English police sergeants of Hong Kong for the Vancouver police force and another for the Provincial force. And these Chinese "crime waves" would mysteriously end.

Years later, when Hong Kong police sergeants did arrive in Canada in the 1970s, they were anything but helpful in the fight against organized crime in Canada's Chinatowns.

Xenophobia, bigotry, and outright repression of minorities were rampant in British Columbia in the period. Overzealous crusaders such as Judge Emily F. Murphy, the police magistrate and judge of the Juvenile Court in Edmonton, fed the flames of racism. Her overwrought account of the slave trade, prostitution, and especially the evil of opium taking and opium-induced corruption in the oriental community was published in a popular book, *The Black Candle*. Most of this book originally appeared as a series of articles for *Maclean's* magazine, under the pseudonym "Janey Canuck." Murphy, the first female judge in the British empire and an early feminist, throughout the 1920s ran a one-person crusade against Oriental and black drug traffickers and for the need for radical new laws and social programs. Although Murphy was an educated and cultured woman who frequently quoted Virgil, Kipling, Whitman, de Quincey, Coleridge, and other greats of classical and modern literature in her articles, she was also a racist. She believed that many Orientals and blacks were inferior to Caucasians, and her racist comments despoil her otherwise interesting studies of drug abuse and its effects on society. Murphy even allowed herself to believe in "the yellow peril," an Oriental plot to take over the white race.

There are even more overtly racist attacks on the Chinese in British Columbia in popular thrillers and the pulp magazine fiction of the time. Much of the material in the media about Chinese gambling and opium dens was exaggerated. The newspapers frequently covered Chinese immigration to British Columbia in an overtly racist manner. For example, the Vancouver *Daily World* published a twenty part series by J.S. Cowper, a former MLA, on the "rising tide of Asiatics in B.C." and its "pernicious" effects on native-born Canadians.

There was a political fall-out to this racism. In May 1922 British Columbia MP W.G. McQuarrie brought a bill into the House of Commons in Ottawa to exclude all Orientals from immigrating to Canada. "B.C. is no longer a white province but the domain of brown and yellow races," exclaimed a 1922 editorial in the *Daily World*. An "Exclusion Act," disguised as "control" on Chinese immigration, was presented by the government. It was passed in 1923 and this racist Act, which prohibited Chinese from immigrating to Canada, remained in effect for the next twenty three years. Still, many powerful people in British Columbia, including the attorney general and the minister of labour, didn't think the Exclusion Act went far enough. They wanted nothing less than the deportation of most of the approximately thirty thousand Chinese (and other Orientals) in British Columbia. Fortunately, their will did not prevail.

Chapter Four

THE KING OF THE GAMBLERS AND THE OPIUM EMPRESSES

Despite the overt discrimination they faced, some early Chinese immigrants to British Columbia actually prospered. Throughout the teens, twenties, and thirties, a gambling overlord named Shu Moy (a.k.a. Shue Moy), who had come to British Columbia from China in 1899, reigned supreme in Vancouver's Chinatown. Helped along with the purchased assistance of the police chief and the mayor, Shu Moy's criminal career in Canada spanned at least four decades. Known by the police and the press as the King of the Gaming Houses and King of the Gamblers, Moy, who was also the appointed postmaster of Mackinnon, British Columbia, was involved in opium importing, opium dens, gambling houses, protection rackets, and Oriental brothels. He was to be the undoing of several important people he was connected with, including the Vancouver police chief, H.W. Long. Even Louis D. Taylor, the mayor of Vancouver in the mid-1920s, with whom Moy was known to socialize on a regular basis and to whom Moy had made generous political contributions, was seriously embarrassed and politically undermined when his connections to Moy were made public.

In 1928 Vancouver City Council was forced to set up a special City Police Commission to look into accusations of corruption at the highest levels of the municipal government. The so-called Lennie Inquiry, under the chairmanship of Police Commissioner R.S. Lennie, and with the able assistance of the promi-

nent Vancouver lawyer, A.H. MacNeill, K.C., kept the scandalous behaviour of the city's highest officials as well as many
policemen in the headlines for several months. Lurid details of
life in Chinese gambling and opium dens were outlined in the
papers daily through the spring and summer of 1928 as Shu
Moy, his underlings, and his associates, as well as many of the
city's top policemen, were paraded in front of the vice inquiry.

Scores of gambling houses in Vancouver's Chinatown were
run by the bosses of a number of syndicates, including Georgie
Chow (Chow Wong Lum), Joe Lem, and, of course, Shu Moy.
The owners of several of the gambling houses, most of which
were in downtown Vancouver, testified that they made system-
atic payments to the police. But the climax of the inquiry was
the testimony of Shu Moy himself on July 3 and 4, 1928.* Asked
on the first day of questioning if he was the King of the
Gamblers in Chinatown, Moy stated that he had never heard
of the appellation, testifying that he was known on the street
as the Potato King, because he owned the largest potato ranch
in Canada and had grocery stores stocked with potatoes in
Victoria and Vancouver. But on the next day, when asked by
the Lennie Inquiry counsel if, "in your experience as King of
the Gamblers," he had found that gamblers were, generally
speaking, "honest" people, his answer was amusing. "Yes,
mostly honest," he replied. Then he hesitated and added as an
afterthought, "Some of them are not honest." Moy, whose main
gambling houses in Vancouver were, for many years, unmolested by the police, was himself less than honest on the stand.
Although he testified under oath that he didn't know anything
about protection money paid to the police by his underlings and
associates, he did admit on July 4, that it was "a Chinese
custom" to give "gifts" to officials. The most explosive part of
Moy's testimony was that he was a close personal friend of
Mayor Taylor, with whom he met regularly at the mayor's
residence, the Granville Mansions. Moy, who was called by the

---

* I found the transcript of Shu Moy's appearances among thousands of
pages of testimony in the closet of the Vancouver Police Museum.

Lennie Commission counsel sarcastically "King, twice in your own right," testified that he talked to Mayor Taylor in weekly meetings "about different things in town. You know, you go to talk to a friend, you couldn't tell what you were talking about after you go there." Moy did admit that very large sums of money were involved in his gambling business, going through his books for one day in 1928, when he made $16,000 in just one of his establishments.

Other witnesses were more specific about corruption. The gift of a diamond ring from Moy for presentation to Detective Sergeant George McLaughlin as part of a protection package was detailed by several witnesses, including Kong Quai, another Chinese gambling boss of the time. Quai told of being ordered by Moy to pay $10 for every share he had in a gambling partnership with Moy. Moy's associate, Ah Kim (described by Shu Moy variously as his cook and as one of his partners in two gambling houses), testified that he paid $300 a month to Mayor Taylor so that Moy could keep his two main gambling houses at 54 Cordova East and West open. (Moy had at least two other places on Pender Street East and other establishments on Main, Carroll, and Powell streets). Georgie Chow and other Chinese gamblers testified to paying money to McLaughlin and other policemen on behalf of Moy and the other gambling and opium den owners. Others, including many police officers under oath, testified that Mayor Taylor himself ordered the police not to raid the illegal gambling clubs run by Moy and the brothels controlled by another of the mayor's social contacts and financial backers, Joe Celona, known then as the King of the Whorehouses. As a result of the inquiry, both Chief Long and Detective Sergeant McLaughlin were fired. Shu Moy, in spite of his notoriety and his admissions at the Lennie Commission, continued on as a major force in organized crime in British Columbia until at least the late 1930s.*

---

* For a detailed look into the Vancouver criminal underworld of the 1920s, the thousands of pages of testimony of both criminals and police at the Lennie Commission are most revealing.

Although Oriental immigration was banned by federal government legislation, the opium traffic thrived throughout the twenties and thirties. The smuggling was organized in Canada by local Chinese with the help of a worldwide network of people in China, Hong Kong, and elsewhere. Since the passage of the Opium and Narcotic Drug Act of 1908 and subsequent criminalization of a number of narcotics (morphine, heroin, marijuana, cocaine, etc.), internationally-based drug syndicates operated secretly in Canada and around the world to provide the now illegal substances to drug addicts in North America. Drug trafficking by the 1920s had become a highly lucrative and organized business. T. Morris Longstreth and Henry Vernon give a slightly bigoted, though nonetheless intriguing, contemporary account of how opium trafficking got going in the twenties.

The oriental still [after World War 1] smoked his opium inconspicuously enough, but others than the slant-eyed began to indulge. Morphine, cocaine, heroin, far worse in their ravages, were being imported to add variety to vice. Mohammed's ancient ban on alcoholic beverages was followed by an increase of drug usage in the train of Islam. . . . In Canada the two great seaports of Montreal and Vancouver vied for supremacy as a drug market. Both cities were natural refuges for national and international criminals. Both sustained a considerable Chinese population.

To both, narcotics could be brought by boat. Vancouver had slightly the edge on Montreal owing to its being nearer the Orient. Already the Mounted police had come to realize the large and sinister ramifications of the traffic. They had laboriously devised new methods and trained trustworthy instruments to aid in the attack. This had been slow work and difficult. The enormous profits of the traffic offered a lure to the morally tainted that most enterprises lacked, furnishing a human chain which started with the pitiful addict, who begged to obtain the stimulation that his wasted body craved, and went straight up through a variety of suppliers, increasing in importance, until the inaccessible, invisible, and nameless heads of the illegal industry were reached. . . .*

Longstreth went on to detail a seven-year-long Mountie investigation into the Vancouver opium trade leading to the case against Sun Yai, Sing Yong, and Leong Kip, who ran a hotel in Vancouver where opium was sold. (There is an amusing illustrative frontispiece that depicts a one-legged Chinese making his way to Leong Kip's hotel under the watchful eye of his intrepid RCMP shadow.) The Mounties, under the able leadership of undercover sleuth Detective Sergeant James Fripps, the longtime head of the RCMP Drug Squad in Vancouver in the 1920s, also deciphered a Chinese code used to describe the operations of drug smuggling from the incoming liners and the sending of the large profits back to China. Leong Kip was eventually convicted, but not before attempting to intimidate witnesses and publicly threatening the police translator.

We get other glimpses of the drug trade in Vancouver in the period through all-too-rare Canadian police memoirs, such as Corporal R.S.S. Wilson's Undercover for the RCMP, published posthumously in 1986, which detailed some low- and middle-level RCMP operations against opium dens in Vancouver in the 1920s. Specifically, he told the story of some of his undercover operations like the one against Vancouver opium dealer Frank Yipp.**

---

* T. Morris Longstreth and Henry Vernon, Murder at Belly Butte and Other Stories from the Mounted Police (The Maclean Publishing Company, Toronto, 1931). T. Morris Longstreth was also the author of the first anecdotal "history" of the North West Mounted Police and the RCMP, The Silent Force.

** Another major source had been the brief accounts in the RCMP annual reports. These are more detailed in the twenties with often a paragraph devoted to each major case. For example, there was the account of the May 1929 conviction of Chin Yow Hing (alias Gee Gim), a wealthy and respected Vancouver doctor who had been an active opium smuggler for over a decade. Other sources include occasional articles on specific cases found in the RCMP Quarterly and the Police Journal, especially in the

Opium was a serious problem in Canada in the 1920s, and Colonel Charles Sharman, the Head of the Narcotics Division of the Department of Health, determined that opium trafficking on the Pacific Coast was "almost entirely in the hands of Orientals." Sharman, a former member of the Royal North-West Mounted Police (RNWMP) from 1898–1904 and a veteran international drug investigator, described the situation in 1930 in an article for the *Police Journal*:

> It is, however, the Pacific Coast, where the illicit opium traffic is almost entirely in the hands of Orientals, which occasions most activity and expenditure on our part. The

---

1930s and 1940s. See for example Colonel C.H.L. Sharman's excellent 1930 article, "Narcotic Control in Canada," in the *Police Journal*, Vol. III, No. 4, October 1930, where several of the Empress cases are discussed in detail. Edward Starkins provides the details of an international drug conspiracy case involving the employer of Janet Smith with a cast of rogues in Japan, England, France, Hong Kong, and Canada involved in smuggling hundreds of pounds of morphine and cocaine hidden in furniture (*Who Killed Janet Smith?*, pages 305–318). His material is from recently declassified documents in the archives of the British government.

The most reliable, objective material for researching the organized traffic in narcotics in the twenties and thirties by Chinese and Hong Kong drug traffickers is the actual case files of the RCMP, the U.S. Bureau of Narcotics, and the League of Nations drug office to be found in the U.S. and Canadian national archives. With the Access to Information Act in Canada and the Freedom of Information Act in the United States, today there are literally tens of thousands of pages of raw U.S. and Canadian law enforcement papers as well as hundreds of boxes and stuffed folders of League of Nations documents available for serious researchers in the archives on the specific nature of drug trafficking in the twenties and thirties. In recovering a bit of this lost history, I shall merely highlight my findings here as they relate to drug-trafficking rings organized by Oriental crime networks with an operating base in or through Canada. I urge the more serious readers to spend some time in the Canadian and U.S. archives for detailed, investigative accounts of specific international drug-trafficking conspiracies, as well as many related alien-smuggling networks, mostly from American, Canadian, British, Hong Kong, Chinese, and League of Nations law enforcement sources.

Oriental, in the very large majority of the cases, also handles morphine and cocaine, so that he is in a position to cater to the addiction both of the Occidental and of those of his own race. In the course of investigations ranging over a period of years, it was, of course, fairly well known who the big operatives were, but they were exceptionally clever individuals; and to transform our suspicion of their activities into such definite proof as would satisfy a jury was a matter of extreme difficulty. When it is realized, however, that within the past three years nearly ninety of these traffickers and smugglers in British Columbia have been given penitentiary sentences ranging from two to seven years, with fines of $1,000, and subsequent deportation, it can safely be said that we have the control of the traffic well in hand.

The drug-trafficking rings generally recruited workers on the luxury liners of the day to import the drugs into Canada and the United States. The Empress ships of the Canadian Pacific fleet, notably the *Empress of Asia*, the *Empress of Japan*, the *Empress of Canada*, the *Empress of Russia*, and the *Empress of France* were infiltrated by such couriers as were the American Blue Funnel boats. In 1929, for example, Tsang Sou, the No. 1 Saloon Boy on Canadian Pacific Empress Steamships was caught red-handed with forty tins of opium. He had been with Canadian Pacific for thirty-seven years. When threatened with dismissal, he claimed he was forced to co-operate with the smugglers and then offered to go undercover to expose Chinese opium smuggling in Canada and the United States. He became an effective police operative.*

The conspiracies were highly organized and each involved a cast of rogues in a number of countries bringing huge amounts of opium, morphine, and other drugs into the lucrative North

---

* For the full story of the No. 1 Saloon Boy case, see the lengthy files on it in the Department of Health Intelligence files in Ottawa (RG 29; Vol. 228 323–12–14). This file also contains reports on Chinese drug smuggling to Canada and smuggling from Singapore.

American market. Many of the opium shipments came off the liners lying at the docks in Vancouver and were picked up by couriers who recovered the drugs under the cover of night, using small boats. One sensational U.S. case centred on the wife of the Chinese consul in San Francisco who was part of a major drug-smuggling ring. In just one shipment, she brought into San Francisco more that a million dollars' worth of opium in her trunk. The ship had come into the United States from the Orient after a stop in Vancouver. But with the help of informers and agents like Tsang Sou, as well as undercover police operatives in both the United States and Canada, the RCMP, with the assistance of the American Bureau of Narcotics, broke up scores of such drug-trafficking networks in the mid- to late twenties. Hundreds of couriers, middlemen, and drug-ring organizers, mostly Chinese who had been living in Canada, many of whom worked on the ships themselves or had associates planted on the ships, were convicted, served time in Canadian jails, and were then deported, usually to China or Hong Kong. Time and again, the major conspirators and traffickers had Chinese organized crime connections.*

Two interrelated worldwide RCMP-led investigations that spanned three years led to a massive crackdown on the opium

---

* The main files on these Empress cases, aside from specific case files in the RCMP archives, are found in the Department of Health Intelligence files, RG 29; Vol. 225 File 3423–9–25 Narcotics, Drug Traffic, and Smuggling British Columbia, Vancouver; Vol. 227 Pts 3 & 4 & 5 International Drug Traffic and Smuggling intelligence files, Vol. 226 323-12-2 pt 1 – 1922–1929; 226 323-12-2 pt 2 – 1930–1936; 227 323-12-2 pt 3 – 1937–1939; 227 323-12-2 pt 4 – 1939–1942; 227 323-12-2 pt 5 – 1942–1950. If you have a few more months to peruse the voluminous files, for more specific case files take a look at Vol. 228 #323-12-3 International Drug Traffic and Smuggling from Japan, which contains a large number of intelligence reports from Canadian, U.S., and British police and military intelligence agencies. See also Vol. 228, 323-12-4, a "General file on Oriental Drug Traffic." There were scores of cases from Toronto, the Maritimes, and even the Prairies. The archives in Canada and the United States have literally thousands of pages of documents relating to each of the cases, reflecting the thoroughness of the U.S. and Canadian authorities to bring the traffickers to justice by carefully documenting their every move.

traffic through the liners. The operations involved undercover Mounties working across North America, using secret Chinese codes and dealing with couriers, middlemen, and drug traffickers in New York, Seattle, Vancouver, and elsewhere.

These operations started in Windsor in early 1927. RCMP investigators made a number of arrests that indicated the source of opium for Windsor was the Chinese underworld in Montreal. But Mounties in Montreal found out after several wholesale buys by undercover operatives that the Montreal supply was coming from Vancouver. Certain that they had identified one of the biggest opium operators in the country, the RCMP began a lengthy operation in Vancouver against one of the wealthiest and most prominent men in the Chinese community there, Lim Gim (a.k.a. Lim Jim), the President of a large Chinese importing house. According to his own testimony, Lim, who had come to Canada at the turn of the century, was making more than $900,000 a year through his various business enterprises. But opium smuggling was the secret source of his fortune.

A Mountie agent, complete with proper letters of introduction, was introduced to Lim in order to negotiate a large opium purchase. The agent, posing as a major New York City drug trafficker in search of a new supply, met with Lim many times and soon found that Lim knew more about the movement of ships along the Atlantic and Pacific coasts than most professional shippers. When the agent tried to buy $10,000 of opium, Lim told him that he didn't have that much Lem Kee opium, the best available quality at the time, but could get it from a ship that was just in Seattle or from other ships coming to the United States. He went on to tell the agent that he had "direct wires pulling in Hong Kong" and the "first option on any stuff coming from China." Lim went on to boast that fifteen years before he and three partners "had the market cornered" in opium, both in the United States and Canada, as he "used to do all the buying, and nobody got any opium except through us." Lim went on to tell how he had made $20,000 profit a year from opium and that he had just sold one hundred cans of good opium to a customer in San Francisco. He explained to the agent that if he (Lim) were out of Lem Kee opium, then nobody in North America would have it in the quantities the agent desired, although he might be able to get him some good No. 2 opium, the next best quality available.

Lim Gim then gave the agent a code to use in correspondence. "Vancouver B" was to represent the numbers one to ten; "George" was to mean "Lem Kee"; "Smith" was No. 2 opium; "Charles B. Young" was to be the agent's name. Lim was working through operators and dealers in New York City, Seattle, Shanghai, Hong Kong, and elsewhere — all using his code. Within weeks of this, the undercover operative received a letter from Lim while in Seattle. It read, *Mr. A.B. Smith is now in town. He will be ready to do business at any time. Let me know as Mr. Smith is going away shortly.* Mr. Smith was the code for the two hundred cans of No. 2 opium that were ready. A coded telegram was sent by the RCMP to Lim in Vancouver confirming that a pick-up would be made shortly. The Mounties faked another telegram in code from a Chinese New York City-area dealer working with the operative okaying the purchase.

Lim met with the Mountie operative frequently. During one of these meetings, Lim fretted about a large quantity of opium he had on a Blue Funnel ship then in Seattle. Significantly, he seemed to know before the cops moved that a police raid was about to take place. Sure enough, a day later more than one thousand cans of opium were seized from the ship by U.S. Bureau of Narcotics officials, but Lim knew that his No. 1 quality opium was still intact. He delivered some opium the next morning, but the price had gone up because of the danger. Payment was made in marked money at Lim's store, and Lim was arrested. The police found all the corroborating evidence they needed — letters in code, marked money, the works. After he was convicted the judge noted the gravity of the offence: "You are what is termed a wholesaler as distinct from an ordinary peddler of dope. The sentence would have been heavier, were it not for the fact that your friends [respectable members of the Chinese community in Vancouver] have presented a wonderfully worded petition of leniency." Lim got only four years, but upon appeal the sentence was increased to seven years.

Since Lim was a naturalized Canadian citizen, the government was unable to deport him after his sentence was served, and he resurfaced in other drug investigations throughout the 1930s. However, shortly after Lim's 1927 conviction, the RCMP developed another lead into a related ring that was bringing drugs in directly off the Empress ships coming into Vancouver. Two non-Chinese Canadians had been discovered by the Mounties to be couriers for the Chinese-run opium smuggling ring were caught unloading a shipment of opium from one of the Empress boats in a small collapsible rubber dinghy. One of these non-Chinese couriers was recruited to operate as an informer and police agent. Shortly thereafter, he reported that Henry Chan, for whom he had worked previously, and another Chinese gentleman he didn't know, had approached him about a shipment of opium coming in via the *Empress of France*. He was told that arrangements had been made for him to pick up the opium for Lee Kim, one of Lim's lieutenants, and to deliver them at a pre-arranged drop site. At midnight the courier rowed up to the *Empress of France* and went to a designated porthole, over which hung a red cloth. There at the end of a rope was half a piece of notepaper. The undercover RCMP agent produced the matching other half and within minutes more than forty cans of opium wrapped in burlap were lowered down to him. He took the opium to the Vancouver Hotel where he was to meet Lee Kim.

After several meetings with Lee Kim, Charlie Sam arrived to actually pick up the dope. Sam was working with yet another middleman, named Mah Poy, who shared his room at the hotel, ironically just opposite the room of the police agent. Police arrested Charlie Sam as he left the agent's room. While the police were searching Charlie Sam and Mah Poy's hotel room, Lee Kim himself as well as Henry Chan came to the door. In searching Lee Kim's hotel room the police found documents that, when translated, were more than enough to convict the lot of opium trafficking.

After the arrests of Lee Kim and his lieutenants in late 1929, the following letter was received by the Chinese court interpreter. It shows how well informed and how brutal the Chinese gang criminals were:

> My friends, Messrs. Lee, Sam, Chan and Mah have been arrested by the Wolf and the Tiger, namely the Mounted Police, and several important documents have been seized. I know that you are employed as a Court Interpreter and therefore beg you to help by not translating these documents. If you agree to do so, please inform Uncle Lee Kay. I will to-night at 8 P.M. present you with a gift of $500 for your trouble. If you refuse to do so, and translate these documents into English, thus revealing these four gentlemen's secret affairs, I am afraid that your life will be in danger. Although these are Mounted Police yet they cannot render you constant protection. Please think it over three times. You know perfectly well that Mr. David Lee has been shot to death.

The request to "think it over three times" indicated triad involvement. The number three is used in triad extortions even today. Shortly afterwards, another letter was received by a Chinese gentleman suspected by the gang of being a police informer. After telling the man to quit his job and to stop working for the police, the letter said, "I heard that you have something to do with the Lee, Sam, Mah and Chan cases. If you do not follow the above instructions we will join together with Lee, Sam, Mah, and Chan and render you a suitable funeral."

Nevertheless, all of the defendants were convicted, most receiving five years in jail, and although no one was murdered in this particular case, several police informants in the Vancouver Chinese community were brutally murdered over the next several years. Among them was a thirty-five-year-old police informer named Quong Quan (Kwong Kong) who was working inside a Chinese gambling house. He was executed on October 15, 1936, on the streets in the heart of Vancouver's Chinatown, just outside a gambling establishment at 102 East Pender Street. For the next few weeks, the Vancouver newspapers were full of lurid accounts of life in Vancouver's Chinatown underworld including "warring Chinese gambling factions" and headlines such as *Police Informer Murdered: 'Gamblers' Revenge'*." In one front-page account Vancouver Police Chief W.W. Foster told reporters that he could not confirm that Quan was on the police payroll because he would have to reveal "police secrets that are too valuable to the underworld." Reporters at the Vancouver *Sun* covering the cases concluded that Quan, "as one of the most outstanding police operatives, was the victim selected by the gunmen to be a gruesome lesson to other informers." The "Chinese gunmen," as the hit men were called, had escaped to the Orient on one of the trans-Pacific liners according to police investigators. No one was ever convicted of the murder.

Even the notorious gangster star of the 1928 Lennie Inquiry, Shu Moy, made an important appearance in the late thirties in the still ongoing investigations of the Empress smuggling networks. As late as December 3, 1937, a secret RCMP report from Vancouver detailed the continuing Empress ship narcotics rings and linked the drug trafficking to Moy. The Mountie undercover operative and interpreter, a Chinese Canadian named Y.D. Leong, had been secretly watching everyone coming to and from the Empress boats for a year. The easy access to such ships by "Chinese of virtually all walks of life," was viewed by the RCMP as a major security problem:

From my observations made during the past twelve months of Chinese who are in the habit of visiting the "Empress" ships, I am not particularly impressed by their character or the nature of their business. Some of these people are as follows: Mrs. Lim Jim, wife of the notorious Lim Jim who served a term of seven years imprisonment under the O. & N. D. Act. . . . Charlie Poy, Notorious Chinese gambler and lieutenant of the more notorious Shu Moy. . . . [Other suspects are named, including respected Vancouver businessmen, some local Chinese actors and actresses with the Jin Wah Sing Theatrical Association, a Chinese interpreter, and other prominent people in the Oriental community.]*

Perhaps the most tenacious and under-appreciated American gang-buster of the twenties, thirties, forties, and fifties, was Henry N. Anslinger, the first head of the Bureau of Narcotics in the 1920s and the first U.S. Commissioner of Narcotics. For years the intrepid Anslinger almost single-handedly led the fight against the Mafia and organized crime in the United States, because J. Edgar Hoover, the longtime head of the federal Bureau of Investigation and later the FBI, seriously downplayed Mafia investigations until the 1960s. Anslinger also offered indispensable assistance to Canadian law enforcement in international drug-trafficking investigations, including many aimed at American and Canadian Mafia-run groups, from the 1920s through the 1950s. In his 1962 book, *The Murderers: The Shocking Story of the Narcotics Gang*, Anslinger described the Chinese criminal control of the opium business in 1930:

In 1930 the Chinese still had a virtual monopoly of the opium trade in America; opium dens could be found in just

_____

* This intelligence memo is dated December 3, 1937, and is found in the files of the RCMP and of the Department of Pensions and National Health, Narcotics Division in the National Archives of Canada in Ottawa (RG 18, RCMP). There are many case file memos that detail intelligence information about a number of prominent Chinese businessmen. Some of the descendents are well known in Vancouver's Chinatown today. Some of these documents can also be found in the United States National Archives in Washington, D.C., as copies of many of these reports were sent to the U.S. Narcotics Bureau. Some of the Empress case files are also among the papers of the federal Immigration and Colonization department (see Immigration branch, RG 76. and RG 7, under the heading, "Chinese").

about any American city. The Chinese underworld of dope
— combined with gambling and prostitution — had its own
special Oriental ruthlessness which fitted the aura of violence and brutality and killing that has always been the
hallmark of the narcotics underworld. Among the criminal
elements, life was the cheapest of all the commodities. The
tongs — the On Leongs and the Hip Sings particularly —
had professional hatchet men who carried out killings on
order; the more important the individual or tong official,
the higher the fee for the execution. The tongs had something of the overtones of an Oriental Mafia, except that
they existed openly and only in the United States. . . . I was
convinced that the tongs, particularly the Hip Sings, were
the distributing agents for opium on a national scale. . . .

Anslinger at least put a damper on things for a while, by
closing Hip Sing-run opium dens across the Eastern United
States, especially in Washington, D.C.'s Chinatown where
opium dens, brothels, and gambling houses were operating on
both sides of Pennsylvania Avenue from Seventh Avenue "all
the way to the Capitol."

Even after the hundreds of Empress convictions in the twenties and early thirties, there were continued arrests and convictions of opium traffickers throughout the thirties and forties.

RCMP Inspector F.J. "Freddie" Mead was a career Mountie
from the RNWMP days who had supervised the undercover
operation against the radical unions, culminating in the Winnipeg General Strike; he had personally arrested the main
Winnipeg strike leaders in June 1919 and was very active in the
1920s and 1930s in breaking up the opium-trafficking syndicates. Mead, who eventually rose to be the deputy commissioner of the RCMP, had worked in senior positions in Mountie
divisions directing operations against subversives, bootleggers,
and drug dealers in Montreal (where in the early 1930s as an
inspector, he led an investigation with Detective Sergeant
Frank Zaneth into the money-laundering and bootlegging activities of the late Sam Bronfman), Toronto, Regina, Vancouver,

and other major Canadian cities. In 1932, Mead was putting his considerable field experience in undercover investigations into educating a new generation of Mounties trying to get a handle on the opium traffic in Canada. Mead wrote a series of lectures, which he delivered in Vancouver to members of the force just starting out on narcotics investigations. He outlined how to develop informers and agents in the Chinese community and how to properly raid an opium den, taking into account Chinese customs and the considerable experience of the RCMP over the past decades. Although his ideas are often simple-minded and stereotypical, Mead's lecture is a good insight into the mindset of a Mountie opium investigator of the early thirties:

> . . . . The Chinese are very suspicious, and in questioning one regarding his connection with the drug traffic, it is very dangerous to attempt to speak to him in his own language, as he immediately suspects that you know too much about him and his people. Another thing to guard against in dealing with Chinese is not to appear too insistent, as if this fact is noted, their suspicion is immediately aroused. In approaching them, it is a good policy to convey the impression that you are a bit stupid and at the same time create an atmosphere of honesty. When attempting to buy drugs never boast of past transactions, or being a "big man" in the game, as it is better to have this information conveyed indirectly through a third party. Do not try to talk to Chinese in Pidgin English, and do not use familiar names, as he resents being addressed by such terms which he looks upon as vulgar. If the party to whom you are talking does not understand English, use the simplest language possible. If you do not know the Chinese by his correct name, it is always the best policy not to use any name at all. The Chinese, as a rule are stoical and, incidentally, revengeful, and in dealing with them kindness and patience will go a long way in obtaining their confidence. When you have a Chinese informant assisting you in getting the evidence to convict a drug peddler, you on your part, should do every-

thing possible for him in the way of affording protection, which is sometimes necessary. . . .*

The *Empress of Japan* was the ship used most frequently by Vancouver-based Chinese opium smugglers in the thirties. Among many others, two names come up again and again as the most notorious drug kingpins in the Oriental community in the trafficking case files of both U.S. and Canadian authorities: Gordon Lim (Lim Fong Duck a.k.a. Gordon Lem) of Vancouver and Goon Lin in Montreal. Gordon Lim had a long career as one of the main drug traffickers working via the Empress ships through and with many couriers and middlemen, and as late as 1937, RCMP intelligence information places Gordon Lim's people meeting and dining with the No. 1 Interpreter of the *Empress of Japan*.

Goon Lin (Goon Dep Bon a.k.a. Goon Kwong Lin and Goon Sham), was the head of the Montreal end of opium smuggling from the late twenties to the early thirties, and his days as a major North American drug trafficker went on until the end of the decade. His methods were simple. A customer would drive into Montreal's Chinatown, stop near Goon Lin's place, and ask a passing Chinese to find Goon Lin. He would then come out onto the front step, check the customer out, and, if satisfied, tell him where the stash was hidden. Goon Lin would then meet the customer at the site of the stash, give him the drugs, and collect his money. But it took until 1932 for the RCMP to have enough evidence to convict him, and that was only after RCMP Detective Sergeant W.H. Styran jumped him as he was

---

* This obviously is just a brief excerpt. A larger chunk of Mead's intriguing, informal lectures appear in the Appendix. This is the kind of police material one rarely finds in the Public Archives in Ottawa, or anywhere else for that matter. I only discovered the Mead lectures accidentally, in the dusty closet of the Police Museum in Vancouver, after the curator, Joe Swan, an ex-Vancouver cop turned historian and true-crime writer, was kind enough to let me rummage through the old files hidden away there on the 1928 Lennie Inquiry.

making a delivery. In the ensuing fight, a deck of opium burst open, and both the Mountie and the dealer were covered in the drug, providing grounds for a search of his premises and for his arrest. But after serving his time and being deported from Canada, Goon Lin popped up again in 1936, organizing drug shipments of morphine, opium, and heroin in New York City. After conviction in the United States, where he had been living and operating for at least two years, he was finally deported back to China in October 1939.

Opium smuggling was not restricted to just Montreal and Vancouver, however; nor was it the exclusive domain of the Chinese criminals. Montreal-based opium smuggler Hum Gar Shing was also active in selling opium in Toronto and worked in partnership with several non-Chinese American drug traffickers. His 1929 arrest in Toronto by RCMP led in the early 1930s to the breaking up of a major mafia-run drug ring operating between Europe, Montreal, and New York City.

During the same period Lee Hee, a Regina grocery store owner, was one of the largest opium traffickers in the Prairies. His supply came from Hamilton, where the RCMP launched an investigation. Sergeant R.E. Webster, the long-serving officer in charge of the Hamilton RCMP detachment, and Detective Sergeant Frank Zaneth, the legendary undercover ace, discovered that Lee Wong of Hamilton conducted a massive opium mail order business across Canada (to Vancouver, Regina, Kingston, for example).* During the 1931 investigation, Jim Lee, a trusted court reporter who secretly worked for Lee Wong, attempted to bribe Zaneth and Webster. Lee was convicted of attempting to bribe both officers and received a sentence of four years in jail. Lee Wong and Lee Hee were both eventually convicted. Lee Hee got only six months in jail, but Lee Wong, who pleaded guilty to the more serious charge of distribution of opium, got a five-year sentence. Another Vancouver-based Oriental drug-

---

* For a look at the career and cases of the ubiquitous Frank Zaneth, see my 1991 book (written with Robin Rowland) *Undercover: The Cases of the RCMP's Most Secret Operative.*

trafficking ring shipped the drugs directly by mail to the Wong On Company in Montreal.

In the forties, smuggling by ship diminished with the war, but the case file on convicted trafficker Chan Chun (a.k.a. Chang Chong, Chang Poon Cho, Chang Poon Char, and Chin Chan) was revealing. The RCMP watched in December 1942 as the recently released drug dealer went from San Quentin prison in the United States to Vancouver, where he had meetings with a number of distinguished members of the Chinese community. When Chan Chun was later arrested in San Francisco, the notorious drug dealer had in his possession a number of letters with Vancouver names and addresses on them as well as twelve tins of opium. The opium in this case was determined by the RCMP and the U.S. Bureau of Narcotics to have come into the United States at Portland, Oregon, and not from Vancouver, though Chan's wide range of Vancouver contacts was certainly a source of RCMP concern.*

It was not just in the west that Chinese criminal networks had been established in Canada. Though at the time they had a much smaller Chinese population than British Columbia, Quebec, and Ontario and to a lesser extent the Maritimes had their proportional share of drug-trafficking, prostitution, gambling, and alien-smuggling activities run by Chinese criminal organizations in the 1920s and 1930s.

---

* The information for the Chan case is from the detailed RCMP case files for 1942 in the National Archives of Canada. There is no evidence that Chan's distinguished contacts in Vancouver were involved in any way in the drug trade.

Chapter Five

TORONTO'S TRIAD
TRADITION

In the period from the turn of the century until the 1960s, Chinese organized crime was much less visible in Toronto than in Vancouver. It wasn't until the 1970s and 1980s that organized criminal activity in Toronto's Chinatown matched and, by the 1990s, surpassed that of Vancouver's more colourful Chinatown. But there is a rich history that has been sadly neglected by both the police specialists and crime writers.

Toronto's main Chinatown was begun by Chinese labourers who moved east after the completion of the CPR in the 1880s. By the turn of the century, a Chinatown had formed in the centre of Toronto along Queen Street East between Yonge and Parliament streets and later expanded westward and north towards Bay and College streets. There were about twelve hundred Chinese in Toronto by the second decade of the twentieth century, only a tenth of the Chinese population out west. But they operated more than two hundred businesses, mostly laundries and grocery stores, and there were plenty of opium dens, gambling houses, and houses of prostitution run by Chinese organized crime figures in Ontario. But in 1912 the puritanical and racist Toronto Vigilance Committee issued a broadside, typical of the times and reminiscent of similar announcements in Vancouver, urging "strenuous efforts to break up Chinese dens of infamy kept for the purpose of ruining young Canadian girls." The Toronto newspapers abounded with stories, often openly racist, about Chinese gambling houses, opium smugglers, alien smugglers, and even "tong wars" in Toronto in the 1920s and early 1930s when the Chinese population climbed to about two thousand.

One of the most detailed accounts of a Chinese gambling house is the transcript of the 1918 trial in Toronto of Lee Chee Yung (a.k.a. Lee Sung and Albert Lee) and Chung Ying.* It provides a unique early look at police operations, the use of informers in Chinatown, and how, as early as the teens, extortion was a way of doing business. Lee Yung had a long history of running gambling and opium dens. His gambling house this time was in the basement of his variety store at 15 Elizabeth Street in Toronto's then tiny Chinatown. The first floor of the building was a small store that sold cigarettes and fruits. Inside, a barricaded door with two latches, a lever, and a peep hole on the side led to a secret basement gambling house containing large padded tables. There was also a table with papers for a lottery. The slips of paper were marked, then put in a dish and drawn. A large placard in the room announced in Cantonese that lottery draws, opening with eighty numbers, were to take place at 3 p.m. and 5 p.m. It also said the place would be open for gambling until early in the morning. It was a thriving business, literally underground, with an entrance from the back street, as well.

When the place was raided by police on November 2, 1918, police discovered eleven men gambling in one room and lots of money on the gambling tables. About thirty-five "Chinamen were running all over the house," according to Staff Inspector Robert Gregory. The games ranged from what was called cow poker (otherwise known as *pai gow*), played with dominoes, to *fan tan*, played with beads. The house raked off ten percent of the money gambled. A number of police informants, including one Jack Pong, testified that they had gambled there a number

---

* The detailed account of this trial is in the Ontario Archives in the files of the Department of the Attorney General. It is truly amazing how many of the different gambling activities of the time still go on in today's Chinatowns in Toronto.

of times, that it was well organized and efficiently run by the two defendants and a third man.

The bombshell in the case was set off when Lee Yung himself took the stand and revealed that the police agent, Jack Pong, was also an enforcer and extortionist for the Chinese National Association, a political group supporting the revolution in China. Lee Yung testified that Pong was trying to extort him to re-join the society. "We will make you pay!" Pong had exclaimed. Lee Yung further claimed that Pong had threatened him a number of times and even came to the club one night and broke some of his tables with an iron bar. Despite Pong's threats that he would expose Lee Yung to the police if he didn't pay the extortion money, Lee Yung still refused. The two defendants were convicted; Lee Yung re-emerged in Vancouver in the twenties as one of the major drug traffickers smuggling opium via the Empress liners. Then working under the name Albert Lee, Yung was arrested by the RCMP in 1929 as he was making a drug pick-up from one of the ships, but he managed to escape back to Toronto, where in 1931 he was once more arrested by the RCMP in a gambling house while playing the traditional Chinese game of mah-jong. He was convicted of opium smuggling in June 1931 and was sentenced to three years in jail.

Jack Pong surfaced again in court in 1923, when yet another police informer in Toronto's Chinatown, one Garnet Wong, was charged with extortion. Wong, who had been a police informant for more than ten years according to police testimony, believed erroneously that he could carry on an extortion business on the side, unmolested by the police because of his assistance to them. The money was collected from the gambling houses as "a price for police protection," according to the Elizabeth Street gambling house owner Yip Tong and two other Chinese men. During his defence testimony, Wong stated that he had been a business partner with Jack Pong in an importing business that turned out to be opium smuggling. When he discovered that the imported commodity was drugs, Wong testified, he tried to get out of the business, and personally "helped to destroy

$50,000 worth of narcotics" in a meeting he had had with Pong in Buffalo. He further claimed that he reported Pong's activities to the police in Montreal, one of Pong's bases of drug activities, but that they did nothing. Pong, of course, was still working for the police. Wong claimed that Pong was "biting the hand that feeds him." A Toronto police inspector testified that Wong was a reliable informant himself and had been a source of information for the police for more than ten years. The case revealed a curious system of police control of the Chinese underworld in Toronto, one that has a certain resonance in some of the otherwise inexplicable events and activities in Toronto in the 1970s and 1980s in relation to the Chinese community and the police.

By the early 1920s, a markedly racist attitude towards Orientals emerged in the Ontario media coverage of crime involving the Chinese. A *Toronto Star* headline in a story about a gambling and opium den case read: "Ching Chang Chinamen Muchee Muchee Glad." The following year, after a raid of an opium den in Hamilton (which, coincidentally, took place the same day as the testimony of Wong Sing in the Janet Smith case in Vancouver), the *Spectator* ran a front page story entitled "The Yellow Peril," indicating a level of racism in the Ontario media that was nearly as bad as in British Columbia.

> Some students affirm that the next problem to face Anglo Saxons and other white races is a monster fight for our very existence against the so-called "yellow peril." The Occidental peoples will have to master the inhabitants of the Far East by force of arms, and only in that way will the hordes of the Mongolian races be subdued. . . .

Toronto newspapers were filled with tales of opium and gambling dens as well as alien smuggling and oriental houses of ill repute in the middle and late twenties, even after the Exclusion Act barred Chinese immigrants to Canada. But it was in 1930 that a mini-hysteria broke out in Toronto about a possible tong war in the city. With all of the tong war violence in the United States, most recently a violent outburst of killing in Chicago in 1929, there was bound to be some spillover in Canada, especially in the media. Toronto newspapers on March 27, 1930, carried a front-page story about a Toronto tong war that was "brewing" with imported American hatchetmen gunning for people in the streets of Toronto's Chinatown. Thirty-five-year-old Low-Hee-faye (a.k.a. Loo-Hey-jeye) had suffered a concussion from a beating as he walked along Elizabeth Street. It was alleged by Low-Hee and some of his followers that he was attacked by outside "hatchet-men brought in by criminals who wanted to get back at those who were helping the police by acting as informers on the criminal activity in Chinatown," according to an interview in the *Toronto Telegram*. A group of Nationalists came to Low's rescue and drove him to the hospital. The Nationalists, who supported Chiang Kai-shek's party in China, ran a police-protected gambling house that was in fierce competition with one run by a pro-Monarchist group who opposed the Nationalists in China and were in alliance with a rival underworld group in Toronto's Chinatown. A member of the Chinese consulate staff in Ottawa was brought to Toronto to help ease the tensions.

What was brewing in Toronto was not a tong war as reported in the newspapers, but a political feud between Nationalists and Monarchists. At the time there was no functioning tong group in Toronto; there were, however, a number of gambling houses run by the various political factions. There were also independently run Chinese whorehouses throughout Chinatown and in the neighbouring "Ward" district, a colourful area of downtown Toronto then teeming with Italian, Jewish, and other immigrants.

On the next day the *Toronto Star* headline blared "Tong War Reports Called Groundless." It corrected the *Globe*'s and the *Telegram*'s erroneous reports of imported hatchetmen and added some details about police undercover operations in the Chinese underworld in Toronto at the time:

There is no tong war among the Chinese in their Elizabeth Street colony, police declared to the Star to-day. . . . Inspector William Johnson, officer commanding the district that embraces the so-called Chinatown, stated to-day he had "never been able to find any evidence of hatchet-men being imported from outside." Inspector Johnson said it was just a small fight between the Nationalist and Monarchist Masonic groups over the recent raids among the gambling element in Chinatown. He said that certain Chinamen are angry because other Chinese have been informing on them to the police.

The Globe itself ran an article on that same day denying the contents of their earlier misleading story. "The tong war which members of the Chinese Nationalist Party feared was brewing failed to materialize," they began their new account. After raiding Chinese gambling houses on Queen Street and Elizabeth Street, police arrested a local hoodlum, Mark Yuen Pan, for the assault.

The Tong War incident in spring 1930 certainly indicated that there were rival factions in control of illegal activities in Toronto's Chinatown and that these factions would use violence to settle scores. The Monarchists probably included triad members since their sacred duty was to restore the Ming dynasty, though, as we have seen, this mission lost its relevance in the earlier part of the century with the revolution of Dr. Sun Yat-sen. The triads did, however, support Chiang Kai-shek and the Nationalists, who were then fighting to retain control of southern China.

These rivalries and divisions soon healed, and although there are isolated reports of problems in Toronto's Chinatown in the thirties and forties, there were no violent manifestations of serious criminal activity. There were, of course, the illegal Chinese gambling clubs and legendary whorehouses as well as drug activity, for which arrests were made periodically during this period. George Wong, a Canadian World War I veteran, was convicted in the early 1930s of importing five decks of opium, and in 1937, Jung How Thun (a.k.a. Jung Jack) got two years in Kingston after police discovered more than a hundred decks of opium in his room, "one of the largest seizures of opium" in Toronto in the 1930s, according to the RCMP Annual Report of that year. The gambling houses, whorehouses, and low-level extortion were under "friendly control," and, generally, the Chinese themselves took care of any problems without bothering to bring in the police, whom many tended to distrust based on their experiences in China or Hong Kong. Some of the criminal activity was undertaken with police complicity in exchange for information about other criminal operations. As we have seen, police informers in the Chinese community seem to have frequently been at the forefront of criminal enterprises in Toronto's Chinatown.

After World War II, the racist Exclusion Act was finally repealed, and new Oriental immigrants were allowed into Canada legally for the first time since 1923. Between 1946 and 1959, approximately twenty-five thousand Chinese, mostly from mainland China, came to Canada, many to the Toronto area, whose Chinese population began to climb rapidly from the levels it had been frozen at since the 1920s. Immigration smuggling and other rackets also began to expand with the influx.*

Alien smuggling had been an ongoing problem in Canada for decades. In the 1920s, the RCMP broke up scores of alien-smuggling rings that specialized in bringing Italians and Chinese illegally into the country by using forged work permits and fraudulent passports. At the time the smugglers charged up to $1,000 per head, though many of the illegal aliens paid extra money for being smuggled into the United States as well, which was usually accomplished by boat across the Niagara or Detroit rivers or by car. Since legal immigration was denied to Chinese

---

* By 1974 there were more than a hundred thousand new Chinese immigrants from China, Hong Kong, and Taiwan in Canada, as well as thousands of Hong Kong students studying in British Columbia and Toronto. By 1992 Metropolitan Toronto's Chinese (and Vietnamese) population was well over four hundred thousand (becoming the second-largest Chinese population in North America after New York City), and Greater Vancouver's was over 250,000.

from the early twenties, the demand to use illegal alien-smuggling networks to get into Canada was particularly high throughout the 1920s and 1930s. Henry Anslinger's U.S. Bureau of Narcotics worked closely with the RCMP in breaking up the many smuggling rings that were operating via Canada.

In 1960, after the RCMP charged a number of people across the country with alien smuggling, the term "triad" appeared in print for the first time in Canada as a designation for an Asian organized crime group, though Canadian law enforcement did not publicly use the term until more than a decade later. On July 28, 1960, *Toronto Telegram* reporter Gerald Waring reported on the front page (under the headline, "Triad Men in Our Top Cities") that "the Chinese immigration racket smashed by the Royal Canadian Mounted Police has been operated under the 'protection' of the most dreaded underworld organization of the Far East. . . . The Immigration rackets were controlled by Triads — Mafia-like groups which have tentacles in rackets all over the world." Although not directly involved in the smuggling of more than eleven thousand Chinese into Canada, the triads were, according to Waring, "taking a substantial slice off the top of payments made to the immigration racketeers." Waring then quotes a "high source" as stating that "triad agents have been identified in the major Canadian Chinatowns" and have "penetrated organized crime in Canada." Waring's story, based on documents seized by the RCMP implicating a number of immigration agents with triads in Hong Kong, was followed up in a major *Maclean's* magazine exposé by crime reporter Alan Phillips. A huge blow-up of the Hung Mun Society symbol accompanied his lengthy story entitled "The Criminal Society that Dominates the Chinese in Canada" in the April 7, 1962, edition. The piece is full of exaggerations and inaccuracies, including the claim that the Chinese Freemasons, the Chi Kung tong (CKT), was nothing more than a front for the triads, that the CKT was "known in Hong Kong as the overseas branch of the Triad society." Although the CKT did practise some triad rituals and sought in the early years to overthrow the Ch'ing dynasty and restore the

Ming, it was not a triad. But it was true that the Montreal CKT president at the time, "Uncle Jack" Wong, known on the street as the King of the Gambling Houses in Quebec in the 1950s and 1960s, controlled a number of illegal gambling clubs, including the notorious Victoria Sporting Club in Montreal, which was later the subject of a Royal Commission into organized crime in Quebec. A rival gang leader in Montreal who challenged Wong's authority by smashing up one of his clubs in an extortion attempt was found brutally murdered just a few weeks later. Wong wasn't brought under control until the middle 1970s, when police, at the initiation of a veteran Montreal policeman, Frank Burns, finally closed all of his illegal clubs. Obviously, some individuals connected with organizations like the CKT were involved in criminal activity, especially alien smuggling and gambling, but that does not make those organizations criminal groups.

Phillips even went on to accuse the Canadian Chinese Consolidated Benevolent Association (CCBA), a strong civil-rights advocate for Chinese immigrants to Canada, of being deeply involved in illegal activity and, through a kind of McCarthyism, cited the fact that one Canadian Immigration agent and his nephew "were associated with the CCBA." There is little evidence to support Phillips's overblown charges against either the CKT or the CCBA as organizations. But Phillips did reveal some new information. He reported that Hong Kong triad leader and multimillionaire, C.S. Wong, was running an immigration scam, and that two Canadian agents, Wong-Lai Yap and Chen Ping-Hsuin, were listed as among those convicted in Hong Kong for running illegal aliens to Canada.

The emphasis in the *Maclean's* piece was on the very real problem of alien smuggling. A June 1960 Immigration study revealed that half the approximately seventy-five thousand immigrants from China and Hong Kong were "probably impostors." As a result of the massive nation-wide immigration investigation, many immigration agents or consultants across the country were charged with and convicted of fraud. Vancouver agent Joseph Hope committed suicide rather than face his trial. In Winnipeg, Lui Pak Yong was found guilty and fined $1,000, and in Montreal, Wilbur Wong paid a fine of $3,000. One illegal immigrant to the Winnipeg area, Yuen Mun, tried to kill a policeman at the border when trying to enter the United States. By January 1962 more than one thousand Chinese in Canada had confessed to being here illegally. The immigration rackets in Hong Kong were definitely controlled by the triads, a criminal force then estimated to be about twenty thousand strong.

Former Toronto-based Immigration intelligence officer George Best, who retired in 1988, spent decades investigating alien smuggling and other triad-connected activities in Canada for both Canadian Customs and Immigration. Best, a short, bespectacled, mild-mannered man, explained how Canada Immigration decided to handle the problem, which they called "Chinese adjustment."

Historically, from an Immigration point of view, when a problem gets out of control, we have a special program. So we had this special program for Chinese Adjustment. The government realized that there were large numbers of Chinese here who were not who they claimed to be. In the sixties the RCMP got involved in the investigations. We brought people in from Hong Kong — police who acted as interpreters. In taking the statements, the Department tried to emphasize "We are giving you an opportunity to adjust your status — tell us the truth and nothing will happen — you may have entered the country illegally, you may have a fraudulent passport — whatever — tell us the truth." We had these Status Adjustment statements, which were a kind of amnesty, though it wasn't called that. . . . The Status Adjustment Program of the 1960s was simply a means for the government to come to grips with the problem of massive illegal immigration to Canada.

Since the government didn't want to miss the chance of losing potential voters, an amnesty was the easiest policy to adopt once they found out how many thousands of people had come here illegally under assumed names and through criminal networks.

Best, like the Metro Toronto police, emphatically states that in his opinion there were no real triads in Toronto before the mid-1970s. "Historically, before the Kung Lok triad, there have been Chinese gangs in Toronto — gambling groups, drug dealers, and youth gangs — but none of these gangs had been structured on a triad principle." With the new wave of Chinese immigration in the sixties and early seventies, which by 1974 had brought the Chinese population in Toronto up to one hundred thousand, new problems emerged. This new group of immigrants from Hong Kong were much more inclined to seek out investments and business expansion. Immediately, Chinatown changed from being a kind of tourist area to a place where the majority of restaurants catered primarily to Chinese tastes. According to George Best, criminals who had come in with the new Hong Kong immigrants almost immediately took advantage of the situation:

Bear in mind we are not saying there was no criminal activity here before. We had gangs before and drugs, gambling houses, and other criminal activities. But with this new wave of immigrants coming from Hong Kong, the criminal element in Hong Kong saw Canada as a land of opportunity. Many of them had been involved in the triads in China and had been forced into Hong Kong when the Communists took over in the forties, because the Communists wouldn't put up with them.

Sergeant George Cowley, who worked in Chinatown at the time, explained that the new Hong Kong Chinese were "a very Westernized Chinese, a very outgoing and gregarious type of people" who had "arrived in Toronto in a very different fashion and with very different ideas from the Toishan Chinese from southern China in the area around Canton," where a good number of the original Chinese immigrants to North America had originated.

Other credible analysts of the crime scene in Toronto agree

with this assessment. The new Hong Kong element that immigrated in the late sixties and early seventies included a small but determined minority of hardened criminals who started new criminal organizations in Toronto. Constable Mike King, one of the first cops on the special Chinese unit begun in 1977, confirmed that the criminal makeup of Chinatown changed dramatically in the early 1970s:

> There were many gambling houses in Toronto in the sixties. They were run by independents who were here before Lau Wing Kui [the Toronto triad leader who arrived in 1974] was even thought of. This included people like Sunny Lem and the old group from Toishan.

The men who ran the gambling houses had informal relationships with the local police. Initially, crimes in the community were simply tolerated. Gambling houses thrived, and some people paid small extortions without reporting anything to the police. In fact for years, each house kept a fund for paying small fines that were imposed on those running gambling houses. Informal liaison officers, gambling house owners who met regularly with the police, would get all the names from the house and pay the fines to the court. Most of the found-ins, those caught illegally gambling in the houses, didn't have to go to court. Many of them didn't even know that they were acquiring criminal records, albeit minor ones. Everything was being taken care of by the police liaison people in the community and the gambling houses themselves.

However, when serious crimes were committed, a system was devised whereby several connected individuals in the community became more formal liaisons with the police through certain trusted police officers who worked in the community. According to Staff Sergeant George Cowley, a former head of the Oriental crime squad, the old Toishan Chinese in Toronto wanted it that way.

> Crimes were being reported not to the police but to an individual officer who was trusted, someone who had established a rapport or trust in the community. That was

acceptable, but it's not very good — because people would then feel that to get to that officer you have to go through someone else in the community. It was not the best way.

The liaison person was generally a local character, such as Sunny Lem or Bill Mar, who himself was often involved in illegal activity, usually running gaming houses. This system, which carried on at least until the mid-1980s, is described by Inspector Barry Hill as occasionally a major headache from the police perspective. Hill was the head of the special police Oriental unit in the early and mid 1980s before Cowley, who at the time was an officer attached to 52 Division in Chinatown. Hill testified in October 1984 as a witness about criminal activity in Toronto before the U.S. Presidential Commission on Organized Crime and is currently one of the most important policemen in Toronto as the Director of the Criminal Intelligence Service of Ontario, which helps the various police forces in the province co-ordinate their criminal investigations:

Reporting to individuals [self-appointed liaison officers with the police who gave police inside information and helped out when there were problems] got me into shit. Because the individual reporting to me was not a very nice person. He'd phone me and I'd go out to meet with him. My name and home number appeared in this person's phone book. But when he was then investigated later on, that got me into a lot of shit. And he was one of the persons who was tipping me off. . . .

This traditional way of dealing with things in Chinatown carried on well into the late 1980s. But by the mid-1970s, with the arrival of the newer, sinister criminal forces from Hong Kong, the old system was under severe pressures. Even before the Kung Lok became established in Ontario after the arrival of a triad leader from Hong Kong in the mid-1970s, a number of former Hong Kong policemen had arrived in Canada and began investing heavily in real estate in Vancouver and Toronto. This was the first major danger signal that a new menace loomed in the Asian underworlds in Canada.

Chapter Six

THE FIVE DRAGONS
AND CLIFFORD WONG

"Half police are Hung brothers" is how a triad leader in Timothy Mo's critically acclaimed 1982 novel, *Sour Sweet*, amusingly refers to the Royal Hong Kong Police in his conversation with another triad leader. But the joke is grimly accurate, if not understated, for much of Hong Kong's history. Until the late 1960s, the infrastructure of the Royal Hong Kong Police Force allowed a small circle of staff sergeants in the Criminal Investigations Department (CID) unlimited power and unique access to graft. The CID sergeants, who controlled whole sections of Hong Kong and wore a red sash when in uniform, functioned more like powerful American sergeant majors. They had power over everyone in their area of control — senior officers (mostly British and Australian expatriates), the major criminals, and the cops on the beat. For a significant and regular sum of money that made many of the otherwise poorly paid staff sergeants wealthy men, they became the main intermediaries between the principal criminals of Hong Kong and the police force. Some of the policemen, like Lui Lok, even became major criminals in their own right, *organizing* rather than attacking the vice in the area under their control.

Staff Sergeant George Cowley, the former head of the Metro joint forces unit on Asian gangs, who had previously himself been a member of the Royal Hong Kong Police, explained how the corrupt system worked:

The "Five Dragons" [five of the most corrupt policemen] were just very powerful people in Hong Kong because of their position. They were one hundred percent connected with members of the triad societies, but they were offering services to all criminals operating within their geographical area. Each of those staff sergeants was the leading ranking non-commissioned officer for a geographical area. So each had his finger in the pie in criminal activity in his area. They would all get together now and again to meet and compare notes. . . . They ran the police force. This was in the days when the government paid very little money to police. There was no budget even for the maintenance of a police station. The painting of a police station was done out of the pocket of the staff sergeant. The staff sergeant would also pay for the upkeep of police equipment. The government knew this was going on, and that they couldn't obviously afford to do this. They turned a blind eye to it. They were running a very low-budget operation.

All Hong Kong policemen were expected to take part in the systemic bribery, not just the ruling staff sergeants. One of the unintentionally funniest moments in the June 1977 "Connections"* television program on organized crime was when Walter Easey, an Englishman who had been an inspector in the Royal Hong Kong Police, explained in a perfectly straightforward fashion how universal the corruption was:

WALTER EASEY: The first bribe that was ever offered to me was two weeks after I left training school. I was never in

---

* The five dragons story was the major news item of the second hour-and-a-half show of "Connections" broadcast on June 13. It created a furore in the newspapers and news outlets across the country and a major uproar in the House of Commons for many days. For the series, on which I was the research director, we had spent years researching in Hong Kong, Europe, Vancouver, and Toronto to track down the story. As one five dragon law enforcement investigator put it to me, " 'Connections' worked. It burned the hell out of those guys. It was the best thing you could have done."

any job in the force where I wasn't being paid off, either by small or large amounts.

QUESTION: Were most of the people being paid off?

WALTER EASEY: Well, the force was about eight or nine thousand strong, and I definitely knew of two people who weren't. One was religious — he was a Plymouth brethren and a very religious person. And the other was just crazy. No one could trust him; so he never got anything. He was thrown off the force shortly afterwards. But he was too unreliable to be paying.

But the corrupt system began to collapse in 1967 when Royal Hong Kong Police Commissioner Charlie Sutcliffe restructured the force so that the staff sergeants were out of the loop for sensitive information. There had been a number of scandals involving cops on the take in Hong Kong after the 1967 riots (partially caused by a sense of social injustice and corruption in high places), which put enormous pressure on the authorities to clean up the notoriously corrupt police force. Among those leading the new anti-corruption drive was Elsie Elliott Tu, a crusading and hard-working Englishwoman who still sits on the Urban Council as an elected member from one of the poorest sections of Hong Kong. Elsie, as she is known affectionately by her constituents and admirers, became a one-person watchdog of the corrupt members and former members of the Royal Hong Kong Police Force. In her memoirs, *Crusade for Justice*, first published in 1981, Elsie Elliott Tu explained how she became familiar with the triads:

> I cannot remember when I first became acquainted with the term "triad." Soon after arriving in Hong Kong in 1951, I became accustomed to hearing the more common term Hak Sei Wooi (black society) [also known as "the dark society"] . . . . I knew from the beginning of my residence in Hong Kong that the triads controlled all illegal operations such as illegal hawkers, the drug trade, and all commercialized vice.

She also learned very quickly the high level of involvement and often open role the Royal Hong Kong Police had in criminal operations in the colony:

> The natural result of this involvement of the authorities in crime and corruption has been an increase in the crime rate. . . . Youngsters see how the triads and some of the police intimidate and extort from the people, and some of them have copied their tactics.

Elsie Elliott Tu had helped many a hawker and street vendor who was being squeezed over the years by corrupt Royal Hong Kong Police and the triads. In 1962, after seeing for herself how poor street hawkers were openly forced to pay bribes to the police, she became a city councillor. Not long thereafter she joined the Reform Club in Hong Kong and helped to write a report on vice and corruption in Hong Kong; she was told by a lawyer that Staff Sergeant Lui Lok had told him that he was "going to get" her and her reform colleagues.

In the mid-1960s the Star Ferry riots rocked Hong Kong. Elsie claimed that Lui Lok had organized the riots to discredit her reform group; RHKP officials, she claimed, planted evidence against her. Others have blamed the Communists for the rioting. But it was always the scandalous and outrageous activities of the corrupt police that infuriated Elsie the most. More than thirty years later, still going strong in her mid-seventies, Elsie was still fuming about the corruption at the highest levels of the RHKP. Although her accusation that today "you cannot get into the RHKP without a triad connection" may be an exaggeration, Elsie Elliott Tu has had years of bitter experience with the RHKP. Many of Elsie Tu's constituents were victimized by RHKP officers over the years, and Elsie herself was subjected to false accusations, harassment, and discredit because of her reform activities.

Courageously, Elsie was one of the first officials to publicly name and denounce the five dragons, the most corrupt RHKP staff sergeants. As early as 1968, she approached the recently appointed head of the Anti-Corruption Branch of the RHKP:

> I particularly asked for action against a policeman named
> Nam (Lam) Kong who had been involved in my frame-up
> in 1967 [the blame for instigating the Star Ferry riots]. I had
> been reporting his activities and he had reason to want to
> get rid of me. I knew that he had some connection to the
> drug trade. He was also quite a senior policeman. "Oh, Lam
> Kong?" replied [the police official], "Yes, I know about him.
> Don't worry, I have thirteen charges against him. We will
> certainly get him."

But when Elsie contacted the same official several months
later, not only was Lam Kong not charged, but the official
denied ever discussing the matter with her. Lam (Nam) Kong
later turned out to be one of the five dragons who came to
Canada in the early 1970s.

Today the chief bulwark against corruption in the RHKP is the
Independent Commission Against Corruption (the ICAC),
which was founded in 1974 after a series of shocking events
took place. Ironically, it was the establishment of this tough
new agency in Hong Kong that opened the floodgates of Chinese triad-connected criminals out of the Crown colony — and
into Canada. In 1973 the old Anti-Corruption Bureau run by
the RHKP had cracked down on criminals, fugitives, and a
number of wealthy ex-Hong Kong policemen; those who were
still at large were leaving the Crown colony in droves. While
under investigation for corruption, RHKP Chief Superintendent
Peter Godber, who had been given notice that he was to be
charged, fled to England to avoid arrest. It was later discovered
that he had millions of dollars in the bank, though he had
earned less than $100,000 total in his twenty years on the force.
Although Godber was eventually extradited back to Hong
Kong, where he was convicted of corruption, his flight and the
exposure of the corrupt staff sergeants' system was a major
embarrassment for the force who, up until this incident, had
essentially investigated themselves.

The new Independent Commission Against Corruption was set up as a powerful civilian agency, separate from the police force, to investigate thoroughly and prosecute corruption in the colony. It had incredible powers of search and seizure and could wiretap without a warrant. Small wonder, then, that so many criminals and policemen decided to flee. Among them were the five dragons. There were many other corrupt policemen from Hong Kong who came to Canada and the United States, but the sobriquet "five dragons" continued to identify the group led by Lui Lok.*

The five dragons named after the hills surrounding Hong Kong, were led by CID Staff Sergeant Lui Lok, who decided to come to Canada in the early 1970s. They were first dubbed the "five dragons" in print by Andrew Davenport of the *Far East Economic Review*, in January 1977. The five dragons was the "nickname they had in Chinatowns in Vancouver and Toronto" as the "wealthiest policemen ever to have retired from the Royal Hong Kong Police Force," according to Davenport. The other four dragons were Nam Kong (Nam Man Kai; a.k.a. Kam Yuen Nam or Lam Kwong); Choi (Tsoi) Bing Lung; Chung Cheung Yau (a.k.a. Lo Kam Tin); and Hon Sum (a.k.a. Hon Kwing-shum). The wealth of these policemen was legendary in Hong Kong, Canada, and Taiwan.

When they came to seek refuge in Canada, the five dragons were welcomed as independent entrepreneurs at a time when this country was seeking serious money from abroad and

---

* For example, there were several former Royal Hong Kong policemen who joined and invested with former RHKP officer Eddie Chan, head of the largest tong in the United States (the On Leong tong) in New York City, and one who worked with Lau Wing Kui in Toronto. Others have retired to the cash-starved Dominican Republic, where citizenship could be bought for a mere $50,000, or to Taiwan, where they cannot be extradited to Hong Kong as no extradition treaty exists between the two governments. This will obviously remain true when the People's Republic of China takes over Hong Kong in 1997. Lau Wing Kui, the Toronto Kung Lok triad leader, had himself started out by working as a graft collector for one of the many corrupt policemen in Hong Kong.

happily allowing moneyed immigrants into the country. Thus, even though several of the five dragons openly declared millions of dollars in assets and cash on their Canadian admittance forms, nobody in Canada questioned how the poorly paid police sergeants acquired their money. Even after the American Drug Enforcement Administration (DEA) learned through street-level sources in Hong Kong the magnitude of what was taking place and issued a worldwide alert regarding the five dragons to all DEA stations in early 1976, Canada was still considered a safe haven for fleeing corrupt Hong Kong officials and other criminals for another two years. And once they had arrived, several prominent Chinese-Canadian businessmen were more than happy to front for Lui Lok and some of the other dragons.

Lui Lok was the most notorious of the five dragons. Dubbed by Hong Kong newspapers "the $500-million man" (because of his reputed worth in Hong Kong), he was the staff sergeant who had accumulated the largest fortune. Lui Lok was also an initiated member of the Sun Yee On triad, the largest and most powerful triad society in Hong Kong. By the time he retired from the RHKP, he owned a palatial home in Hong Kong. When he arrived in Vancouver, he lived for a few months with a member of the RCMP Security Service before buying a modest bungalow on West 44th Street.

Once landed in Canada, the five dragons began to make massive investments in the country, primarily in real estate — apartment and office buildings, restaurants, and businesses in Vancouver and Toronto. At least one of the five dragons, Nam Kong, invested money in the private Florence Nightingale Hospital in Vancouver. Nam Kong's wife and children had been patients of Dr. K. Ting Yue, the hospital's managing director, who had known them for some time. When Dr. Yue was interviewed for "Connections," he seemed surprised when told about the nature of Nam Kong's background, particularly the allegation about possible involvement in drug dealing.

Yet Canadian Immigration officer Brian Harrington had told of meetings at the Asia Gardens Restaurant in Vancouver with some of the five dragons and Dr. Yue, who, Harrington said, was not only a part owner of the restaurant, but had himself set up the meeting. When asked about whether he had met with any "government" people at the restaurant, Dr. Yue was baffled.

YUE: Government? . . . What you mean?

MARTYN BURKE ("Connections" co-producer): I mean have you ever had any meetings with government people over at Asia Gardens?

YUE: Government people . . . . What government people?

When asked about the possible involvement of some of the five dragons on the board of the Asia Gardens, Dr. Yue was again extremely hesitant and quizzical.

BURKE: Don't you have some ownership in the Asia Gardens?

YUE: Yes, I do.

BURKE: . . . . There's a company called Trans Global Investment where there's an ex-sergeant for the Hong Kong police?

YUE: Come again? I couldn't get the name.

BURKE: Are you also involved in a company called Trans Global Investment?

YUE: No.

BURKE: Not at all.

YUE: No.

The screen then filled with the corporate papers of Trans Global Investments. It showed a Dr. K.T. Yue of Vancouver as a director along with a former Hong Kong policeman. The five dragons also had a piece of another large Vancouver restaurant.

Dr. Yue, Immigration official Brian Harrington, the five dragons and their families, and businessmen associated with the dragons were not the only people to be embarrassed by the section on the five dragons on "Connections." The Canadian government seemed totally unprepared for the controversy about the admission of the five dragons. In the uproar in the House of Commons in the days following the program, Immigration Minister Bud Cullen said that the five dragons were legally admitted to Canada even though they claimed assets of up to millions of dollars.

The one dragon who remained in Canada by that time, Hon Sum, who lived with his family on West 54th Street in Vancouver, was ordered arrested in March 1978. He was to be extradited to Hong Kong to face the charges, but the wily Hon Sum was one step ahead of the authorities. He jumped bail after his arrest and fled to Taiwan. Only the lawyer for dragon Choi Bing Lung was arrested in Hong Kong where he had moved. He was charged with stealing $185,000 worth of jewellery from Choi Bing Lung's palatial home in the Shaughnessy area of Vancouver.

Stanley Wong, a Hong Kong drug trafficker turned DEA informer interviewed for "Connections" in 1977, had been in Vancouver importing heroin when Lui Lok and Nam Kong arrived. He explained how Lui Lok made his fortune:

> The money he made he received from drugs, from the gambling shops, from all sorts of activities, mostly illegal. I mean the people that are smoking opium in Hong Kong, they pay Lui Lok and the police every night one thousand Hong Kong dollars (two hundred U.S. dollars) .... Also the massage parlours, they paid about seven hundred Hong Kong dollars per night to operate. ... Lui Lok was clearing about forty thousand dollars a day [as his share of the criminal proceeds in Hong Kong].

Wong went on to explain that when Lui Lok and Nam Kong retired, they came to Vancouver where they bought, according to the word from mutual friends in Hong Kong and Vancouver, "ten blocks of prime property in the business area of Vancouver."

Lui Lok found some savvy Canadian partners to front these real estate investments in Canada. Among them was Clifford

Wong, a Canadian-educated former Hong Kong architect and developer who was making quite a name for himself in Hong Kong and Canada. He is one of the heroic entrepreneurs of *China Tide*, journalist Margaret Cannon's 1989 book on Hong Kong immigration to Canada. Cannon, who is well-known for reviewing crime fiction in her weekly "Murder and Mayhem" column in the *Globe and Mail*, focused on Wong's business acumen and his family life, but overlooked the intrigue and mystery in his story. In Hong Kong, Wong is best known as the brains behind the $750 million HK Fairview Park private housing estate in the New Territories, which he financed through a Canadian company, Canadian Overseas Development. His partners in this massive development project included the Royal Bank of Canada, through an affiliate in Amsterdam called Roy-East, and such distinguished Hong Kong businessmen as Sir Albert Rodrigues, CBE, the former senior unofficial member of the Executive Council of Hong Kong, Alex Wai Tse-hang, and Dr. Peter Lee Chung-yin, JP.

Clifford Wong was one of the people Lui Lok chose as a chief front in Canada. Through Barony Estates, a Canadian development company incorporated in Ontario in 1967, Wong bought a number of buildings in the mid seventies, including the then elegant, $50-million LuCliff Place office building and adjoining apartment complex at the corner of Bay and Gerrard streets in downtown Toronto.* According to the official version, that given out by Clifford Wong himself, the building, which included an office building wing, commercial stores on the first floor, and an apartment building section further down Gerrard Street, was an acronym for his first name and his wife's first name (Louisa). But police intelligence later learned that the "Lu" also stood for Lui Lok, who had put up a major amount of money for the building. Wong maintained that Lui Lok was just

---

* This address was just across the street, ironically enough, from Toronto Mafia leader Paul Volpe's natal home on Walton Street, which remained standing until the late seventies in spite of all of the development in the area.

one of many financial partners and, furthermore, that he was not aware of the source of Lui Lok's money.

Inspector Barry Hill, then head of the Toronto police's Asian crime unit, testified in 1984 before the U.S. Presidential Commission on Organized Crime that the five dragons in Canada "joined with other ex-Royal Hong Kong officials and a prominent architect from Hong Kong, and purchased a large office building in downtown Toronto. . . ." He was referring to LuCliff Place.

In fact, the original incorporation file on Barony lists fourteen Hong Kong directors named to the Board between 1969 and 1971, six of whom were former Hong Kong police sergeants, four of whom were part of the five dragons — Lui Lok, Nam Kong, and Choi Bing Lung, and Chung Cheung Yau — as well as two other former Hong Kong policemen, Cheung Sau and Kwong Tui. Also on the board was James Cheung, a legitimate Toronto real estate manager.

A fully documented case of a business which was secretly owned in part by the five dragons surfaced in the "Connections" series. Centrepoint East consisted of two high-rise apartment buildings on Sherbourne and Dundas streets. Complex manager James Cheung, who was ambushed on the street by the determined "Connections" co-producer Martyn Burke, admitted on camera that Lui Lok and three of the dragons had been on the board, but that he was now "the sole director." Although Cheung admitted that he had "heard the rumours" about a warrant out for the arrest of his former fellow director Lui Lok, he said that he "hardly ever" saw him or the other dragons; however, he admitted he had been involved with them as associates "in a couple of things."

Clifford Wong also stated that the staff sergeants were brought in by some of his business partners — he named Eddie Hoy and Jimmy Cheung. He added that he met Lui Lok only twice, that the sergeants rarely came to board meetings, preferring to operate in Toronto through their lawyers. Cheung added in an interview that when they became partners, "they had retired with honour" from the Royal Hong Kong Police. "Three and a half years ago [1974], when they became notorious, we wanted to buy them out, but we couldn't get in touch with them." It would have spared Cheung and his associates a lot of embarrassment had they been able.

In the late seventies and early eighties, police had Clifford Wong under surveillance. At the time he maintained a closely guarded secret office in the penthouse of LuCliff Place, which many senior members of the Metro police Chinese unit were convinced acted as a headquarters for a major drug ring. Though there were never any charges, informants insisted that Clifford Wong was the chief money man behind the big heroin deals in Toronto at the time. Unable to penetrate the extremely tight security of the penthouse to put in a bug, police finally gave up, although one police source has stated that they didn't try very hard to get the evidence.

Metro Toronto police also linked Lui Lok to ownership of a major restaurant in Toronto. A so-called "source of previous reliability," who was described as a former RHKP officer himself, maintained that the principal owner of the well-known restaurant was a corrupt former corporal in the RHKP and was both a first cousin of and front for Lui Lok. Curiously though, the same restaurant was later mentioned in a mid-1980s Royal Hong Kong Police report; it seems that a number of Hong Kong immigrants had come to Toronto to work at the restaurant as a way to get into Canada in an immigration scheme run by Kung Lok leader Danny Mo and his triad colleagues. Whether this intelligence information about the restaurant was correct was ultimately impossible to determine, and there was not enough evidence to firmly link Lui Lok to the restaurant, in spite of the Metro police source and the many rumours in the community.

The five dragon connection had even tainted Wong's Fairview Park development project when in 1977 Wong transferred his shares in the project to Favorable Investments, Inc., a Panama-based company. Suddenly, people began to wonder who Wong's other secret partners might be. When asked in early 1977 by the Independent Commission Against Corruption (ICAC) in Hong

Kong, Wong refused to divulge their identities. This development embarrassed the Royal Bank, which in June 1977 said that its Panamanian company had been formed simply for tax reasons.

But the connection to the five dragons isn't the only matter in the substantial file that the ICAC compiled on Clifford Wong. In 1977 Wong was formally charged with bribing a public official when David Wilkerson, an English surveyor working in Hong Kong, admitted to the ICAC that he had accepted the bribe. At the time Wong was the principal officer of a development company called Tsun Sheong Ltd. and Wilkerson was a professional architect with the Public Works department. Wilkerson was found guilty, was charged in April 1977 under section 10 of the Bribery Ordinance, and was fined $102,000 HK, but received only a suspended prison sentence. As a result of Wilkerson's testimony, Wong was then charged with one count of conspiracy to pervert the course of justice and two counts of bribery. But there were long delays in the trial as Wong's lawyers used every trick in the book, including appeals to Magistrates Court and even to the Privy Council. The entire Crown case was built around Wilkerson's testimony. But after his disgrace, Wilkerson left Hong Kong and returned to England. He refused to come back for Wong's trial; by the time the trial actually began in late 1978, the Crown was without its chief witness. As a result, the judge, the Honourable Collier McLeggatt, Q.C. couldn't proceed, and on December 9, 1978, a verdict of *nol-pros* was issued, and the case was dropped.

"The justice system was manipulated throughout" claimed a senior ICAC prosecutor, "to the point that the main prosecution witness couldn't appear." Edward "Ted" Winnington, the ICAC investigator on the case, was very disturbed at what happened — particularly at Wilkerson's suspended sentence and his subsequent disappearing act. Winnington died shortly thereafter, extremely bitter about Clifford Wong getting off scot-free, according to a high-level ICAC colleague. Although it was never proven, the feeling at the ICAC was that Clifford Wong had got to the witness.

But there was some negative fall-out for Wong, who was fairly well-connected. One of Wong's lawyers in Toronto, incidentally, was Bill McMurtry, the brother of the then attorney general, Roy McMurtry. Although this certainly unnerved a number of police officials at the time, it was a perfectly open and above-board business relationship. When Premier William Davis was on an official visit to Hong Kong in the early 1980s, he was advised by the police not to meet with Clifford Wong, who had returned to the Crown colony to live. A senior Toronto police officer explained that this was a deliberate "slap in the face" because the deputy minister in the attorney general's office had had the police file on Wong read to him. This included the serious allegation of being involved with Lui Lok and the five dragons. A Chinese member of the police's Asian crime unit had previously thought of Clifford Wong as simply naïve, but he read the file to the deputy minister and concluded that he had been wrong, and that Clifford Wong "really was a bad guy."

The broadcast of the story of the five dragons on the "Hong Kong" segment of the second "Connections" show broadcast in June 1977 had a devastating effect on them. Much of their money was quickly moved to the United States and Asia, and although several had families and palatial estates in Vancouver, the dragons all eventually left Canada. Lui Lok and two others now live in Taiwan.

Nam Kong is the only one of the five dragons who actually sued the CBC for being mentioned in the "Connections" series. Amazingly enough, on June 7, 1982, the CBC apologized to Nam Kong for "any inference drawn by our viewers that you were one of the principal leaders of a criminal organization which controlled the illegal drug trade in Hong Kong, Vancouver, or elsewhere, or that as a member of the Hong Kong Police force you in any way interfered with the administration of justice which would have in any way benefitted those involved in the drug trade." The apology by the CBC in June 1982 was sent without the signatures or even knowledge of the show's producers. When co-producer Bill Macadam received a copy of the text in the mail, he denounced the move in a letter to current affairs head, Bill Morgan: "I am unalterably opposed to sending any letter to Nam Kong without the matter being further thoroughly discussed with me, Jim Dubro, and the lawyers in question."*

Shortly after the apology was sent, it was learned that Nam Kong was a partner with Eddie Chan in two restaurants in New York City, and, at the same time, the DEA had arranged through U.S. Immigration to get Nam Kong included on a permanent list of undesirables who could no longer legally visit the United States. Nam Kong, after years of hiding in Taiwan, died of natural causes in exile in the Dominican Republic in 1990. Along with Hon Sum, Chung Cheung Yau, and Choi Bing Lung, Lui Lok took refuge in Taiwan.

Although there has been an ICAC warrant out for the arrest of Lui Lok under section 10.1b (corruption) for a number of years, there is little chance of getting him to Hong Kong, which does not have an extradition treaty with Taiwan. However, Lui Lok was also the subject of civil litigation in Hong Kong after his name surfaced in the trial of drug kingpin Ng Shek-ho, known in the street and the newspapers simply as "Limpy" Ho because of an injury to his leg acquired in a triad fight in his youth. Ho had a special relationship with the five dragons, as they were all Chiu Chao, descendants of the original brotherhood of people (from the Swatow area about 170 miles up the coast of China from Canton) who had organized opposition to the Manchu invaders in the seventeenth century and who to this day, though dispersed, often use their own dialect rather than Cantonese. In 1982 Ho offered to become a crucial witness against Lui Lok in a Hong Kong civil action against him to recover some of the illicit money. Limpy Ho and others testified in the High Court case in 1984. According to a *South China*

---

* But Morgan had already posted the apology, simply to clear his desk. So much for the courage and backbone of some CBC executives. Morgan has been promoted to a new job and is currently the arbiter of journalistic ethics at the CBC.

Morning Post account of the proceedings, the court was told Lui Lok collected the money because he "could have the heroin and gambling stalls 'dead or alive,' " and because gambling and drug kings, including the well-known drug trafficker "White Powder" Ma (Ma Sik-yu, one of Hong Kong's most successful and wealthy heroin traffickers from the 1960s through the 1980s who himself had escaped to Taiwan when things got too hot for him in the mid seventies) "had to pay tribute to him because he had information about police raids on illegal establishments and he could give them prior warning."

After lengthy negotiations with representatives of the Government of Hong Kong, on May 21, 1986, Lui Lok made a settlement with the Crown colony. He gave eight properties to the Crown with a market value of $14 million HK. He claimed he wanted to reveal the full scope of corruption in Hong Kong in exchange for an amnesty and immunity, but there were no takers. There is still an ICAC warrant out for his arrest on criminal charges, so he is not expected back in Hong Kong in the immediate future.

A bitter man, according to those who have seen him recently, Lui Lok today runs a restaurant/bar in southern Taiwan and says that he is broke after his settlement with the Hong Kong government. Limpy Ho, the notorious drug kingpin and friend of Lui Lok, Lau Wing Kui, and a host of corrupt Hong Kong policemen, who had been sentenced to fifteen years in jail in 1983 for drug trafficking was given a special leave from prison in 1990 because he was terminally ill. He died in Hong Kong in mid-1991. Clifford Wong died in Hong Kong in March 1988. Wong had maintained his respectability in Toronto as an architect, developer, and entrepreneur in spite of his self-professed "embarrassment" over the five dragons affair; a million-dollar legacy left in his will to his alma mater, McGill University, completed the process of sanitizing his image in Canada.

PART TWO

The Rise and Fall of Chairman Lau

Chapter Seven

ENTER THE DRAGON HEAD

In mid-1974 a short, unassuming, middle-aged gentleman stopped at the Canadian Commission in Hong Kong to pick up an application to enter Canada as a landed immigrant. Lau Wing Kui (Keung) was coming to Canada to open a restaurant in the Toronto area.* Canadian immigration policy has always favoured immigrants coming in as independent entrepreneurs. When a routine check by Canadian Immigration and the RCMP Security Service revealed nothing untoward, the Canadian Commission approved Lau's application for landed immigrant status. Significantly, when asked, the Royal Hong Kong Police said absolutely nothing about Lau. He did not have a criminal record, and apparently there was nothing in the police files to indicate any problem. He was given a pink Immigration Form 1000, which allowed him six months to enter Canada as a landed immigrant.

On December 22, 1974, Lau Wing Kui took up the generous invitation of the Government of Canada. He arrived in Toronto after a flight from Hong Kong with his wife, two sons, and two daughters. His British Hong Kong passport with his legal name written out in the international telegraphic code for Chinese characters, Lau (0491) Wing (3057) Keung (1730), had been stamped routinely in Vancouver, his port of Canadian entry

---

* For many years, Lau has frequently used "Kui" (pronounced "Koy" as in toy) as his third name, though Lau Wing Keung is his legal name.

after the day-long flight from Hong Kong. Lau was admitted to Canada with virtually no questions asked.

The five-foot-two, 123-pound, forty-five-year-old, brown-eyed Lau was not physically impressive. Soft-spoken, polite, and well-dressed, he was a slightly bald, emaciated little man with short black hair greying at the sides. "The type of person you simply wouldn't give a second look" was how Immigration intelligence officer George Best, described him. Lau was also an international traveller who spoke fluent Cantonese, English, Portuguese, and Spanish.

On his arrival in Toronto, Lau said he was going to stay with a niece, but he soon bought a house at 6 Fernside Court in Willowdale, which in 1992 was still listed in the phone book as his Toronto residence. Within a year, in November 1975, Lau opened up the Fair Choice Restaurant on Lombard Street, on the site of the old Firehall Theatre.

He kept up his international travels with trips to Hong Kong, Macao, the Dominican Republic, and elsewhere. Each time he came back to Canada, he filed returning resident statements to protect his landed immigrant status. On one return in September 1978, he told Immigration that he was going to be working for a company called Wingscope. He was granted re-entry as a landed immigrant. Later investigations determined that the company never existed. On another return, Lau indicated that he was employed by Donald Lee (Lee Chee Wah) of Hong Kong Overseas Travel, but it is unlikely he ever worked for him.

George Best, who later headed an Immigration investigation into Lau, was amazed at how Lau carried himself when Best ran into him once at Toronto's airport:

He was completely surrounded by an entourage of about a hundred men. I probably exaggerate, because at the time it seemed to me there were about fifty people accompanying him — all young men. Probably there were no more than half that with him, but he looked like a visiting king. I just couldn't help but wonder, how did this little old man manage to do it? How could such an insignificant-looking man have so much power and authority? Obviously he must have some kind of charisma. They were impressed by him in some way. Maybe it was simply because of the fact that he was a triad member in Hong Kong. Maybe he made them some great promises, and they were just overcome by the thoughts of what they might achieve here.

Lau's ambitions in Canada were clearly of a criminal nature, and in this his achievements were daunting. In less than a year, Lau had set up a major new triad in Canada. By mid-1977 Lau was at the height of his powers, with the Luen Kung Lok triad (literally, the house of mutual happiness) firmly established in Toronto; a cell of the Kung Lok in Ottawa under Cheang Chi Wo (a.k.a. Danny Cheung) was operating smoothly; and associations with other criminal organizations across the continent had been established.

Lau's early followers included a mixed lot: the hot-headed, Hong Kong-born kung fu practitioner, Danny Mo (Mo Shui Chuen), who arrived in February and became the new triad's 426, the red pole, in charge of enforcement and recruiting; the intimidating "Big John" Yue (Yue Kwok Nam), who became a landed immigrant on April 2, 1974; and his younger brother, Ringo (the brothers were personally inducted into the triad by Lau); mild-mannered Jimmy Kan (Kan Ka Tim); Peter Leung (Leung Kin-hung), the straw sandal for the Kung Lok; Paul Kwok (nicknamed Chiu Chow Por, now in jail for drug trafficking); and Chan Ching, like Danny Mo a major kung fu expert; and Charlie Kwan (Kwan Yee Man), the Kung Lok treasurer. There were also regular New York City visitors such as Kit Jai (Hat Chuey Chan) who participated in crime in Toronto. Other members of the triad included a Eurasian named Paul Bittick, a Macanese named Richard Castro, as well as Raven Tsoi and Victor Cheng — people who hung around Centennial Billiards or Derby Billiards on Yonge Street. The Kung Lok, with close ties to similar triads and gangs in Hong Kong, Boston, and Los Angeles, soon had a major criminal monopoly, including control over lucrative (illegal) gambling clubs, legal and very profitable entertainment businesses, brutal extortion and protection rackets, and a host of other both criminal and quasi-legal enterprises operating across the country, with a relatively safe base in Toronto.

Although he had no criminal record in the Crown colony, Lau had indeed been well-known to Royal Hong Kong Police, who had a thick file on him. He was known as an initiated member of the Hong Kong-based Tung Lok Society, part of the Luen (Kung Lok) triad family. Lau ran underground gambling, loansharking, and drugs in Yau Ma Tei, the crime centre of Hong Kong. In his early days there, he had been a graft collector (*kap sui-jai*), handing over graft to senior, corrupt Royal Hong Kong Police non-commissioned officers. Lau later became a partner in the Jumbo floating restaurant in Hong Kong, and in the red light district of Wanchai, he was the owner of a night-club called the Fay Choi Lau (Precious Jade Restaurant). This had allegedly been a front for gambling, drug, and prostitution activities according to the Royal Hong Kong Police. He was an associate of the notorious drug dealer Ng Shek-ho (Limpy Ho), who died in Hong Kong recently after serving more than ten years of a thirty-year sentence for heroin trafficking; Lau was known as having a protector (*bo-gar*) named Poon Lam (a.k.a. Poon Lam Jai), a notorious Kowloon-based drug trafficker and triad dragon head who acted as Lau's criminal mentor; he was an associate of Lui Lok and Hon Sum, two of the five dragons, and he was close to Eddie Chan, the corrupt former Hong Kong policeman who became the leader of the On Leong tong in the United States. In addition, several credible police sources had information that Lau was either the son or nephew of the late Royal Hong Kong Police Staff Sergeant Lau Fook, described as one of the mainstays of corruption in the police force in the old days. None of the information from the Hong Kong intelligence files on Lau made it to Canada until 1977.

Lau was a lion in sheep's clothing. He had also been involved in legitimate enterprises, including casino gambling, with several very prominent Hong Kong-based businessmen. For years Lau had been a director of security at the best casino in

Macao, the Lisboa. He later rented several very active gambling tables at this elegant casino.

Soon after Lau arrived in Toronto as a landed immigrant in December 1974 and the Kung Lok triad was established in Canada, strange things began to happen in Toronto's Chinatown. There was a sudden rash of nasty extortions and beatings of Chinese restaurateurs and students. There were kidnappings, and there suddenly appeared new "protectors" for several of the gambling houses. People inside the community began talking about a new force, a Hong Kong triad operating in Toronto, and an emergency meeting was held at the Cecil Street Community Centre in late 1976. Many voiced their concern over the changing face of Chinatown resulting from the massive new immigration from Hong Kong. The Toishan Chinese felt that they were being displaced, and new, more violent methods were enveloping Chinatown. Community leaders invited the police to attend the meeting to witness the community's alarm over this violence — things were so bad that one old man in Chinatown almost had his arms broken by a couple of new toughs. Sergeant Ken Cosgrove was one of the first to be alerted to the change. He told his colleague, Constable Mike King, who had just finished a special project with Vancouver police investigating the five dragons affair, that there were "all kinds of movement" and changes afoot in the community.

Constable King, who had started his police career in London in the late 1960s before going on to a very disillusioning stint in Hong Kong, had been working in Toronto on a special assignment for police intelligence. Conversant with Cantonese, the highly energetic and resourceful King checked out street reports in Chinatown on the presence in Canada of the five dragons, as well as reports of savage extortions and robberies. King developed a number of sources in the criminal and business communities and was soon in a position to inform the brass of the scope and depth of the problem in Chinatown. A special police task force was immediately set up. Two Metro Toronto police intelligence officers, Ken Cosgrove and Dave Saville, had begun investigating Lau after a number of new, highly organized gambling houses opened in Chinatown and after a series of extortions occurred, reportedly under the authority of the leader of "a new triad in Canada."

This new police operation, Project Quay, begun in the first months of 1977, was the first joint forces police operation in Toronto on organized crime in the Chinese community. Cosgrove, Saville, King, and Metro Constable Henry Chan were all assigned to it. A request went out to the Royal Hong Kong Police for background information on Lau, and this time they replied with one paragraph of their criminal intelligence on him, which included the information that Lau had been criminally active in the colony and had close associations with other crime figures there. By the fall of 1977, two Mounties and two OPP officers had joined Project Quay, which now included a full joint forces investigation into gambling, extortion, alien smuggling, assaults, and drug trafficking in Chinatown. Lau Wing Kui quickly became one of Quay's first major targets, and now Immigration intelligence officer George Best, a dogged criminal investigator, annoyed at how easily Lau had slipped in, joined in the all-out police effort to undermine Lau's growing power.

The first thing the new unit found out through their sources was what everyone in Chinatown already seemed to know: the Kung Lok triad, which was posing as a kung fu club, was very active in Toronto, and Lau Wing Kui was somehow at the centre of it all. His Fair Choice Restaurant was essentially a front acting as a recruiting ground for new triad members, and in the more than two years it was opened, many Kung Lok novitiates came through its doors.

Lau's genius was as an organizer and talent-spotter. He put the Kung Lok triad together with the nucleus being the young toughs who hung around the poolhalls. "Lau saw a power vacuum when he arrived and decided to exploit it," one knowledgeable observer has explained. "Then he decided he could take over Toronto." Most of the Kung Lok members were already somewhat established in Toronto in one way or another, though many of them hadn't arrived until the early to mid-seventies. The original followers then were ordered by Lau to go out into the community to recruit "49 boys" (soldiers) in any way they could.

The Kung Lok never was a totally homogeneous group under a strict hierarchy. Many of its leaders ran their own autonomous groups outside the triad itself. Big John Yue, like other original Kung Lok leaders, had his own loose-knit gang in Toronto before Lau brought everyone together. And there was even some friction between some of the leaders — the Kung Lok was not always a co-operative, cohesive unit, a fact it took the police some time to learn. According to the former head of the Chinese joint forces unit, Inspector Barry Hill, "We started hearing of fights within these groups in the Kung Lok. For example, there was talk of problems between Mo and Yue in the early 1980s. That is, there were fights going on between their boys." But then this sort of internal conflict is characteristic of most organized crime groups; the Mafia is notorious for its treacherous, deadly in-fighting.

According to Mike King, violence in Chinatown accelerated soon after Lau set up shop in Toronto. The first tangible evidence was the activity of one of Lau's earliest Toronto recruits, Chan Ching:

> At first, Chan Ching's name came up very early on in connection with a shooting incident in Chinatown in 1974 that was reported to police. But no charges were ever laid — because no one wanted to talk for the record. But Chan Ching was behind it. Ching was very good at the martial arts and a thug of the first order. He worked directly for Lau. But he was only on temporary status in Canada, and it wasn't renewed. So back he went to Hong Kong. That was the last of Chan Ching, but not the end of the problems in Chinatown.

Chan Ching was, however, just a symptom of a larger problem. From 1975 on, Lau began shakedowns in the community. Businessmen and restaurateurs were being extorted, either to join the new triad or pay protection money. "Lau wanted to get into gambling in a big way," according to Mike King, who was warned by several of his informers in the community that Lau was the one man the police should be watching.

Danny Mo, as the enforcer and recruiter for the Kung Lok, was the next of Lau's "boys" to be sent out to terrorize the community and bring it into line. He and his colleagues extorted people for money and in some cases to join the triad. Constable King put it this way: "Lau insulated himself naturally. He sent people out like Mo to teach them respect." A number of break-ins were also attributed to the new triad. But in 1976 serious trouble began. At that time, according to King, Mo, acting for Lau, tried to get "a throttle-hold on the gambling in Toronto."

Old-time Toishan Chinese in Toronto, like gambling king Sunny Lem, who for decades had run gambling joints in Toronto without too many problems, were worried. Lem came from the old school, and like many of the Chinatown gambling-club owners, he co-operated with the police. The police had long relied on such people as a vital source of information in the community. Lem was one of those figures the police could count on when there was trouble and someone whom people in the community had for a long time considered an unofficial liaison between the community and the police. According to police, Sunny Lem was no hero. He had his own muscle. But he didn't realize what he was up against in the Kung Lok. And Lem, while he resented the likes of Lau coming in and taking over, was "not made of heroic proportions," according to a former friend.

Sunny Lem was also deeply in debt. As well as running his restaurant and his gambling clubs, Lem was himself a heavy gambler. Suddenly, he couldn't get credit in Chinatown to cover his debts. He went to a friend, a Japanese-Canadian accountant who took him to Mafia loansharks associated with the Commisso crime family run by Remo and Cosimo Commisso. When he couldn't pay them back, there were threats. Finally, on May 3, 1977, Sunny Lem's restaurant, the Wah Kew Chop

Suey House at 111 Elizabeth Street near Dundas in Toronto's Chinatown was bombed by Commisso family hit man and enforcer Cecil Kirby, who was offered $15,000 by the Commissos for the job. Kirby had been told that the Commissos were also doing a favour for some of the Kung Lok triad people who wanted Lem out of business. Kirby had been instructed to level the Wah Kew at 6 a.m. when it would be empty — the bombing was supposed to be just a warning. But Kirby's bomb went off at 5:30 a.m. when Sunny Lem and his cook were still there. The cook, Chong Yin Quan, was killed. Lem, although severely shaken, escaped with just a broken arm.*

Although Kirby thought the Kung Lok were behind the Commisso contract, the police did not. As one old Chinatown hand on the force put it, "Dynamiting a man's restaurant is not the Chinese way of doing an extortion. Going over to the restaurant and cutting him up — that is more the Chinese [criminal] way." Whether it was the Kung Lok or just the Commisso mob, Lem was terrorized by the bombing. He got the message and disappeared for a long time. It was years before he emerged from hiding.

In the summer of 1977, the Kung Lok overreached themselves when they boldly tried to extort the Chinese Opera in Toronto visiting from Peking. According to Constable Mike King, "There was trouble with the Kung Lok making a nuisance of themselves by threatening shakedowns with the actresses and actors backstage. We were tipped off to that right away, so we went around every night and watched the show. We made our presence very obvious to keep the assholes away." It worked,

---

* Police uncovered who was behind the bombings only in 1981 when hit man Cecil Kirby became an informer and police operative and was promised immunity for all crimes he told them about. Before his confession, the police didn't have a clue that either Kirby or the Commissos had anything to do with the bombing. Kirby was never charged with the manslaughter, though Remo and Cosimo Commisso went to jail for it and a number of other extortions, bombings, and beatings. To this day, Cecil Kirby maintains that he tried to warn Lem by calling before the bomb went off. He now regrets the loss of life.

and there were no major extortions of members of the company reported. Later, when the Chinese Opera went to New York City, Kung-Lok affiliated gangsters were thwarted in a similar manner when the captain in charge of the police unit in Chinatown saturated the hall with uniformed police, and no extortions were attempted.

By the middle of 1977, the Kung Lok triad controlled the protection rackets in the gambling houses in Chinatown. Lau decided to have another all-out recruiting drive, and he brought in an associate from Hong Kong, a famous singer and actor in Hong Kong, who had been a lieutenant with Lau in the mother triad, the Tung Lok Society in Hong Kong. The singer's appearances in Lau's Toronto club, The Fair Choice, gave him a lot of respect in Chinatown and helped enormously his new recruiting drive.* As Mike King, who was watching Lau and his restaurant around the clock, put it, Lau "was saying to his troops to get members. 'Go raise money; shake them down. Bring in more 49s.'" Many forcible recruitments took place during that period. But Lau kept up appearances for those who were watching, including police like Mike King:

> I kept the restaurant under close observation. I used to drop in and have a cup of tea at a table. Of course they'd all be very pleasant. Lau would invariably be there. We'd sit there and have a little chat. Everything between us was very polite. I never had any ill feelings toward the man, personally, but it was obvious to me who he was and what he was up to. . . . But the club was a front — a recruiting front mostly. I don't believe he intended to make money out of

---

* Today this prominent Hong Kong actor and singer is the dragon head of the Hong Kong version of the Kung Lok. He is still close to Lau Wing Kui, who sees him frequently and lives nearby in the Mong Kok area of Hong Kong. When I was in Hong Kong in 1990, the dragon head/actor came to a disco where I was meeting a friend for drinks. Unfortunately, I had to leave to catch a plane and didn't have the opportunity to attempt an interview with him. Lau Wing Kui himself had earlier declined to answer my hand-delivered, written request for an interview.

that place. The location was all wrong — it was out of Chinatown, for one thing.

Most of the early Kung Lok extortions were of Chinatown businessmen, mostly restaurateurs, and Chinese students who came to study in Toronto from Hong Kong. By 1980 there were approximately twelve thousand visa students from Hong Kong in Canada, about half of them attending high schools in Ontario, and they were particularly vulnerable to triad extortion. Generally they had money (their tuition fees alone were more than $4,000, and their parents often regularly sent them living expenses), they were less familiar with the Canadian legal system, and, most importantly, they had families back in Hong Kong. They became prime targets for extortion.

Finally, in the late seventies, the police made two important, precedent-setting cases against Kung Lok members in Ontario for extorting students. Both cases offer a unique look at life inside the new triad.

The first real courtroom glimpse into the new triad's extortion *modus operandi* came in a case in St. Catharines. In November of 1977, two young students newly arrived from Hong Kong, Roger Szeto and Rene Chang, were living together and attending Denis Morris High School. In December two men from Toronto visited their apartment and asked Szeto to pay $1,008. He refused. The two Kung Lok enforcers came back and threatened the couple with dismemberment. Later, the two Kung Lok members beat them up and threatened further beatings if the $1,008 was not paid immediately. (The number $1,008 was significant for two reasons: it is divisible by three, recalling the three elements in the triad world view — Heaven, Earth, and Man — and it recalls the legendary 108 monks who had originally started the Hung Mun Society, according to triad mythology.) Finally, Roger Szeto agreed to pay in two instalments of $708 and $300.

When police learned of the incident from an informant, members of the Chinese unit questioned Roger Szeto and his girlfriend, who confirmed the extortion — one of the first times that someone had the courage to come forward and point the finger at Kung Lok members. Five weeks later Ed Law (Law Ah Fat) was arrested in Toronto and was charged with extortion. On the day before his bail hearing, Ronnie Ma (Ma Chun Fai) visited Szeto and Chang in their apartment. Later that day, Szeto and Chang accompanied Ma to Toronto, where their lawyers Gordon Grant and Michael Hardy had drawn up an affidavit stating that statements made by Szeto and Chang in relation to the alleged extortion had been made to the police under pressure and were false. Under duress, Szeto and Chang signed the affidavit. The lawyers had no knowledge of the falsity of the statements contained in this affidavit.

Later that same day, however, Szeto and Chang repudiated their newly signed false statement, and Ronnie Ma was charged with obstruction of justice. Ed Law was convicted and sentenced to one year in jail for extortion, and Ronnie Ma was eventually found guilty and sentenced to two years in jail (less a day). Admitted into evidence in the case was the fact that Ronnie Ma was a member of a criminal organization, known as the Kung Lok triad. Sergeant Ken Cosgrove and other members of the Chinese unit regarding the triad was allowed by the judge. Cosgrove had testified that there were about 150 to 250 members of the triad in Toronto and that it was involved in extortion, robbery, drugs, prostitution, gambling, and corruption. Cosgrove also told the court that there had been between 75 and 125 crimes of violence in Toronto in the past year involving members of the Kung Lok. "Fear was the instrument used in seventy to eighty percent of these crimes." Constable Mike King, who had frequently seen Ma in the company of other known Kung Lok members, testified that he found important triad documents in the possession of Ronnie Ma, and that Ma had proudly told him he was a member of the Kung Lok.

The lawyers for Ronnie Ma and Ed Law attempted to appeal their convictions in 1978 on the basis that evidence put forward by the police on the Kung Lok triad and its documents should not have been admissible. But the three judges in the Supreme

Court of Ontario's Appeals Court found the police testimony of relevance and dismissed the appeal in 1979. Evidence of the existence of the organized criminal group known as the Kung Lok triad in Ontario had become an established fact.

As a result of the St. Catharines cases, the Kung Lok triad lost a lot of face in the community, particularly because triad documents had been admitted successfully as evidence in a court of law. But the witnesses in the case, Rene Chang and Roger Szeto, though they lived in fear, were never harmed and subsequently moved to the United States.

Another early and precedent-setting extortion case involving the Kung Lok took place in Ottawa where a chapter of the Kung Lok had been established by 1978.[*] In this case, the police were able to introduce in court evidence of triad rituals and initiation ceremonies and prove once again, through the use of documents and expert witnesses, that the Kung Lok triad existed as an ongoing, structured criminal organization in Ontario.

In 1978 Tony Wong and several other students just arrived from Hong Kong and Singapore to attend school in the Ottawa area were approached by several Kung Lok members. The students were asked by Marvin Ko, 43, and Cheung Kwong Hung, 24, two triad members, to pay $10 a month and to join the Kung Lok triad or face the consequences. But Wong, cleverly, was able to convince the Kung Lok enforcers that he was already a member of a triad in Hong Kong, and he thus managed to avoid being initiated himself. Nevertheless, he did witness the initiation ceremony, called Cho Hay held at 67 Adelaide Street in Ottawa, which he described in court on September 24, 1979. Candidates stripped to their underwear and stood or kneeled in front of an ornamental altar draped in red paper. The man running the show tapped the back of each

---

[*] According to recent RCMP (1990) intelligence reports, the Ottawa branch of the Kung Lok remains significant even today, especially as the focal point for the importation and distribution of heroin in Canada. The RCMP drug squad has been investigating this group and their Toronto connections (who are also Kung Lok people).

novitiate with the blunt edge of a chopping knife as incense rose from the altar. They then passed through the heaven and earth cycle, which in this case was a rope on the floor. Next came the traditional thirty six oaths; the thirteenth oath stated that if a member ever left, or even tried to leave the triad, he would be killed; the sixth oath ordered that anyone who "betrays" his brothers in the society would be "killed by five thunderbolts"; and the thirty-fifth oath stated, that "I must never reveal Hung secrets or signs when speaking to outsiders. If I do so, I will be killed by a myriad of swords." Incense was then thrown on the floor to punctuate the deadly point. A live chicken was decapitated and its blood put in a bowl and mixed with some blood from a prick in each person's finger. After adding a little wine to the mixture to make it more palatable, everyone drank the mixture. Members were now united as blood brothers with heaven and earth.

Two of the victims in the case, Frank Chiu and Jimmie Kwok, testified they were forced by Ko and Hung Cheung to join the secret society as forgiveness for their poor behaviour in failing to pay an alleged debt. They testified that during their initiation, as Ko tapped each of the initiates on the back with a knife, they were warned they would suffer the same fate as the chicken beheaded during the ritual. Chiu and Kwok also explained to the court the numerical equivalent for Kung Lok triad office bearers (e.g., 49 for soldiers, 426 for the "red stick").

Another witness Vincent Cheung, was asked by senior assistant Crown attorney Mac Lindsay in cross-examination whether an oath had been taken at a ritual ceremony in February 1978 at which a chicken was beheaded. Cheung, who testified in Cantonese, which was being interpreted, replied, "What's an oath?" Judge Elmer Smith who was presiding, expressed concern whether Cheung had appreciated the seriousness of his sworn oath to tell the truth when he took the witness box. "He says he doesn't know what an oath is, and he's just been sworn under one," Judge Smith exclaimed. "That concerns me." Cheung then testified that he had been "asked" by three University of Ottawa students — Tony Wong, Frank

Chiu, and Jimmie Kwok — to mediate on their behalf with Hung Cheung, one of the accused, over the payment of a small pool debt.

The defendants had a different story, though they didn't deny the initiation ceremony took place. Cheung and Ko testified that the ceremony was intended to form a brotherhood of men devoted to the re-opening of Tung ching, a recreational sports club, which had been forced to close the previous year due to financial difficulties, and to help each other in business. "For example, if one of the brothers was unemployed, one of the others would hire him. . . . The brotherhood makes it easier to work together." Cheung said he had been given the nickname "Chicken" at the ceremony because, he said, the Chinese word for chicken sounded similar to his Chinese name, Ah Shing. Cheung maintained that Wong, Kwok, and Chiu had not been forced to join the group, and that others who had been asked to join refused without consequence. He said the brotherhood was still in existence, although it had not met since the ceremony. In other words, this wasn't a sinister triad, but more a benevolent tong association (others have compared the triad to a harmless Shriners' or Kiwanis club). The court, however, did not believe Cheung and Ko who, along with three other Kung Lok members, were convicted and sentenced to jail terms for extortion. The case created a stir in the media and in criminal and police circles throughout Ontario in the Fall of 1979.

The overall mandate of the Kung Lok triad in its early years had been, much like the local police, "to serve and protect." They protected the numerous gambling houses in Chinatown, mostly along Dundas Street in downtown Toronto, and through various entertainment companies run by Danny Mo and others. They also protected visiting singers and actors from Hong Kong who performed at Massey Hall and elsewhere. The protection, then, at least in the mid- to late seventies and early eighties, was primarily against themselves, the major criminal force in the community.

Chapter Eight

UNDERCOVER
IN TORONTO

Gambling is an intrinsic part of the culture of Chinese overseas. As Constable Mike King had observed during his police work in Hong Kong, England, and Canada, gambling was a staple of life in Chinatown:

> The tradition of gambling is there. It's a cultural phenomenon. It was the same in England, but it's legalized there now. For some reason the Chinese gamble extensively, heavily, and excessively. Atlantic City goes all out to attract Chinese gamblers. So does Vegas. It's there, so you have to deal with it.

Gambling is widespread among the Chinese and has a lot to do with the Chinese concept of "joss" — how your life can change based on whether it's your lucky day or not; whether your "joss" is good or bad. Chinese social scientist Lynn Pan put this popularity into its North American and European context in her book, *Sons of the Yellow Emperor: The Story of the Overseas Chinese*. In the early days of massive emigration of workers overseas, "when they were not smoking opium, the Chinese immigrants, especially the ones who toiled the hardest, were likely to be gambling." Pan offered other reasons for the passion for gambling in overseas Chinatowns:

> The men loved to chance their luck. . . . The native enthusiasm for gambling did not merely survive the journey from

EDDIE GONG: Leader of the Hip Sing tong, pictured here in 1930. "Tongs are as American as Chop Suey," Gong wrote in his 1930 book *Tong War* – a rare insider's look at the early Tong rivalries.

Right:
This is a red envelope for "lucky money" or "lomo" of the kind used in many extortions in Hong Kong and elsewhere. Many businesses in Hong Kong and Chinatowns across North America are used to paying criminal gangs protection money on a regular basis to avoid problems.

DANNY MO: 1980
Metropolitan Toronto police
mug shot of the Kung Lok
triad leader.

LAU WING KUI (KEUNG):
The founder of the Kung Lok
triad in his 1974 passport
photo. Lau established one of
the largest triads in Canada
before being ordered out of
the country in 1980.

Lau Wing Kui's condo at 32 "D" Braga Circuit in Mong Kok – a placid section in a congested area of Hong Kong. The inconspicuous-looking Lau commutes from here to Macao where he has several tables at Stanley Ho's Lisboa Casino.
JAMES DUBRO COLLECTION

The Lisboa Casino in Macao. This landmark casino is owned by Macao billionaire and gambling magnate Stanley Ho.
JAMES DUBRO COLLECTION

Ambulance attendants rush one of four victims from Toronto's A Dong Restaurant on Mar. 3, 1991 after Vietnamese gunmen burst into the restaurant with automatic weapons blazing. Three of the four died.
CANADA WIDE FEATURE SERVICES

Emergency crews exchange information outside Toronto's Kim Bo Restaurant where members of the Vietnamese Born to Kill gang staged a daring daylight raid Dec. 27, 1990 that resulted in three deaths.
LEE LAMOTHE/CANADA WIDE FEATURE SERVICES

The funeral of Thung Ta, one of the three innocent bystanders who were felled by bullets during the notorious A Dong raid in Toronto in 1991.
CANADA WIDE FEATURE SERVICES

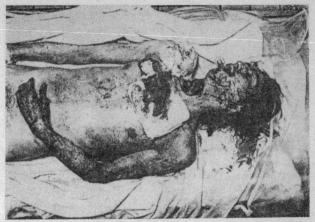

Autopsy photograph of Kung
Lok triad treasurer Richard
Castro, who was murdered
outside a Chinatown restaurant in Toronto by a man who
thrust a broken bottle into his
jugular vein. METROPOLITAN
TORONTO POLICE

RICHARD CASTRO:
Born in Hong Kong and of
Chinese and Portuguese
extraction, Castro ran
Kung Lok gambling houses
in Toronto's Chinatown for
several years before
his murder.

After being arrested in Vancouver for an extortion, Vietnamese gang boss ASAU TRAN (left, in handcuffs) is taken into custody in the mid 1980s by veteran Toronto police Asian crime fighter Sergeant Benny Eng. FROM THE BENNY ENG COLLECTION. PHOTO BY ROB LAMBERTI.

KING FONG YUE:
Police mug shot of one of
the ring-leaders of a major
Big Circle Boys gang of
alien smugglers uncovered
by the RCMP in the late
1980s joint forces operation
called "Project Overflight."

CHIU SING TSANG:
The ringleader of the Big
Circle Boys gang of alien
smugglers. The Big Circle
Boys gangs, made up of
refugees and immigrants
from mainland China, are
one of the major threats to
the Asian communities in
Canada in the 1990s.

NG KWONG YU (EDDIE WU): Convicted in 1982 of
defrauding an insurance company for a claim on his BMW.
Kung Lok leader Danny Mo and New York City Ghost
Shadow gang member Kit Jai assisted Ng in the fraud.

TRUNG CHI TRUONG:
Extremely mobile and violent Boston-based Vietnamese gang leader who came to Montreal and Toronto in the late 1980s and temporarily established himself as a serious criminal figure in both Canadian cities.

NGUYEN THANG QUANG:
A Toronto Vietnamese gang enforcer with connections to other gangs in Boston and New York who is currently wanted by Toronto police for allegedly stabbing another man during an argument on the sidewalk near Dundas and Spadina in Toronto's Chinatown on Feb. 22, 1992. Police have issued a Canada-wide warrant for Nguyen's arrest, and if anyone spots him they should call the police at (416) 324-5200.

the home country; as an antidote to boredom and loneliness it blossomed. . . . There is also this, that the man who emigrates, who goes abroad to seek his fortune, will be a gambler at heart, a seeker after quick money. . . . It doesn't matter where they were — in Singapore, Bangkok, London or San Francisco — the Chinese played the same games.

Unfortunately, as Pan detailed, "deeply enmeshed in all of this were the secret societies," because of "the huge profits to be made from running gaming houses and from the associated racketeering."

In 1978, as the battle against the Kung Lok was intensifying, particularly because of their hold over many of the gambling houses in Chinatown, the hand of the police was strengthened from an unlikely source. Dave Fu, a senior American tong official who had been secretly working undercover for law enforcement, was invited by the RCMP to set up a gambling club in Toronto and to use his unique talents and connections to go after the growing power of the new triad.

Dave Fu (Fu Lo-Jen) literally represented the old traditions in North America's Chinatowns. As the vice president of the Hip Sing tong in Washington, D.C., he was privy to the inner workings of criminals involved in alien smuggling, gambling, payoffs to the police, and drug trafficking. He also had ties to the triads as a former lieutenant colonel, adviser, and garrison commander in President Chiang Kai-shek's (and his son's) corrupt and triad-influenced Taiwanese government. A short, grey-haired, distinguished-looking gentleman, Dave Fu had seen them all — straight and crooked. But Fu had never been entirely what he appeared to be.

Dave Fu was born in Liao Chen, Shantung, China, on December 6, 1928, and remained in China, mostly in the Shanghai area, until 1949. His family was respected, wealthy, and well-connected; he was related by birth and marriage to both Chiang Kai-shek and Mao Tse-tung (his mother's cousin was Mao's first wife and another cousin married Chiang's grandson), and his father was a general in Chiang's army. At the age of just twenty-one years, after completing his education at the military academy in Whampoa (in Canton province), Fu fled China with General Chiang Kai-shek's party after the Communist victory in December 1949. General Chiang first sent Fu to Hanoi to help the Nationalist troops that had retreated to Indo-China.

Via Hong Kong, Fu finally arrived in Taipei, Taiwan, where he worked in the inner circles of General Chiang Kai-shek's government, first as a garrison commander, then as an aide to General Chiang, and later as a senior police official who acted as a key liaison with the U.S. military and the CIA. He was photographed with U.S. presidents (he guided President Dwight Eisenhower when he visited Taiwan in the late 1950s) and escorted CIA directors around Taiwan (John McCone in 1962). In 1960 Lieutenant Colonel Fu covertly supported a coup of middle-ranking officers against Chiang because of what he called widespread corruption, which also included massive organized drug smuggling. The coup failed, and although his role was never revealed, he finally left Taiwan permanently in September 1970 because he was involved with the CIA in planning yet another coup, this time against Chiang Kai-shek's son. He emigrated to the United States, becoming a citizen in 1980.

According to his own account, as well as that of a law enforcement source close to him, Fu was asked by the CIA to infiltrate the tongs after his arrival in California in 1970. There he began to work undercover for the Drug Enforcement Administration (DEA) on immigration and drug cases. The CIA had recommended Fu to the DEA. As a well-connected Chinese expatriate who was a former senior military officer in Taiwan, as a tong official, and as the "godfather" of Nickie Louie, one of the most colourful young gangsters in New York City's Chinatown of the 1970s, Fu was singularly well-placed. Later, he became a senior Hip Sing tong official in Washington, D.C. This city served as his base of operations and cover for a host of undercover operations involving the international drug trade for the CIA, the Justice Department, the DEA, French police, and the RCMP. During the seventies and early eighties, he travelled to Thailand, France, Germany, Taiwan, Holland, and other locations (including significant operations in Buffalo, New York City, Montreal, and Toronto with both federal and local police forces) on behalf of his U.S. government employers.

The story Fu tells about his CIA work in Taiwan and elsewhere, for which he has documentation, is all the more credible when one looks at the long-standing connections between the CIA and Chiang Kai-shek's KMT, some of whom were among the most prominent drug traffickers in Asia. For both sides, it was a marriage of convenience that continued for decades. The CIA covertly supported General Chiang and his triad cohorts, first in their battle against Mao, and then in establishing a stable (by which was meant dictatorial) government in Taiwan as a bulwark against Mao's Communist China. KMT officials and CIA operatives worked together for years with opium growers and drug traffickers in the golden triangle, both to generate a secure base for running operations and to finance the CIA's covert activities against the Communist incursions throughout Asia. Planes from the CIA's covert airline, Air America, were even frequently used for major drug drops and for smuggling arms to the drug traffickers. These activities were aimed not just against China, but in the sixties and later, against Vietnam, Cambodia, Laos, and other countries — all the possible dominoes in Asia that might fall to the Communists. Even the most notorious of the warlord drug smugglers, the Burma-based brigand General Khun Sa (Chang Chi Fu) was an important CIA asset for a long time.*

---

* Two particularly good, book-length investigative accounts of the CIA role in drug trafficking and its active recruitment for the drug world of bankers (the Nugan Hand Bank being the most infamous), politicians, and businessmen around the world and a must-read for anyone interested in pursuing this fascinating, though labyrinthine, topic, are Professor Alfred McCoy's classic 1972 book, *The Politics of Heroin in Southeast Asia* and *Wall Street Journal* investigative reporter Jonathan Kwitny's more recent, 1987 book, *The Crimes of Patriots: A True Story of Dope, Dirty Money, and the CIA*.

Fu had originally been invited by the RCMP to come to Toronto to help gather intelligence on Chinese criminal groups involved in drug trafficking. The RCMP had asked the DEA to loan them an undercover operative for this sensitive international Chinese drug-smuggling investigation, and they gave the RCMP Fu. When he initially came up to Toronto in late 1977, he set up a small real estate outfit with a Toronto mob-related figure and rented a small apartment. His first major operation with the Mounties, in early 1978, was run from Toronto. It was a fiasco, from beginning to end. The target was a Chinese Taiwanese heroin trafficker in France who was working with people in Toronto. The RCMP flew a crack team from Toronto to Paris to supervise the operation and to work with French intelligence. Fu made calls from Toronto — all of them taped — offering to sell "stuff" to a number of criminal figures in the Chinese and Italian community in Toronto. Almost everyone he called was interested in the "stuff." Oddly, according to Fu, several of the RCMP officers in Paris spent most of their time drinking and were often too drunk to follow through on any of the drug deals he set up through his extensive contacts. At the same time, two Mounties who were there deny Fu's charges and point out that Fu was not in Paris with them. More importantly, two of the target's couriers had been arrested in Bangkok en route to Paris, tipping the Taiwanese drug dealer off that he might himself be under police scrutiny. Thus, the entire operation was terminated. (It seemed to Fu that the failure was a result of RCMP incompetence, but really it was just a bit of bad timing.) At least two of the RCMP officers who worked on the Paris end of the doomed operation have verified that Fu's intelligence information was very accurate.

Then the RCMP had another idea for using Fu in Toronto. According to Constable Mike King, "There was a lot of intelligence about heroin coming through Toronto from the Orient with important Toronto connections." Fu also knew of specific drug dealers operating between Holland and Toronto. As well, according to King, there were credible reports of police officers on the take in Toronto police Division 52 in Chinatown. Through his connections with the Hip Sing and his "godson" Nickie Louie, David Fu easily mixed with Lau Wing Kui, Danny Mo, and the other major leaders of the triads, the gambling houses, and the drug trade in Toronto. It was a major coup for the new unit to have Fu at their disposal, or so it seemed at first blush.

Since there was also a lot of illegal gambling activity then going on in Chinatown, it was decided that Dave Fu should have, as a cover, his own illegal gaming house. It would make him look like an influential man in the community and allow him to set up major international drug deals. A former senior tong officer himself, Fu had experience in running a gambling house in the States where the tongs controlled many of them. The tongs were the only ones with the kind of money needed to finance a gaming house in major cities such as New York, Washington, and Boston. Fu explained:

> Just to open a gambling house in any city, you have to grease some palms and you have to buy certain people out. Just for a small gambling place, the overhead for one week should be somewhere between twenty-five and thirty thousand dollars. So you're talking a lot of money. In fact, each night, since the gambling stake is pretty high, you should have at least a quarter to half a million dollars to operate a Tong gambling place.

In Toronto, Fu rented a place at 150 Dundas Street, on the fourth floor, and called it The Fraternity Club. He was to establish the place as the meeting place for drug deals. Although the Mountie drug squad wanted this club as a base of operations, they did not want their role known in case things went wrong. The operation was organized by Constable Mike King with the able assistance of veteran intelligence officer Gabe Marion of the RCMP. Since he knew Fu already through a DEA friend in New York City who had previously used Fu on an undercover operation there, King was the only Metro Toronto officer let in on the operation.

As Fu and Mike King tell the story, at the time Fu opened up his gambling club there were three other major gambling clubs operating in Toronto. These other clubs were unmolested by police because of an informal corruption scheme that involved free dinners and $500 payoffs to certain officers at 52 Division. However, when Fu opened his club he was raided four times a day by the cops at 52 Division. Mike King informed 52 Division to no avail that an operation was going on. One uniformed sergeant came to the club and "couldn't wait to close it," according to King. Both King and Fu strongly felt that the 52 Division officers did everything to "screw" the operation. Fu was not in a position to bribe the officers for fear of being charged himself. King and Gabe Marion went to senior officers, who ordered the 52 Division officers to co-operate, but they didn't. A direct order was given by a senior Mountie to an inspector in 52 Division, but it was ignored, though the club was allowed to stay open for an additional thirty days. King reported that there was panic at 52 Division. The police raids began again in the fourth week. In exasperation, Fu himself went down to 52 Division, and told them that the money for the club was from the RCMP. Still the raids continued.

After just five weeks, Fu had to close down the club — there were no patrons because of all the police heat, and the operation was a total failure. Mike King (with the support of his RCMP colleagues) wrote an "explosive" internal report on alleged police corruption in Chinatown, the only result of which was that King was himself eased out of intelligence and the Chinese unit in January 1979. He eventually left the force.

The account of the incident by Inspector Barry Hill, then a sergeant at 52 Division and currently one of the most senior police intelligence officers in Ontario (as the head of the Criminal Intelligence Service of Ontario and a former head of the Chinese unit), was very different from that of King and Fu. Hill stated that the club, whether an operation or not, was "pretty obvious," and that to make matters worse, Fu was going around saying that he had "taken care of the police." (This, according to King and Fu, was part of the cover of the sting, just like other operations in Chinatown that had been run by the police over the years.) Hill steadfastly maintains that the reason the Fu undercover operation was closed down is that everyone in the Chinese community would have assumed the 52 Division officers were on the take if they let it continue. Speaking of Fu's club, Hill was circumspect:

There were arrangements made to leave one gaming house [The Fraternity Club] alone because the person [Dave Fu] operating it had convinced certain police personnel [Mike King and his RCMP colleagues] that he would come up with certain drug information if his gaming house was left alone. But the situation became so untenable as far as we were concerned we had to close it [The Fraternity Club]. . . . Because we were closing other places and didn't close the place run by Dave Fu, the other plainclothes officers and myself were accused of being on the take. We couldn't go around saying, "No we're not on the take because these police officers have an arrangement with this place, that it is an operation." It became so bad we went back and said we can't put up with it any longer — we'll give you one month. Then after thirty days we went in.

Hill was flabbergasted at how his raid was greeted by Fu and his colleagues. "Nobody even moved back from the bloody tables." Hill couldn't believe it. "They were so confident that nothing was going to happen to them. They just allowed us to walk in." But Hill was to feel the repercussions of the raid for some time:

I am still suffering from the consequences of that. There are still people who have a different impression of what was happening. That's one of the reasons that when I came to the [Chinese] unit. I was determined that I wouldn't let the gaming houses stay open — the police cannot be seen, or believed to be, actively avoiding closing a place. I was adamant about not letting the gaming houses stay open. . . .

George Cowley, who succeeded Hill as the head of the Chinese unit in 1986 and stayed there until 1990, agrees with Hill's version of events and of the tactics used against Fu. One of the problems with the Fu operation, according to Cowley, was that Fu made no secret that he was operating a gambling house (as he had done before when he ran a gambling joint in Boston for the police). Cowley reiterated that 52 Division felt they had to close the Fu house to avoid being accused of corruption.

> You have too much to lose if you let the gambling houses stay open, ever. One of the main problems we have in speaking with the community, so that they trust us and co-operate, is the spectre of corruption. One of the things that is constantly being pointed out is, if the police aren't corrupt, why aren't they stopping the illegal activity? And the number one illegal activity that everyone points to is the gambling houses. "If the police aren't on the take, why are these places still open?" they ask. And of course the operators of the gaming houses perpetuate the myth — be it true or false. They employ go-betweens — a police liaison officer who is known and trusted in the community by all sides. They are employing this guy in that position — and everyone knows about it. They say, "If you gamble with me, you are not going to get raided. We've got somebody on the police side, and I'll look after it for you." So you see, for the gaming houses to stay open, and at the same time for us to go out to the community and say, "Of course you can trust us, we're not involved in any game, tell us everything." People are going to be worried that we're being paid off by the gang members, and that we're going to go back to the gang . . . .

Even though Hill and Cowley consistently explained that they had to close the Fu gambling house to preserve their own integrity, Fu, King, and some of King's colleagues still interpret events more darkly, concluding that some of the 52 Division officers were on the take. King and others have pointed out that other illegal gambling houses had been allowed to stay open if they were run by agents controlled by 52 Division officers and, later, by officers on the special unit. It was true that several gambling clubs on Dundas Street were known to the police and, in fact, were partially run by police sources of information, right up to the middle 1980s when Barry Hill was in charge of the unit. One of these was operated in part by Bill Mar. But what some didn't know is that the police were also running an operation *against* Bill Mar, to nail him for attempting to bribe the police! Whatever the true reasons behind the débâcle, the Dave Fu undercover operation in Toronto was not an example of brilliant police work. There was too much distrust and subterfuge on all sides.

Nevertheless, the Mounties paid Fu handsomely for his work — according to Fu himself, between ten and twenty thousand dollars. Fu stayed on in Toronto for a short time, during which the RCMP helped him get his brother into Canada and then into the United States, where he sought refugee status from mainland China. Later in 1979, Dave Fu moved to Buffalo, opened a restaurant, and continued to help the RCMP and DEA with small jobs. According to Fu, some OPP officers came down to see him in Buffalo in December 1981 to tell him not to talk about his aborted operations in Toronto and to keep away from Mike King, who, like many police undercover handlers, had come under suspicion by higher-ranking policemen because of his close relationship with his operative.

In a September 1982 interview for "The Fifth Estate," Fu had a lot to say. While working in Toronto, he had learned a great deal about how the Chinese underworld there operated at the time, as he met with and mixed with some of the key players, including Lau Wing Kui, Danny Mo, Nickie and Eddie Louie, among others. Nickie Louie even hid out with Fu after a contract was put out on him by the On Leong tong leader, Eddie Chan. Fu stated categorically that Clifford Wong was "key in drugs in Toronto" and that Wong "worked closely with Lui Lok." Although unsubstantiated, this puts the ICAC investigations of Wong in a different light.

As a senior tong official, Dave Fu was also able to describe in detail for "The Fifth Estate" interview how the gambling clubs were run with the help of the tongs and gang enforcers. The On

Leong tong, headquartered in Boston and New York City, had some control in Toronto according to Fu, who stated that he had heard that Lau Wing Kui was assigned to Canada by the On Leong of Boston who gave him a grant to set up operations here. "All the tongs help with one-shot drug deals and sponsor gambling clubs in various cities," Fu explained. Fu had other revelations about the tongs. The On Leong, according to Fu, had $400 million in assets in the United States and owned four or five banks and credit unions. The On Leong, which had at least four major gambling houses on New York City's Mott Street, had wanted to establish a base in Toronto for the future, mainly in Mississauga, Scarborough, and in the downtown Chinatown. Fu stated that the On Leong tong leader, Eddie Chan, had "considerable clout with gangs here in Toronto." Fu went on to state that "in 1979, after Lau was kicked out of Toronto, he was sent to Santo Domingo after a big meeting in New York City of tong, triad, and gang officials." At that point, "Eddie Chan took more of an interest in Toronto."

As for the Hip Sing tong, for which Fu had served for years as a senior officer, Fu said it had major gambling houses on Pell Street in New York's Chinatown and was controlled by a good friend of his, Benny Ong (a.k.a. Eng), a seventy-four-year-old known affectionately as "Seventh Uncle." All the gambling houses had been protected by the youth gangs — the On Leong ones for years by Nickie Louie, and the Hip Sing houses were protected for a period in the 1970s by Nickie's brother, Eddie. According to Fu, "Eddie Louie was sent to Toronto by the Hip Sing in 1973 after a big bust. They gave him $100,000 and he opened a restaurant and bought a house." Nickie Louie became a major gang leader in New York City, the head of the Ghost Shadows, with "business connections in Toronto."

Little of Fu's intelligence information about the tong role in Toronto can be substantiated. It is known that Eddie Chan did own a piece of a theatre and a funeral home in Toronto at one point. But there is no corroboration of Lau's being controlled by the On Leong in Boston, though a relationship between former On Leong president Eddie Chan and Lau certainly existed. Certain senior members of the Ghost Shadows in New York and the Kung Lok in Toronto used to make regular visits to each other's cities, and while Fu's depiction of Nickie Louie is fairly accurate, there is no supporting evidence that Eddie Louie was "sent" to Toronto by the Hip Sing or that he was given the money by them for his Toronto restaurant and home. In a recent book by journalist Yves Lavigne, it is reported that Eddie Louie is the 14 K triad leader in Toronto, and in another book it is categorically stated that he was sent to Toronto by the Sun Yee On triad in Hong Kong. But Eddie Louie has maintained a low profile in Toronto over the years, operating his E-On Restaurant in the centre of Chinatown and running a few floating gambling houses. *Nickie* Louie has always been the major criminal organizer and trouble-maker of the two brothers.

From his unique perspective of a tong gambling-house organizer, Fu was able to outline the structure of a typical Chinese gambling house, which, he maintained, are the major locations for drug deals. In the United States, the houses are highly structured "twenty-four-hour banks" controlled by the tongs:

> There are three levels of *paos* in a house. (1) *Tow Pao* is the owner of the house who never appears in the house. He is totally insulated from drug dealing and gambling. (2) *Er Pao* is the No. 2, the manager in charge of the club, [this is what Fu was in his Fraternity Club in Toronto]. (3) The *San Pao* handle the money; these are the footsoldiers [e.g., Nickie Louie and Eddie Louie were to be Fu's *san pao* in his Toronto house].*

Fu also described a complex system of hand signals and movements used inside clubs when dealing in drugs. "Drugs," according to Fu, "are never mentioned by name." For instance, when ordering a coffee, the chopsticks are placed in a certain

---

* The spellings here are phonetic equivalents of what Dave Fu said in his interview.

way to indicate "I have some stuff to sell." The *san pao* goes to the *er pao* for $100 bills to purchase the drugs "after some negotiations with hand signals." Fu believed that this system of talking in codes and sign language, used by the triads in one form or another for hundreds of years, was the reason that "Chinese dope traffickers, especially the upper echelons, are so very hard to penetrate." In addition, "all the top drug dealers know and trust each other." According to Fu, there was little chance that they would betray each other. Everything, especially phone conversations, was in code — simple and very flexible to the initiated, but meaningless to outsiders. For example, a code for heroin arriving might be, "Good news! We have a fourth son." This could mean, "The number four heroin [the purest heroin] is ready for delivery."

Fu also charged in his 1982 interview for the "Fifth Estate" piece (called "Lomo" and broadcast on November 8, 1983),* that there was systemic police corruption in Toronto, mostly arranged through Chinese "go-betweens," and often the payoff was simply free Chinese meals to cops:

> The go-between will come in at a certain time, at a certain hour. They go in and they'll leave some money on the table, two, three hundred dollars. The police will then come in and pick up the money. The gambling house owners also have certain older people, some seventy or even eighty, manning the [gambling] table. When the police come in, they take the name down of the old people working there and charge them with operating a gaming place. They are

---

* The final piece that aired on "The Fifth Estate" had none of the Dave Fu interview in it. This was because the powers that be at the "Fifth" wanted a narrow focus on specific extortion on students in Ontario by the Kung Lok, rather than the broader picture of criminal activities in Chinatown that Fu outlined. It was also felt by the producer that there wasn't enough back-up to support many of Fu's charges, including that of police corruption at 52 Division. A short television item generally does not have the luxury of time to get into lengthy explanations and varying points of view.

fined a small amount — $100. The gambling houses just pay it and everybody's happy.

Asked by Eric Malling if he was "alleging serious police corruption," Fu asserted that he was merely "stating the true facts." He added that he did not see policemen paid off, but he knew about the payoffs from the go-betweens who arranged them. Asked how he knew for certain of the payoffs if he had never seen them, Fu replied that the same go-between would approach him while he ran his club to make payments for two or three cops at $200 a week each. This paid for "entertaining" the cops as well as for meals for the cops on the beat. Fu also charged that the go-betweens were offered one or two shares in the illegal business itself. He said the shares were worth about $4,500 apiece for a total of about $9,000 per month. To prove that some policemen broke regulations, Fu also offered to show "tickets" that police signed for free meals at his place.

The system of police payoffs in Toronto described by Fu matched in almost every detail revelations that came out in the testimony of Chinese gambling bosses at the 1928 Lennie Inquiry in Vancouver, which Fu was unlikely to have known anything about. There the Chinese gambling-house owners described a similar use of go-betweens and the collecting of a small sum from each gambler to pay off the police. There were also gifts to the police and free meals. This system also existed for years in Hong Kong and China.

It wasn't just the police who had to be taken care of in Toronto; the triads and the gangs operating in the area were also paid off. Asked whether Chinese in Toronto's Chinatown lived in fear of the gangs, Fu gave a surprising answer:

As a whole, the Chinese are very pessimistic. As a race, they are fatalistic. They're not really concerned about giving a little bit of money here and there, just to make things easy-going. And I don't think they are in fear. But, of course, when you open a gambling house you need protection. And if you don't pay, and if you don't take care of the people that you have to, including your [criminal] sponsors, you can expect some trouble.

Fu also alleged that in the late 1970s and early 1980s, Toronto was used as a major transit point for heroin shipments destined for the United States: "Toronto was becoming a major drug centre and will be getting far worse in the future." Today, in 1992, when the RCMP and the DEA steadfastly maintain that a large percentage of the quality heroin coming into the United States is trans-shipped through Toronto, Fu's remarks seem prophetic.

Fu listed a number of other criminal activities run by Chinese criminal groups in Toronto in the early 1980s: a profitable Toronto-based protection racket in the entertainment businesses that bring in touring Hong Kong singers to Toronto and across North America, the opening up of a number of new Chinese brothels in Toronto over the past decade, increased heroin trafficking through Toronto, and the increasing gambling activity, now mostly at professionally organized floating games across the city. According to Fu, Canadian Immigration officials were the most important target for corruption. A number of arrests and convictions of Immigration judges and officials across the country over the past decade has borne out Fu's assessment.

One of the last operations Fu undertook for the Mounties, in May 1982, again ended badly for him. An officer in RCMP intelligence asked him to renew his connection with a Toronto area loanshark with whom Fu had had a previous relationship. This traditional organized crime group had a number of criminal operations planned, including the starting of a major bank in the United States and an arms deal involving a well-known Toronto arms dealer and a respectable Toronto hotel owner. In order for the RCMP to gather evidence of fraud, Fu was to be brought in as a partner with the loanshark in the bank as well as in the arms deal. A major meeting to be set up by Fu was scheduled to take place at Eddie Louie's E-On Restaurant in Chinatown. Fu and the loanshark's representative arrived at the restaurant, but the arms dealer was in Washington, D.C., meeting with the Argentine ambassador to sell that country desperately needed arms including Exocet missiles for a probable war with Britain. The arms deal in Toronto was aborted. Although Fu passed all information on the arms and bank deals to the RCMP, they were unable to pursue either of the projects, as the main Mountie on the Fu project had his hands full with another major organized crime investigation involving two Toronto Mafia families.

Suddenly, Fu was at loose ends, and soon he got into serious trouble. He met at Eddie Louie's E-On Restaurant with Chiang Yu Min, the son of a Taiwanese general who was assigned by the KMT (Taiwanese Nationalist Party) to immigrate to the United States and go to a school in New York City. Fu apparently offered to help him in his mission. It was a big mistake, as now Fu, the longtime DEA and RCMP operative, himself became a target of an undercover Mountie operation — one going after the massive alien-smuggling business into the United States via Canada.

Fu allegedly paid $400 to Richard Barber, a thirty-five-year-old Windsor man, to get Chiang to the United States by boat from Windsor. In May 1982, after accepting Fu's money, Barber took Chiang across the Detroit River in a small boat that Barber piloted without running lights. What Fu didn't know was that Barber had gone to the RCMP as soon as Fu, who had introduced himself as Frank Wong and said that the Taiwanese was his nephew, gave him the first payment. When Fu met the pair at a marina on the U.S. side at Belle Island to pay Barber the additional $200 for bringing Chiang illegally into the United States, he was arrested. (Fu had met the boat at the marina in his Oldsmobile, which the RCMP had shadowed from the Detroit tunnel to the marina.) Barber later testified that Fu was setting up an alien-smuggling ring and that Fu had bought him a new motor for his boat to be used in future smuggling operations. His fees would have gone up to $2,000. A few days later, on May 17, Barber was severely beaten in the parking lot of a Windsor shopping mall by a gang of Orientals. Fu was charged with alien smuggling. Fu asserted that it was a setup. Ironically, the Taiwanese illegal, Chiang Yu Min, was eventually allowed to stay in the United States in return for his testimony against Fu.

But this wasn't Dave Fu's only foray into the alien-smuggling world. He was charged in April 1982 along with a Buffalo area resident named Dennis Harkins, with arranging the illegal smuggling of yet another Taiwanese into the United States. This time the illegal alien, said by Fu to be a KMT agent on some sort of assassination mission, was hidden in the trunk of his car and brought in over the Peace Bridge. Fu and Harkins were charged with conspiracy to smuggle aliens into the United States. At the same time as the two separate indictments for alien-smuggling, the U.S. Immigration Service was moving to deport his older brother, Fu Li Le, who had come to the United States as a visitor from mainland China.

Why Dave Fu became an alien-smuggler after all his work for law enforcement is puzzling. Clearly he was no longer of any use to the RCMP. The RCMP in Windsor told the *Windsor Star* that Fu was part of an alien smuggling ring that was big business: "We face alien smuggling every year but it's becoming bigger and bigger." Alien smuggling has been big business, particularly the smuggling of Orientals into Canada and the United States, since both countries officially prohibited legal immigration in the mid-1920s. Even today, thousands of illegal immigrants from China, Taiwan, and Hong Kong and other countries who cannot or will not go through legal channels pay top dollar to get into Canada and the United States illegally, by whatever means. Fu, with his long experience in undercover work, may have been attracted by the allure of easy money and may have felt that he would be protected by his previous connections with U.S. and Canadian law enforcement agencies. But Fu did not need the money. He had made a great deal of it legitimately helping Taiwanese businessmen get contracts in the United States, particularly in Pennsylvania, where he was commended for his work for the state by then governor and former United States attorney general, Richard Thornburgh. Fu stated flatly that the charges against him were to discredit him — probably because he knew too much, particularly about police corruption and incompetence.

Fu was eventually convicted in both cases and spent six months in jail in 1983. Former Toronto police constable Mike King, who had worked with Fu for some years in a professional capacity, was the only one of Fu's law enforcement contacts to publicly help him during his trials, and he still stands behind Fu. But none of Fu's conspiracy theories for his legal troubles is totally convincing. The most logical answer is that, once discarded by law enforcement, he probably decided to make a few extra bucks on what usually was a relatively risk-free endeavour. Still, to this day, Mike King believes Fu was innocent of alien-smuggling and was set up in both cases. *

When Fu emerged from jail, he settled in Pennsylvania and went back to his investment and development consulting business, Trans-Orient Ltd. Today, in his mid-sixties, Fu continues to work as a consultant for Taiwanese and other Asian businessmen, including those from the People's Republic of China, where he has been allegedly spending a great deal of time recently. One person close to the Asian underworld in Toronto has even maintained that Fu is living in the People's Republic, but this has not been confirmed. Fu has also been considering writing his memoirs. It should make interesting reading.

With his unique access to the top leadership of Chinese organized crime in both Canada and the United States, Fu could have been one of the best undercover operatives in the war against the triads, tongs, and Asian gangs. Instead, he had become a foolishly wasted resource, especially in the much ballyhooed "war against drugs" in both the United States and Canada. This loss could easily have been prevented, particularly in his big operation in Toronto that offered Fu, the public, and the police's new Chinese unit a unique chance to triumph

---

* In a bitter letter to me in October 1982, just after his conviction in the Detroit case, Fu stated that the government went after him and set him up because they thought of him as "the public enemy No. 1."

in the early part of the war against the Kung Lok triad. Why Fu's full potential as an undercover operative in Toronto was never realized is still a mystery. It may have been simply that Toronto police officials didn't trust him. Ironically, one senior Metro Toronto officer has seen to describe Fu as having been "one of the biggest figures in the Chinese Mafia in North America."

Chapter Nine

THE KUNG LOK
GOES CARIBBEAN

In 1979, the police joint forces Chinese unit moved directly to cut off the dragon's head. While Lau Wing Kui was insulated from prosecution for the numerous extortions and other Kung Lok criminal activities going on in Toronto's Chinatown, as a landed immigrant not yet a Canadian citizen, he was still very vulnerable. But since it was nearly impossible to catch Lau committing a criminal act, though everyone knew who he was, the police were puzzled as to how to proceed. It was Immigration intelligence officer George Best who suggested the solution to the police:

The question was, of course, "What do you do with this man? How do you attack it from an immigration point of view, if he is a landed immigrant and not a citizen?" Of course we might have been able to take action if he were convicted, but he never was. So we had problems. Eventually we suggested considering section 40 of the Immigration Act to get rid of Lau. [Under section 40, a person's landed immigrant status can be revoked and he or she can be deported based solely on criminal *intelligence* information that the person is a threat to Canadian society.] It [section 40] had never before been used based solely on criminal intelligence; it had been used only for cases under national security grounds.

In early 1979 the Metropolitan Toronto Police's Chinese unit (with the able Mike King as the main point man) and the Immigration Department in Toronto (under George Best's methodical direction) began to establish their case. Slowly but surely they collected evidence from informants on the streets of Toronto and Hong Kong, police sources in Hong Kong and the United States, and other community and international sources on Lau's criminal connections. As King explained, little existed on paper about Lau: "I had to use mainly informer evidence. Show a pattern — his reputation, his position; the fact that he had no discernible income; his links with various people here and in Hong Kong and the United States."

In April 1979 the report was ready to go to the solicitor general of Canada and the minister of Employment and Immigration. Since this was the first time section 40 had been invoked in this way, they referred the matter to the Immigration Advisory Board (IAB) which at the time was under the chairmanship of a former Supreme Court justice. The three board members took their work very seriously — after all they were dealing with life, liberty, and the very essence of democracy. Members of the Board were civil libertarians, not rigid authoritarians, and they were willing to give the subject the benefit of the doubt. They heard the arguments from Best and the police, who explained the problems that they were having in relation to Lau — the difficulty of getting witnesses to speak out against him, the widespread fear in the community. Finally, the Board agreed to proceed with the case.

The Immigration Advisory Board then called a special hearing for May 1979 to discuss the best way to inform Lau of the situation. It was considered only fair that Lau be told the gist of the case against him and that he be allowed to respond. The problem for Best and the police was how much information to give out without betraying important confidential sources and informants. It could be a matter of life and death for some of them. The police, Immigration, and the three-person board determined that Lau would be told of the grounds for the action, but that the specific sources of the information would be withheld for security reasons. There were at least three drafts of the final decision, as the lawyers for the board and Immigration went over it several times.

Finally, in early October a registered letter was hand delivered, and Lau's son, Joseph (Lau Kai Dik) signed for it. Joe Lau was not an office-bearer in the triad, since, according to Mike King, he "was too stupid to cut the mustard in the Kung Lok." The letter stated that a special hearing was scheduled for October 17, 1979, to decide whether Lau should be deported from Canada on the basis of criminal intelligence information about him. On the scheduled day, the hearing was held, but Lau didn't appear. A few days later, Lau's lawyer, Samuel I.C. Yang, finally contacted the Special Advisory Board, but by then it was too late, as the board had already made its decision.

George Best was subdued in his victory over Lau:

> In some respects it's fortunate and in other respects it's unfortunate that Lau didn't turn up for his special hearing. He saved us a lot of trouble by not turning up and he certainly indicated his guilt. Yet it would have been interesting to take the thing through the system to see how it would have all turned out. Maybe he just decided to cut his losses.

On October 25, 1979, all three members of the Special Immigration Advisory Board signed a letter to the Cabinet explaining the circumstances and making the recommendation that Lau be deported from Canada. On January 11, 1980, an order-in-council (P.C. 1980–122) by which Lau was ordered deported, was signed by the governor-general. But by then Lau was no longer in the country. He was not without options, after all. In addition to retaining his Hong Kong/Macao passport and papers, he had in 1978 become a citizen of the Dominican Republic. But since the order-in-council lasts forever, Lau can never legally return to this country. His name is in the Immigration Department's and Customs' computers as an undesirable subject, liable to arrest. If he is ever caught here, he would be subject to immediate deportation.

Perhaps surprisingly, Lau's family — his wife, two sons and two daughters — has remained in Canada. His wife and grown children still live in Willowdale. Since 1980 Lau has tried, at least twice, to come back to Toronto. In 1983 he applied from Hong Kong to visit his family in Canada, but the Immigration Department denied this request because, as George Best pointed out, his family could travel to see him anywhere in the world at any time.

A second attempt was made in 1985, when Lau's son, Joe, made an application for his father in Toronto. The Immigration Department instructed Joe Lau to have his father make the application himself from Hong Kong, but the matter was never pursued.

George Best, now happily retired, says today, "Somehow I feel we haven't seen the last of Lau Wing Keung [Kui] in Canada." People have allegedly seen Lau in Toronto over the years since the deportation order; he is alleged to have a concubine in Washington, D.C., and he has also been seen in New York City. Today he lives in an elegant condominium complex in Mong Kok, Hong Kong, and operates from Hong Kong and Macao, where he rents several gambling tables at Stanley Ho's largest casino, the Lisboa.

The section 40 formula that was so successful with Lau Wing Kui was never used again. By the time the police and Canadian Immigration thought of using it on Danny Mo, who became the leader of the Kung Lok soon after Lau's untimely departure, it was too late; Mo had already become a Canadian citizen. Subsequently, section 40 has been eliminated by the government and replaced by an almost impossible-to-use section.

Lau's great ambitions and designs for Toronto were never fully realized. He was bitterly disappointed at his own failure to take over criminally in Toronto's main Chinatown. He realized, according to former Constable Mike King, that "there wasn't quite as much money in Toronto as New York City, which is where all good Chinese criminals tended to go. We knew he was doing deals with New York City and other places all along. Lau was not getting from Toronto what he fully expected to get.

He thought there was going to be a lot of money here and that he would be the undisputed overlord of Toronto's Chinatown. And he probably would have, had the police not been there."

On the very day that Lau Wing Kui was ordered deported by Canadian authorities, he was already building a new life in the Dominican Republic, the West Indies country which shares the island with Haiti in the Caribbean Sea and that until 1992 was what law enforcement officers called "a bookie paradise." (In January 1992 the FBI and the Dominican Republic police closed down a $100-million Mafia-run off-shore bookie ring, arresting a number of the organizers. Scores of American mob bookies based in the Dominican Republic would communicate their bets by phone, fax, and the latest satellite technology.) Mike King had heard from an informer inside the criminal Chinese community in Toronto as early as 1978 that Lau was "moving to South America," where he was going to take over the management of a hotel that had a gambling casino. The Toronto police soon found out the name and address of Lau's hotel. It was the Hotel Embajador (Spanish for Ambassador) in Santo Domingo, the Dominican Republic; the hotel had been built in the late 1950s as a showpiece by the dictator of the country, President Rafael Trujillo. The hotel had been owned by the Intercontinental group, but in the late seventies it had been sold for a relatively low figure to a man named Simon Yip (Yip Chung Ling), an old friend of Lau's from Hong Kong. Yip was a wheeler dealer originally from Shanghai. It was Yip who convinced the government of the Dominican Republic to institute an unusual program whereby Chinese from any country in the world could buy citizenship for $50,000 U.S. (after a six-month waiting period). Up to five thousand Chinese families have been brought into the Dominican Republic by Simon Yip's team, many of them people who were desperate for legitimate travel documents. All became Dominican Republic citizens and got Dominican passports. The program helped the Dominican Republic as well, bringing in much-needed cash for the starved economy.

But Yip brought something else as well — the Kung Lok triad.

It was Yip who extended an invitation to his old friend Lau, whom he knew had run many underground gambling businesses in Hong Kong, to come down to "manage" the new casino in the Ambassador Hotel. Lau was chosen too because it was hoped that his high-level, well-heeled contacts in the Far East, Toronto, New York City, and San Francisco would come down and gamble. Lau was to pay the owner an annual licensing fee for the rights to run the casino in Yip's hotel. He was then to be on his own, to make or break the new gambling establishment.

What neither Yip nor the Dominican Republic government anticipated was that Lau would bring with him some of his tough young hooligans, Kung Lok extortionists and thugs, many of whom were happy to get away from the heat of the Toronto police's Chinese unit. Joining Lau in Santo Domingo in 1980 were Danny Mo, Big John Yue, Danny Tse, Paul Kwok, and a host of other tough boys from the Toronto triad. They were given apartments near the Hotel Ambassador. For a while they just strutted around with Lau, who by this time had become a citizen and was carrying a Dominican Republic passport. Wherever Lau went in Santo Domingo, six or more of his young gangsters following in his footsteps.

For a short period, the casino seemed to be doing quite well. Lau had brought in all the games — roulette, blackjack, baccarat, *pai gow*, and *fan tan*. And he had organized some junkets from Toronto and the States. Things were looking very good. But then Lau lost control of his Kung Lok crew, and everything became unstuck. The young thugs had unleashed a reign of terror, and Lau had started to proclaim himself publicly as a gambling king, rather than maintaining his usual low profile. Word got out all over the island that the "Chinese mafia" was in Santo Domingo "doing funny things." According to Mike King, who went down to the Dominican Republic to observe the happenings first hand after authorities there got worried, "Lau played on the fact that he was a gangster, and that he had his gangster friends with him. It seems that he wasn't content to do legitimate business. He had to get involved in more things than that. All he wanted to do was rake off profits wherever he could get them, legally and illegally." None of this was popular, with the government, the people of Santo Domingo, or even with Simon Yip's people, including Yip's son Bernard, who acted as his general manager. They were running a respectable hotel. Lau was supposed to be running a reasonably legitimate gambling casino, though, of course, there's always a bit of stealing, skimming, loansharking, and other illegal activity around any casino. But Lau and his Kung Lok hoodlums went overboard, making it apparent to everyone that his was an underworld operation of the worst kind.

Although Lau allegedly already did have some high-level police officials in the country on his payroll or in his debt, he did not control the country. The democratically elected government of the born-again Christian Antonio Guzman was not in his pocket. For a while the police and Yip's staff tried to look the other way and tolerate the unruly behaviour, the assaults, and the extortions of Lau's gang. At one point, sensitive DEA intelligence documents on his activities there were given to Lau by friendly Dominican Republic police sources. The country was more than used to corruption and crime, but Lau was rapidly outstaying his welcome. Two of the most unruly of his entourage, curiously enough, were Danny Mo and Big John Yue. To this day, in Santo Domingo, Danny Mo particularly is remembered as one of the principal troublemakers, assaulting and insulting the local patrons in the hotel.

Things became totally untenable for Lau in early 1981, when Bernard Yip decided that he'd had enough. According to a source close to the investigation in the Dominican Republic, Bernard went to his father in Hong Kong (Simon Yip still spent most of his time there running his many business enterprises, including a trust company, and left Bernard in charge of things in the Dominican Republic). Bernard said bluntly, "Either you get rid of Lau and his people, or I will leave the island myself, and not come back. I am a married man and I have a child, and I can't tolerate these gangsters in this hotel, strutting around like they own this place and the whole island. We must try to maintain respectability and credibility. Either he goes or I go." The next day Simon Yip arrived from Hong Kong and fired his old friend and colleague. He told Lau, "You and all the guys with you have to go."

From the Dominican Republic, Lau went directly back to Hong Kong to lick his wounds. Soon he was back in business there and in nearby Macao, running gambling in both underground and legitimate casinos. Lau was now in his element, though he continued to keep close ties with triad and gang leaders in Canada and the United States. Lau's boys, the Kung Lok troublemakers of Santo Domingo (Paul Kwok, Danny Mo, Big John Yue, Danny Tse) didn't return immediately to Toronto, but went to New York City where they made new alliances with triad, tong, and gang leaders.

There are different views in law enforcement circles about the significance of Lau's interlude in the Dominican Republic. Many, including several top U.S. DEA investigators, believed that Lau's casino was a front for a massive heroin-smuggling ring. The heroin was allegedly coming from the Far East through the Dominican Republic in bales of shrimp and then into North America, mainly directly to New York City. Since Lau was the master of the operation, or so the theory went, he didn't care about the success of the casino. The Yips had nothing to do with the heroin and, in fact, knew nothing about it. It is unlikely that Danny Mo or any of the other younger toughs with Lau would have had any role in the drug business. But, while the DEA tried very hard to get evidence on Lau's involvement in the drug business, they were not successful. One of the major flaws in the DEA theory, of course, was that Lau would hardly import the toughs to the Dominican Republic, thus bringing even more attention on himself and his operations, if he were secretly running a major heroin-trafficking ring. On the other hand, the Kung Lok gang reign of terror could have been a diversionary tactic which kept the police busy.

Ironically, it was Simon Yip, the apparent victim of Lau's activities in the Dominican Republic, who ended up in jail. In the early 1980s, the Dominican Finance Company in Hong Kong, which Yip owned, became involved in a major fraud of the Overseas Trust Bank. Millions of dollars were missing, and Yip had made a series of unsecured loans. Yip was arrested in the United States and extradited back to Hong Kong where he was sentenced in the mid-1980s to eight years in jail for fraud.

Lau's enterprises in the Dominican Republic, like his ambitious criminal plans for Toronto, had ended up as a humiliating, personal failure.

Chapter Ten

THE DRAGON HEAD TALKS

In 1981, after the Dominican Republic débâcle, Lau Wing Kui returned to his old life in Hong Kong. A brief excerpt from a mid-1980s Royal Hong Kong Police "confidential" report on the connections between Hong Kong triads and North America, centring on the activities of Lau, is revealing — certainly a lot more frank than the RHKP was when Lau arrived in Toronto in 1974:

> Perhaps the best documented information link between Hong Kong and Canada concerns a Mr. Lau Wing-Kui. He first came to the notice of the Police here as a major casino operator in the early 1970's. He was at that time a major official in the Luen Kung Lok Triad Society. . . . He and his family left Hong Kong for Canada in 1973 [sic; it was really December 1974] and was granted landed immigrant status in 1975. He either set up or took over a Triad organisation in Canada known as the Kung Lok which is the equivalent of the Luen Kung Lok in Hong Kong. Whilst this Society in Canada prospered, LAU was spending considerable time away from Canada . . . . In January 1980, LAU was deported by the Canadian authorities for his Triad activities. However he is still in touch with the Kung Lok in Canada. A son, Joseph LAU married the daughter of the Kung Lok's accountant in 1982 and LAU himself was known to be sympathetic when one of his closest associates in Canada

failed to be elected to a powerful position in the Kung Lok in the same year . . . . In January 1983 LAU held a meeting with Danny MO the supervisor of the Kung Lok in Toronto, William TSE the Los Angeles head of the Kung Lok and Vincent JEW of the U.S. based Wah Ching, a major Chinese organised crime group and similar to a Triad Society. This meeting took place in Hong Kong. There were a few other figures from the U.S. and Taiwan present. What the meeting was about no one knows.

What this report, sanitized no doubt for distribution to Canadian and U.S. authorities, neglected to state, is that Lau had been brought into police headquarters for questioning in Hong Kong after the 1983 meeting. In a series of follow-up discussions in Hong Kong and Macao in 1984, the Royal Hong Kong Police learned a lot more about Lau and the triads in Canada and the United States. For after his embarrassing return from Canada and the Dominican Republic in the mid-1980s, Lau himself had become a police source of information.*

There is another, more detailed report in the Royal Hong Kong Police force's files about Lau's activities and his co-operation. The following confidential police report was sent to North American law enforcement officials on June 13, 1984, by Senior Superintendent Brian Merrit of the intelligence section as a reply to persistent DEA and Metro Toronto police queries in early 1983 about Lau's activities in Hong Kong. Entitled "Alleged Triad Meeting," it concerned a secret meeting in

---

* Lau Wing Kui, incidentally, is considered by some to be the person referred to in a scene in the 1985 film, *The Year of the Dragon* (scripted by Oliver Stone and based on Robert Daley's 1981 thriller of the same name) in which the triad boss in New York sinisterly mentions "the big man in Toronto" taking care of things. There were howls of laughter in the Toronto theatre where I saw the film when this serious line was delivered, as many in the audience obviously found it inconceivable that a Toronto crime figure could loom so prominently on the world crime stage. A closer reading of the book indicates that the "Toronto connection" is a composite figure of Lau Wing Kui and Danny Mo.

January 1983 at the Miramar Hotel in Hong Kong between Lau Wing Kui and certain leaders of the North American triad and Chinese gang movement. It revealed a great deal about the interconnections of triads and gangs in Toronto, New York City, San Francisco, and Hong Kong in the eighties. It also includes rare police debriefings of Lau Wing Kui, based on two formal interviews with Lau by the RHKP:

> . . . the meeting occurred in January 1983 in the Miramar Hotel, Nathan Road, Hong Kong. The RHKPF was tipped about the reported meeting and conducted an investigation, by responding to the meeting site. Many of the meeting participants were found in the hotel's Tsui Hong Village Restaurant, where they were detained and questioned. Those detained included:
>
> LAU WING KUI, Triad leader in Hong Kong of the Luen Kung Lok Triad and former Canadian Kung Lok Triad leader.
>
> DANNY MO, Canadian Kung Lok leader and the individual that arranged the meeting at Lau's request
>
> MICHAEL PAK and PAI SHING PING, Nightclub owner, Monterey Park, California.
>
> VINCENT CHU, a.k.a. Vincent Jew, leader of the Wah Ching gang in San Francisco and purportedly of the Wah Ching in North America as well.
>
> LEE YOO TING, Motion Picture actor in Taiwan with unknown affiliations to organized crime.
>
> PETER MAN a.k.a. Man Kam Fai, San Francisco restaurant owner.
>
> In addition, TONY YOUNG, Wah Ching leader in Toronto and San Francisco had been at the hotel, but left prior to the raid. Finally, Tin Lung, leader of Boston's Ping On group, was to attend the meeting, but cancelled out.
>
> Lau Wing Kui gave a statement to the RHKPF at the time he was arrested in which he identified other lieutenants of his

in North America, who were not at the meeting. Among these were William Tse, who heads up the Wah Ching in Los Angeles, but who Lau described as also being a Kung Lok leader. Charlie Kwan Yee Man/a.k.a. Kwan Yuk Shum/Toronto a.k.a. Sum Kwan Kan/Jimmy Kan Ka Tim, Yue Kwok Nam, Peter Leung Kin Hung and Tyrone Pau Hing On were also identified. It is speculated by the RHKP that these associations may not be Lau's most important lieutenants, but rather group members in lesser positions, that Lau surrendered as an accommodation to the RHKPF.

It is believed that many of these individuals have Hip Sing Tong connections or are connected with Tongs allied to the Hip Sing.

The agenda for the meeting and the activities of the meeting were not learned by the RHKP. However, it is speculated that this meeting represents a general trend on the part of Triads to return to a more tightly controlled and traditional structure, that has been dissipating in recent years.

It is suspected that the meeting may have discussed attempts to shakedown Raymond Chau of Golden Harvest Film Company for free rights to distribute his films in various Asian and North American cities. In Taiwan this activity is reportedly being carried out by a faction of the Green Pang gang called the Chuk Luen Bong. In North America the Wah Ching seems to control the effort and in Hong Kong the Luen Triad seems to control the effort. The ties between the Taiwan Chuk Luen Bong and the Hong Kong Luen appear to exist, but are not clearly understood.

TRANSCRIPT OF CONVERSATIONS WITH LAU WING KUI

The following notes are taken from the transcripts of two conversations with Lau Wing Kui.

(i) Herbert Lui describes the ceremony, when he joined the Hip Sing Tong, in an American magazine article. From his description it is fairly certain that the ceremony is, or is derived from, a proper triad initiation ceremony. The "Original Chinese Freemasons" referred to by Lui, in his recent news conference, are not part of the Masonic movement as we know it but, in fact, refers to the original triad movement.

(ii) Danny Mo Sui Chuen of Toronto alleges that the Golden Star Restaurant shooting in New York was the result of the dispute between the Kam Lam Chai and the Hip Sing Tong.

(iii) The mass murder in the Seattle recreation centre involved a dispute between the Bing Kung Tong and the Chi Kung Tong.

(iv) The shooting of Michael Chan in the Hip Sing Tong recreation centre is seen as a direct challenge to the Hip Sing tong. The victim was the right hand man of Chat Suk and was the de facto operational leader of the Hip Sing Tong. He was responsible for wresting control of Pell St. from the On Leung and Tung On. He was responsible for collecting all protection monies in Pell Street and by *his own* estimate the sum collected was approximately US $1.5 million per annum in Pell Street alone.

For anyone wanting to wrest control of Pell St. from the Hip Sing Tong, then Michael Chan was the obvious target. Whilst it was initially felt that Herbert Lui and the Kam Lam Chai were the obvious suspects, William Tse, the Kung Lok leader from Los Angeles states that the consensus of opinion amongst gang leaders throughout North America is that [Eddie] Chan Chu Chi, was responsible. [Eddie] Chan it is said, felt that Michael Chan was a threat to his own safety. The gang leaders are afraid that further escalation of trouble is inevitable.

(v) William Tse, the Kung Lok leader in L.A. was recently in Hong Kong in connection with a new import/export business he has which involves partners in Mainland China.

(vi) The Hip Sing Tong has about 60,000 members — but this figure is misleading in that all persons paying protection fees are themselves considered members. The operational membership, i.e. those responsible for enforcing the Hip Sing Tong's control is only about 50–60.

(vii) Casinos are operated by the various Tongs but loansharking [in North America] within the casinos is on a much reduced scale compared with a Hong Kong casino for example. This is because of the geographical size of the U.S.A. and Canada, such size enabling a debtor to easily disappear. For this reason only known customers are able to borrow from the casino's loansharks.

(viii) Lau Wing Kui claims he established the Kung Lok in Toronto in order to promote Kung Fu. *Danny Mo Sui Chuen started collecting protection fees and Lau claims that he became worried and withdrew from running the Kung Lok.* The Kung Lok are active in L.A., Toronto and Ottawa. The Ottawa leader is Danny Cheung Chi Wo. Canadian PP. BG 407151, Canadian Certificate of Identity 1477989. His D.O.B. is 5.1.48. Cheung was arrested, in Hong Kong, in 1978 and was charged with Criminal Intimidation following an incident in the China Night Club, Sheraton Hotel when about 200 persons occupied all the tables in the club and totally disrupted business. The incident occurred because the club staff had refused to allow him to sign a bill the previous evening. Cheung was subsequently acquitted on the benefit of the doubt.

[Cheung's name was actually spelled Cheang. He died of natural causes in the late 1980s, though his group in Ottawa is still criminally active.]

(ix) [a Hong Kong government consular official overseas] of the Consulate in Hong Kong, is a triad member in H.K. He is an ex. H.K. police officer and was retired in the public interest. His telephone number was found in Vincent Jew's notebook.

(x) Lau confirms the Kung Lok Membership of the following: [Lau named seven of the most prominent Kung Lok members including Danny Mo, Big John Yue, and Charlie Kwan.]

(xi) Lau has heard that Danny Mo Sui Chuen and Charlie Kwan Yee Man are in possession of forged Canadian immigration documents and assist immigrants to go to Canada. Fees payable are not known. The • Restaurant, Toronto was known to be used as a short cut for people wishing to emigrate from Hong Kong. Despite the fact that the restaurant was losing money, the restaurant continued to recruit large numbers of staff from Hong Kong.

[This intelligence information on the • restaurant in Toronto is interesting in that for a long time it was erroneously thought that this restaurant was partly owned by Lui Lok. I am not naming the restaurant here as this was simply unconfirmed intelligence information, not hard fact.]

The last part of the Alleged Triad Meeting memo presented some new intelligence information on Lau:

. . . Lau Wing-kui (0491–2837–1730) DOB 19.4.29 res. 32-D Braga Circuit 3/F, Kowloon. tel. 3–7158073, H.K. Passport A046437 issued in Hong Kong on 15.10.81. was interviewed on 31.1.83. . . . Lau has been a notorious illegal casino operator in Hong Kong and for two years after his deportation from Canada he ran a casino in the Dominican Republic. Lau states that he was deported because a magazine called "Covered Ups" alleged that he was a triad member and engaged in drug trafficking in Toronto. He claims he was in the Dominican Republic when his immigration hearing took place. . . .

Lau, who was considered by many DEA intelligence analysts as one of the top ten heroin traffickers in the world, was the subject of many DEA investigations, though none has been successful. In fact, it is entirely likely that the DEA is wrong about Lau, and that he is what he appears to be, a successful gambling operator with excellent triad connections.

One of Lau's best connections was with Eddie Chan (Chan Tse or Chi Chiu), a corrupt former member of the Royal Hong Kong Police who had relocated to New York City in the 1970s. Chan quickly became the head of the powerful On Leong tong. The RKHP asked Lau about his relationship with Chan:

> Lau claims that he is neither a good friend nor an enemy of Chan Chi-chiu, Eddy, but does state that after his deportation from Canada he was in possession of a large sum of cash and he used Chan's bank, the Oriental Bank of New York to transfer the funds. Chan is allegedly a vice president of the bank. Lau states that the gang leaders in New York are:

> (i) Chan Chi-chiu — head of On Leong . . . . *Chan Chi-chiu* is engaged in the operation of casinos. Always carries a revolver.

The "Lau Report" then gave a detailed rundown of a dispute between the leader of the Hip Sing tong and a rival gang, which ended in the shooting of a number of the rivals' gang members in a downtown New York City bar. Lau was quoted as telling the RKHP that the Flying Dragons, the youth gang associated with the Hip Sing, were responsible for the shootings. The RKHP report concluded with a list of "other areas" of information from Lau:

> (i) Toronto — the head of the Luen Kung Lok after Lau's deportation in Toronto was a man called Sum Chai who is now in Houston.

> Lau was not prepared to say that Mo Shui Chuen, Danny was the current head of Luen Kung Lok in Toronto but he did admit that he and Mo visited Macao for 3 *hours* when Mo supplied the version of events leading up to the shootings in Grandpa's Bar.

Lau was prepared to say that so far as he knew the Luen Kung Lok's main business in Toronto was gambling (pai gow and fan tan) with casinos at the basement and first floor of a premises previously housing the Hoi Tin Restaurant, Dundas Street.

(ii) Los Angeles — William Tse is head of the Luen Kung Lok there.

(iii) Boston — Tse Toi Mo, Stephen, [a.k.a.] 'Tin Lung' is a member of the Hung Mun.

(iv) New York — [two New York City restaurant owners] . . . are gang leaders but Lau Wing Kui professes not to know their affiliations. . . .

15. Lau Wing Kui is currently in Macau and efforts will be made to re-interview him on his return to Hong Kong with a view to obtain more definite information on the gang situation in North America/Canada and the connections with Hong Kong.

Today Lau Wing Kui is back where he was before he set off for North America supervising, among other things, several rented gambling tables at the famed casino Hotel Lisboa, the largest and most luxurious of all the casinos of Macao, the Las Vegas of the Far East. The Lisboa is perhaps the number one architectural oddity among the old world charm of Macao's more traditional buildings — its Moorish-looking turret garishly covered with light stands as one of the dominant symbols of Macao. The Lisboa casino, with its seventy-three tables on three floors, offers gamblers every type of game — baccarat, blackjack, roulette, boule, *fan tan*, *dai siu* (a Chinese dice-based game), slot machines, jai alai, 12 numbers, tombola, mah-jong, and *pai gow*, a type of Chinese dominoes (Lau Wing Kui has several *pai gow* tables). Unlike Las Vegas and Atlantic City, there is no entertainment offered here, just many rooms full of people seriously gambling around the clock.

All the casinos in Macao, including the Lisboa where Lau had once been a director of security, are owned by billionaire and sometime Toronto resident, Stanley Ho. The grand-nephew of Sir Robert Ho Tung, the legendary comprador for Jardine Matheson & Co. (the founding trading house of Hong Kong and the model for the Noble house of taipans of James Clavell's very popular novels), Ho is the scion of one of the oldest, wealthiest, and most prestigious families in Hong Kong. The debonair, aristocratic looking Ho, now in his late sixties, is a Canadian landed immigrant, but he lives most of the time in Hong Kong and Macao, where he enjoys a complete monopoly on gambling. Ho became a high-profile resident of Canada in the late 1980s by buying one of the most expensive mansions in Toronto in the posh Bayview area of the city and by becoming the chairman of International Semi-Tech Microelectronic Ltd. in Markham, a powerful international conglomerate that now owns several major U.S. companies, including Singer Sewing Machine Corporation and the U.S. branch of Consumers Distributing.

Ho's fortune is conservatively estimated at $2 billion. Allegations of his membership in the triads have been fairly widespread. A 1988 United States Justice Department "top secret" report erroneously stated that Stanley Ho was a member of the "Unk" triad. The document, which was conveniently made available to many journalists in Canada and the United States, was misinterpreted by some journalists and local police who thought that "Unk" was Ho's triad affiliation. But what the FBI meant was that he was suspected of being a member of some triad as yet unknown ("unk") to them.

Other allegations of Ho's membership in the triads were published in the 1988 book, *Warlords of Crime: Chinese Secret Societies — The New Mafia* by Gerald L. Posner, a journalist and lawyer. Posner quoted unnamed Hong Kong police intelligence sources who flatly stated that Stanley Ho was a triad member and that the eighth floor of the Lisboa was where "triad loan-sharks operations were headquartered." DEA sources told Posner that other triad people used the Lisboa on a regular basis for loansharking and enforcement shakedowns.

In March 1990 I asked senior Macao law enforcement officials about the accusations of Ho's triad membership. When shown a photocopy of the Justice Department report, they laughed about the Americans' naïveté about life in their neck of the woods. They explained that Ho was certainly *not* a triad member or leader. He was far too prominent and successful a businessman for that. After all, Ho is from one of the most prestigious and wealthiest families in Hong Kong. Moreover, Macao, which has a resident population of only about five hundred thousand, ninety percent of whom are Chinese, receives one-half of its annual revenue from taxes on Ho's casinos. Rather, the senior Macao police officials explained, Ho had neutralized the triads in his spheres of influence by bringing in people like Lau Wing Kui. One of Lau's jobs, they explained, was to make sure that the triads were happy and created no problems in Ho's casinos. Money was also paid to the three triads that operated in Macao, to keep the gambling casinos quiet. Ho's casinos did not get extorted because an accommodation has been made between the triads and the casino management.

Lau was very well-known to the Macao police. One senior officer said he talks regularly to Lau and that he spoke excellent Spanish and Portuguese. He also said that Lau and most of the others who rent tables at Ho's Lisboa don't generally rent the tables under their own names. Lau commutes regularly by the hydrofoil ferry between his home in Mong Kok, Hong Kong, to Macao. According to the senior Macao police officials, Lau simply gives the Lisboa "face."

As the Macao police eloquently and frankly put it, "The triads are a natural part of our landscape." They identified another local resident as the triad boss in Macao. (They added that most of the impoverished rickshaw drivers who crowd around Macao's seedy docks are heroin addicts whose supplies come from triad dealers.) They also revealed that Ho has had only one known rival for the casinos in Macao. He is Yip Hon, described by the police as "a respected member of the Macao community" and a former business partner of Stanley Ho in Sociedade de Turismo e Diversoes de Macau (STDM), a travel and casino conglomerate owned principally by Ho, which operates all the casinos in Macao under a unique government-sponsored franchise. But Yip Hon had a falling out with Ho, and for a long time he was trying to get his own casino. Yip Hon now runs the largest race track in Macao, the Macao Trotting.

Though he has had a virtual monopoly on all casino gambling in Macao since 1962, Ho has had his share of problems over the years, with both criminals and governments. On July 15, 1987, his personal secretary and the manager of STDM, Thomas Chung (Chung Wah-tin) was brutally murdered, savagely chopped to death as he walked to his automobile in a carpark near Victoria Park in Hong Kong. The casino tycoon offered a million dollar reward to anyone who could offer facts about the murder. Police in Macao and Hong Kong believed the killing was related to triad-run loansharking rackets at the Hotel Lisboa, where Lau Wing Kui was a prominent renter of tables.

But it wasn't Lau or his triad that was fingered by the police as the most likely culprit, rather it was a crime syndicate in Macao known as Mor Dang. Several Hong Kong-run loansharking rings had tried to infiltrate Mor Dang's control in the Macao area. This action, according to some police sources, "led to a show of strength" and the murder of Chung. But neither Chung nor Stanley Ho were part of the loansharking network, and other police sources denied that Chung's death was the result of this rivalry as, according to the *South China Morning Post* of October 27, 1987, "these clashes had been foiled by the police before rival groups could embark on a full-scale triad war." They speculated that there might be a connection between Chung's death and that of Wong Ti-ho, a wealthy businessman who had been shot nearby a few months earlier. To this day neither murder has been officially solved, though many now believe the Chung killing was the result of a feud between Ho and another syndicate.

Ho's other problems have come from the Hong Kong government, which, for a short time in the late 1980s, allowed floating casinos to operate in Hong Kong waters, jeopardizing Ho's business monopoly on gambling in Macao. But Ho fought back by bringing his own gambling floats into the Hong Kong area. Finally, in March 1990, Hong Kong capitulated and banned floating casinos altogether, and Ho's casino monopoly for Hong Kong/Macao was once again secure.

As 1997 and the mainland Chinese takeover of Hong Kong approach, the likelihood of Lau Wing Kui leaving the Hong Kong/Macao area once again grows greater. Of course, since he still carries a Dominican Republic passport, he could return to that Caribbean island, where some say former On Leong tong leader Eddie Chan now lives.* It's possible but doubtful since he is a citizen, that the Dominican Republic would refuse him entry. Once there, he might, of course, like his old casino back, but the chances of that are very slim. He is also still in close touch with his wife and family in Toronto. It may be we haven't seen the last of Lau in Canada.

---

* In fact, one recent intelligence report from the DEA states that Eddie Chan is the new manager of the casino at the Ambassador Hotel in the Dominican Republic. This would certainly be ironic if it were actually the case.

Chapter Eleven

THE TEFLON DRAGON HEAD
Danny Mo and
His "Lucky Money"

The Kung Lok triad continued to blossom even after Lau Wing Kui was unceremoniously tossed out of Canada in 1980. One of the main figures to emerge in the vacuum created by Lau's untimely departure was his faithful follower, Danny Mo (Mo Shui Chuen) who through a skilful blend of personality and brutal force as the triad society's red pole (the enforcer and recruiter), simply took over. Mo, who came from a well-to-do Hong Kong family, "wanted easy money and to become big very fast," according to one of his former associates. The lean and mean Mo, known to have a short temper, soon became the dragon head of the triad in Canada, controlling or influencing the rackets in Chinatowns large and small, new and old, in Toronto and throughout Ontario. At public functions in the 1980s, Mo, who has an excellent command of English, simply introduced himself as the "President of Kung Lok,"* which, of course, as most in the community knew, was not just a kung fu club, though Mo himself was an avid and experienced kung fu enthusiast and practitioner.

---

* Mo was officially "president" only on and off, since each year a new president was elected. Under the society rules, one cannot be president for more than two years in a row. For example, Big John Yue was president of the Kung Lok in 1980–81 and Raven Tsoi in 1987.

As well as taking over as the leader of the Kung Lok, Mo became a major deal maker and liaison figure with other triads and Asian gangs as far away as San Francisco, Los Angeles, Montreal, Boston, Vancouver, New York City, and, of course, Hong Kong. Mo, who started out as a part owner and maître d' in a restaurant on Eglinton Avenue, was also quite close to a number of legitimate and well-known restaurant owners in the Chinese community who have supported him when he has been in trouble.

Even today, after two decades in the Kung Lok extortion and protection rackets, the still youthful-looking Mo remains an imposing figure on the Oriental crime scene. Police intelligence officers in New York, while watching his New York City gang associate Kit Jai, identified Mo as the driver of the getaway car at the scene of the 1979 gang hit of rival concert promoter Tony Chow. Royal Hong Kong Police also placed Danny Mo in key meetings with the triad leadership in the Crown colony, and Metro Toronto police have placed him at the heart of many extortion and protection rackets in Canada. Yet Mo is one of those people who seem to have the uncanny ability to make all the right moves, often just in the nick of time. His ability to slip away from trouble makes him the Teflon dragon head — the John Gotti of the triads. For like Gotti, the boss of the Gambino Mafia family in New York City who was nicknamed "the Teflon don" because he avoided going to jail for so long, Mo, though charged several times with serious offences, has managed to keep out of prison. No serious conviction against Mo has ever stuck.* He is, according to people who have worked with him and top cops who have worked against him, capable of being both totally ruthless and absolutely charming.

---

* Prosecution persistence against Gotti, however, did pay off in the long run. He was imprisoned in 1990 after being charged with a number of murders under the American RICO Act. No less a person than Gotti's own number two, Sammy "the Bull" Gravino, has flipped over and emerged as the chief witness against him. Gotti was finally convicted in April 1992. The still "Dapper Don," his Teflon gone, was sentenced in June 1992 to jail for the rest of his life.

Based in Toronto, but working closely with criminal and entertainment figures in New York, Boston, Montreal, and Hong Kong, the wily Mo has had a virtual monopoly on bringing into Canada and protecting major Hong Kong and even mainland Chinese singers, actors, and entertainers for the past two decades. A shrewd politician, he astutely adapted to the rapidly changing circumstances by trimming his sails to the prevailing winds — from the mid-seventies when he was working as a partner with Lau Wing Kui to the late 1980s and early 1990s, when he was doing business amicably with Asau Tran, the pre-eminent Vietnamese gang boss of Toronto, as well as with the mainland Chinese gangs. Mo was a chameleon, surviving the ups and downs of the treacherous life he had chosen. He always appeared to be where he wanted to be — moving with ease and grace around the criminal underworlds in a number of locations. Even in today's radically changing Oriental crime scene, Mo, now in his third decade of activity in Toronto, perseveres as one of the major dragons of crime in North America while others have been killed, jailed, deported, retired, or are simply content to watch from the sidelines. "Sponsored by some rich and powerful people both in and out of the crime world," according to Benny Eng, a veteran Asian crime fighter, Mo now appears almost legitimate, running a prosperous entertainment business and, until recently, operating a Scarborough restaurant.

Police who have spent years investigating Mo find him a determined and formidable foe. Inspector Barry Hill, who was "determined to stop Mo and his people right from the start" and feels he knows him better than any other investigator because of the years spent listening to Mo on hundreds of police wiretaps, described Mo as a "cold and calculating" individual. According to Hill, Mo also had an enormously inflated ego:

> He was very much "I'm Mo. Everyone in Chinatown knows who I am." He's very full of himself. He's the one with all of the connections, with New York City, Hong Kong, everywhere.

But this arrogant strutting of Mo's was also a source of his power; it was true — he was the one with all the connections and everyone in Chinatown did know who he was.

Over the years police have laid charges against Mo and his organization, many of them between 1980 and 1984, when the Metro Chinese joint forces unit (called the "Oriental Unit" at the time), turned up the heat and succeeded, at least for a time, in breaking the victims' code of silence, which had all too frequently been the norm in Chinatown. The testimony given by the witnesses, as well as extensive surveillance and wiretapping investigations, resulted in a number of charges against Kung Lok members. Mo himself was charged with extortions, illegal possession of guns, frauds, assaults, and an immigration scam and bribery. But in one way or another — witnesses would mysteriously disappear or change their testimony or identification — Mo managed to emerge unscathed from all the trials and tribulations of the period, though many of his underlings and colleagues were less fortunate.

But in the summer of 1981, a savage killing in Chinatown shook Danny Mo and the Kung Lok leadership. On July 12, 1981, the Macanese Richard Castro, the Hong Kong-born son of Chinese and Portuguese parents who ran a Kung Lok gambling house, had just finished a lunchtime business meeting with three of his Kung Lok brothers — Francis Ching (Ching Chun Chung), Walter Ip (Ip Heung Wing) and Big John Yue — at the then elegant China Court Restaurant on Spadina Avenue in the heart of Chinatown. Castro was the treasurer of the Kung Lok. He walked out with Ching and Ip towards the parking lot. Four acquaintances of the trio, known as Jimmy Lau, Michael Wu, A Chan (or A Chou), and Hon Jai, had been sitting at another table in the restaurant and followed them out. As Castro walked slightly ahead of his colleagues in the parking lot, A Chan, who had been carrying a beer glass, suddenly broke it on the end of a nearby post, then he and Hon Jai jumped Castro and viciously assaulted him. The two others, Jimmy Lau and Michael Wu, backed off, held at bay by Francis Ching and Walter Ip. Finally, the four assailants fled, A Chan screaming,

"It is none of your business." Castro's throat had been ripped open by the force of the savage attack, and his jugular vein was severed. He died within minutes, as his shocked Kung Lok colleagues looked on in disbelief.

The attackers were not simply a rival gang, rather they were tough street guys, one of whom owed money to Castro, who was also a loanshark. The money had been borrowed in one of Castro's Chinatown gambling houses. All four attackers were known to Ching and Yue. The man they knew by the street names of A Chan and A Chou (a.k.a. Sam Chan, also known by his nickname "Woo-ying-bei" or "fly on the nose" — he had a mole on his nose) was actually thirty-year-old Lo Wing Chou. He was in Canada illegally and had a record for robbery, illegal possession of drugs, statutory rape, and escaping custody. Hon Jai, or Hon Chi, was actually Edmund Yu (Yu Wing Hon). After the killing, Yu managed to escape to Hong Kong via Buffalo, clearly helped by influential connections. Paul Richard Bittick, a Eurasian member of the Kung Lok, was later charged for assisting in the escape by driving Lo and Yu to the American border at Fort Erie, where the pair swam across the border.

Big John Yue was one of the witnesses at the trial. At the time he was the Kung Lok president and ran several gambling houses, some for the Kung Lok and some for himself. He testified that he had just had a meeting with Castro, whom he described as a "keeper" of a gambling house on the southeast corner of Dundas Street West and Elizabeth Street. Yue testified that Castro managed the house and had an interest in the profits. After Castro left the restaurant, Yue joined his wife who had been sitting at another table in the restaurant. He noticed that the other four men also left the restaurant just after his Kung Lok associates. Five to ten minutes later, Walter Ip returned and told Big John that Castro had been beaten up. When Yue went to the parking lot, he saw Castro lying on the ground in a pool of blood. The two main attackers, Lo and Yu, were later identified by Yue in court, although he, like Francis Ching, knew them only by their street names.

Although Edmund Yu had managed to escape to Hong Kong

and Lo Wing Chou to New York State, both men were eventually caught, extradited, and brought back to Canada by October 1981. During their brief 1982 trial, Crown Attorney Chris Punter stated that Castro was a member of Kung Lok, which he likened to the Mafia. In his summary of events, Punter explained the background for the killing. Castro had previously arranged for Lo to be beaten because of an unpaid gambling debt. Castro just happened to be eating lunch and having a meeting with his Kung Lok colleagues at the same time that Lo and Yu were in the restaurant. Castro approached Lo as he left the restaurant, threatening him again over the debt. Lo reacted by breaking a bottle and killing Castro. There was no need for a full trial as both Lo and Yu pleaded guilty. Lo got six years, Yu got three years. Paul Bittick, who was born in Hong Kong and had a previous record for mischief, was convicted of being an accessory after the fact.

Although the guilty men were eventually caught and convicted, the bold daylight attack on a leading Kung Lok figure in full view of several other Kung Lok members cost the Kung Lok more than their treasurer. It cost them face in the street world of Chinatown, and face is everything in the world of Asian gangs.

Soon people in the community were coming forward to the police to reveal information about Kung Lok extortions. Francis Ching, who was an eyewitness to his friend and colleague's grisly death, was, in late 1982, one of two defendants in the first of a series of cases brought against Kung Lok members by the Metro Chinese joint forces unit.* Ching and Tang Tai Loong (known as Paul Tang), both in their thirties, were charged with a series of extortions and assaults that had occurred between March 1981 and May 1981, just weeks before the Castro murder. During the later trial, the police were able to introduce in evidence some triad books found during a raid on Ching's home.

---

* In rapid succession over the past decade, the unit became the "Oriental Unit," later the "Special Unit," and finally the "Asian Investigative Unit" or the "AIU," in a desperate search for the politically correct tag.

But had it not been for the courage of one of the extortion victims, there would have been no case at all. Charles Chan (Chan Wai Hung), who lived with his family in Toronto and worked as a waiter, not only testified several times in court but also appeared without a disguise on the lead item of the November 10, 1983 "Fifth Estate" program on the Kung Lok. Although police knew about the many extortions going on in Chinatown, till then they had been powerless to do anything about them until victims stepped forward. As Barry Hill put it:

> People won't come forward in Chinatown. It's an old tradition, a way of life in Chinatown. In one particular case, a youth that we did charge with a couple of extortions, the word was out that he'd earned $20 to $30,000 within a couple of months from various students. But all we were hearing about [from victims who came forward] was about $3,000 worth [of the extortion take]. So it's a case of maybe six to one, as far as victims coming forward.

Yet Chan openly discussed in court and on television the concept of *lomo*, or "lucky money" that was paid to the gangs in Toronto in a red envelope, just as it was to the triads in Hong Kong. Chan had been beaten several times in 1981 and generally terrorized by the Kung Lok to pay *lomo*. In an interview, Eric Malling, then one of the hosts of "Fifth Estate," asked Chan about an episode in 1981:

ERIC MALLING: The night they came for the money, Chan was with a friend in Chinatown. They were ordered into a certain restaurant, and once inside, the gang shut the doors and told Chan to get rid of his friend.

CHARLES CHAN: One of the guys locked the door right away and then a Chinese boy named (bleep) call [to] my friend. "Get out, get out on the street right away." . . . If I didn't tell my friend to get out on the street, they would have beat us like dogs. . . .

ERIC MALLING: That night Chan remembered seeing Johnny Yue, who was present at the earlier beating. Chan didn't know he was an important man in the gang. But he was there in the locked restaurant. He was the one who told them that they would be beaten like dogs if the friend didn't leave. Among the six or seven other gang members in the empty restaurant were Francis Ching and Paul Tang. They had roughed him up before, and now wanted some money.

CHARLES CHAN: Paul Tang and Francis Ching tell me to go to a small table. They ask for a thousand and eighty dollars for *lomo*.

ERIC MALLING: *Lomo*, what does that mean?

CHARLES CHAN: Like this kind of money, like I give it to them. Put it in a red pocket, a thousand eighty dollars for settle down this thing.

ERIC MALLING: And if you didn't pay them the thousand eighty dollars *lomo* what was going to happen to you?

CHARLES CHAN: They give me trouble. I working, when I get out of restaurant, maybe some kid going to beat me up.

ERIC MALLING: Did you think they meant business, that they'd do it?

CHARLES CHAN: They do it for a living I think.

Eric Malling asked Chan why he stepped forward when he could have just paid the money:

CHARLES CHAN: No, like if I owe them money, I pay, right. This kind of — I don't owe them money. If I pay, what for?

ERIC MALLING: Weren't you afraid that they'd come after you if you didn't?

CHARLES CHAN: The policemen would help me, you know. I report to police.

Another witness in this Kung Lok extortion case, Ricky Woo (Woo Chuen Fung), the assistant Manager of the Golden Country Restaurant in Scarborough where Chan had been working as a waiter, confirmed the extent of the injuries Chan received during a severe beating from Tang and Ching on March 29, 1981. Though he did not confess to extortion as such, Francis Ching admitted in both his statement to the police and in court that the money he collected from Chan at the restaurant in Scarborough was to be paid in "a red envelope for lucky money." Ching's Kung Lok colleague and co-defendant, Paul Tang, had told Chan that he had to pay "old hair," a triad slang term meaning, as Chan well knew from Hong Kong, money wrapped in a Chinese red envelope.

Furthermore, on questioning about the two triad books seized from his apartment by Sergeant Chuck Konkel* of Metro police, Paul Tang admitted that they were given to him by Danny Mo, "to study and read," though, of course, he would not admit that they were triad books. He remained silent when asked what they were by Asian crime fighter Constable Yau Pat, but the Hong Kong-born Pat, who testified in court as an expert witness on the triads, described the first book as a 442-page study on triads in general, and the second was a book on the operation of the Kung Lok triad. Pat also called the Kung Lok "the most infamous gang" in Chinatown which was "spreading fear and violence through the community."

In their defence, Ching and Tang told the court that they were simply trying to collect "an old gambling debt." But in finding both Francis Ching and Paul Tang guilty of the charges on September 8, 1983, Judge Stephen Borins called the defendants liars and warned of the growing danger from the Kung Lok triad:

> Never in my career on the bench have I encountered the accused to give such false testimony [their alibi about a gambling debt]. . . . The beating and violence was con-

---

* Detective-Staff Sergeant K.G.E. Konkel, who had served as an inspector in the Royal Hong Kong Police Force, is the author of the critically-acclaimed novel, *The Glorious East Wind*, a highly readable detective thriller about the triads in Hong Kong. Now at work on his second detective novel, Konkel still works full time as a policeman in Toronto.

nected with the request for money. It was a preview of things to come. *Lomo* is the word used by the Kung Lok when they are asking protection money. It was known to Chan and it is known to have this meaning in the Chinese community.

Inspector Barry Hill, Head of the Oriental unit at the time and now the officer in charge of the Criminal Intelligence Service of Ontario, a body that co-ordinates all police intelligence in the province, explained to Eric Malling the significance of Chan's testimony:

[It was] the first time somebody came forward in a charge involving who we consider some of the important people in the gang. And he came to us at a very early stage of what was happening to him. Some of these extortion attempts take place over a matter of weeks. We were able to get in at the ground floor and observe what was going on and could lay the appropriate charges.

Hill believes that the case was a watershed: "I guess my breakthrough was Ching and Tang because finally there were people on the bench who were realizing what was happening. Most of the time we had just been hitting our heads against a brick wall." Asked on "The Fifth Estate" program why it had been so difficult to get victims in the Chinese community to come forward, Hill detailed the very real and psychological pressures on the victims:

They go through an awful experience — something which they carry with them for the rest of their lives. . . . It takes a tremendous deal of courage to finger some of the people who are extorting them. [In order to come forward] they have to deal with the facts and deal with the legend. The legend seems to be that if I go to the police I'm going to be killed. The fact is that that's not true. And the fact is that we've been very successful in our prosecutions in the last couple of years. There have been no problems to any victim and they have to realize that. You have to realize that, as with any organized crime, it's a problem that grows unless you're prepared to deal with it.

In a follow-up extortion case in 1983, the victory came a lot more easily for Barry Hill's Oriental unit. This time the case involved two Kung Lok members named Ricky Kot (Kot Yiu Kei) and Kam Man Ho, and a seventeen-year-old visa student from Hong Kong named Frederick Pow (Pow Siu Ki). Pow had been introduced to Kot and Ho in April 1983 through a mutual friend, named Tony Poon (Poon Shiu Cheong). Immediately, Pow was directly told by Poon that Kot and Ho were members of the Kung Lok Triad Society. The extortion began right away. Once again, the Kung Lok extortionists told the victim that the "lucky money" was for protection, this time from a shadowy triad personality they identified only as "Duck Jai," a Chinese-Canadian member of one of the most powerful and feared triads in Hong Kong, the 14 K triad.

Adapting to the new technology, the Kung Lok pair managed over the next six months to extort from Pow a lot of cash as well as money through possession of his Green Machine automated teller card and secret bank PIN number. But in late September 1983, Pow told his school principal at the exclusive Rhenish Church Collegiate about the extortion. At first this act increased the pressure on Pow, because Kot and Ho found out about the principal's knowledge. They told Pow that because of him they were having trouble collecting "lucky money" from other visa students at the school and that therefore Pow would now have to pay a lot more to the Kung Lok. Finally the police were brought in. After Pow's detailed statement and photo identification of the pair, Kot and Ho were arrested on October 1, 1983. Once again the police introduced in court the Kung Lok as one of the triads that "anyone of Chinese descent growing up in Hong Kong would be aware of and scared of." The triads, the Crown maintained, were "criminal in nature and use violence, fear, and corruption to prey upon their innocent Chinese victims." Kot and Ho were convicted the following year.

The heat on Danny Mo and the Kung Lok throughout the early 1980s, and especially in 1983, didn't come from just the police and the courts. In May 1983 the *South China Morning Post* in Hong Kong carried headlines about the Kung Lok's extensive extortions in Ontario: "Chinese Gang Terrorising Hong Kong Students in Toronto." Then in November 1983, "The Fifth Estate" ran a piece called "Lomo" on the Kung Lok extortions in Ontario. Members of the Chinese community, organized by alderman Ying Hope, attempted in vain to stop the airing of the program so as to preserve the image of their community rather than to protect the criminals. They called an emergency meeting with several prominent Chinese businessmen in Hope's office to tell the executive producer and senior producer that there was no crime in Chinatown. Unfortunately for alderman Hope, one of the businessmen present was an owner of the China Court restaurant; he reluctantly agreed that the grisly murder of Richard Castro had occurred just outside his restaurant. The producers decided to go ahead with the story.*

In "The Fifth Estate" program, Eric Malling confronted

---

* When the *Globe and Mail* ran a series of front-page articles about Chinese organized crime in Canada in 1986, they were soundly condemned as racist in a letter campaign organized by the Chinese Canadian National Council and the Toronto Chinese Business Association. I wrote one of the few letters of appreciation for the series; it was published as the lead letter on October 27, 1986. It said, in part, that "it is not racist to expose organized criminal organizations.... It is a sad fact of life that criminal organizations exist, and that many of these organizations are restricted to criminals of the same ethnic background." I went on to emphasize that it was also a sad fact of life that most of the victims of this criminal activity "are people in the Asian community, primarily students and immigrants who are not familiar with the Canadian legal system.... It is not in the interest of the public or the Asian community to pretend that organized crime groups do not exist and to protect extortionists and murderers from exposure." The Chinese Canadian National Council has since modified its position and has publicly admitted that organized criminals are operating in the Chinese communities.

Danny Mo for an interview outside Massey Hall while inside a Hong Kong singer who was being protected by Mo and his boys was performing. Because there were three cases pending in the courts against Mo at the time, one of them an extortion case that was due to be heard in days, CBC lawyers advised that we black out Mo's face and not identify him. So Mo's voice was heard, denying membership in the Kung Lok and claiming that the triad had nothing to do with the concert, but his face was covered up and his name removed by bleeps. With Mo was Andrew Tsang, who was a partner in Mo's company, Oriental Arts and Promotion. Tsang, who had worked in Hong Kong and the United States with Mo, called the concert "one of the biggest events of its kind in town." (Within months of the interview, Tsang was killed in an airline accident in China.) "The Fifth Estate" item also showed a triad initiation and interviewed a number of victims of the Kung Lok, several in disguise, and one brave soul without a disguise.

But the police were not very successful in a series of cases they brought against Danny Mo in the period from late 1980 through 1985, though not for want of trying. Charges of assault, gun possession, and immigration fraud were withdrawn, dismissed, or hopelessly bogged down in court bureaucracy. Then, in 1984, Mo was charged and, in June 1985, convicted, on two counts of armed robbery, one of which was by far the most serious case against him to date. But the key witness soon made himself scarce, and Mo was acquitted on appeal.

For several years the only case successfully sustained against Mo was pitifully trivial. In August 1982 Ng Kwong Yu (a.k.a. Eddie Wu) approached Danny Mo for help in disposing of his 1981 BMW so he could then make a fraudulent claim on his insurance company. Mo moved quickly to help his friend. He first contacted two of his New York City associates, Kit Jai and another. Arrangements were made by Mo and his co-conspirators for Ng to take his car to New York City on September 4, 1982, leave it in the parking lot at La Guardia Airport, and then report it stolen at a later date. On September 15, 1982 Ng reported the theft and, on September 21, 1982, made a claim for $32,262 from the Commercial Union Assurance Company of Canada. But after insurance and police investigations, the company did not pay Ng's claim, as the extensive police wiretaps and surveillance helped prove the fraud.

Mo was charged with conspiracy to commit fraud over $200 and attempt fraud over $200. No expense was spared in building the case. There were wiretaps, mostly on Mo's phones at home and at the Kung Lok sports club at 538A Dundas Street, as well as physical surveillance of the various targets. At least fifteen officers in Toronto alone worked on making the case. Police intercepted dozens of calls between Eddie Wu (Ng) and Mo, making the various arrangements for the car's "disappearance" in August and September 1982. Among other calls taped by the police for this case were calls from New York-based gang leader Kit Jai to Danny Mo and Charlie Kwan, the Kung Lok treasurer, making arrangements for taking care of the car in New York.

The preliminary hearing took place in June and July 1984. Mo and Ng were both committed to trial. In June 1985 the trial finally took place, and Mo and Ng were found guilty and fined — hardly a major coup for the special police unit, which had spent thousands of dollars and hundreds of man hours tracking the fraud. Mo paid the fine and carried on with his criminal work. Danny Mo alone, of all the Kung Lok membership, seemed invincible and untouchable, and for this he was respected throughout the Oriental underworld in Toronto.

In their continuing war against Mo and the growing stature of the Kung Lok in the Asian community, the Toronto police's special joint forces Oriental unit went after the gaming houses that the triad either owned, protected, or robbed. As we have seen in the Dave Fu case, gambling houses were a major problem for the police. If they closed the places, they were damned by the many in the community who wanted to gamble and by their important sources of information, many of whom profited by running gaming houses. If they didn't, they were damned by those who felt the police were on the take, as well as by the law-and-order types who like to have the laws of the province enforced. In order to diminish the power of Mo and the Kung Lok, the police mounted an all-out assault on the gambling houses, closing five of them in the mid-1980s. In some cases they even used police informers or operatives to close down gambling houses run by former police agents such as Bill Mar (Mar King Foo).

There had been an armed robbery in one of Mar's gambling joints in 1983. Johnny Hau (Hau Ho Ming), a Kung Lok associate, robbed Wai Situ of $4,000 in cash at gunpoint on March 28, 1983 as he played *fan tan* at one of the longest-running gambling houses in Chinatown, on the second floor of 127A Dundas Street. This was right in the heart of Chinatown in a block that has been the home of several Chinese gambling houses over the years. The many gambling houses that used to operate openly in fixed locations in Chinatown were a major source of criminal activity, as there usually was a lot of money around, and technically the gambling houses were illegal. Many of the houses were protected by a gang, in this period usually the Kung Lok. Later, the Vietnamese gangs and mainland Chinese gangs filled this function, though by then the gambling houses had frequently become floating businesses, moving from place to place and often using hotels. Because he sometimes helped the police, any gambling house in which Bill Mar had an interest was generally allowed to stay open. Mar acted as the interpreter for Staff Sergeant Barry Hill when he arrived at the illegal gambling house to question the victim of the armed robbery, restaurant owner Wai Situ who, like many Chinese gamblers, carried lots of cash on him. Hau was convicted of armed robbery and illegal possession of a firearm, in this case a .410 gauge sawed-off shotgun.

Over the years there have been many accusations of corruption against police officers of 52 Division, which has for a long time included Toronto's main Chinatown in its sprawling and densely populated downtown beat. In one curious case in the early 1980s police busted an illegal gambling house, only to have some of the officers later accused of stealing cash from the tables. This incident was known in Chinatown as the infamous "money burning," where police from 52 Division allegedly simply stole the cash on the tables and later said that it had been burned. Charges were brought against several officers after the owner of a gambling house complained to senior police officials. At least one officer was eventually convicted. This wasn't long after the Dave Fu operational fiasco in 1980. None of this exactly inspired confidence in the police at 52 Division, especially bearing in mind what Fu and others, including some of the police themselves, said about the former corrupt system in 52 Division. Though the fact that the Metro Toronto police acted against the tainted officers once allegations were made does speak in favour of the police brass. It still calls to mind the corruption of the Vancouver police in the 1920s and again underlined the close, often unhealthy, relationship between the police and people running illegal gambling houses.

Bill Mar caused major problems for the police in another matter concerning an illegal gambling house. Mar, who had come to Toronto from Victoria decades earlier, had been for years a kind of unofficial liaison between the community, the gambling houses, and the police, the kind of fixer figure, as we have seen, that many in the old Toishan Chinese community in Toronto preferred to use, especially since the rise of the Kung Lok triad and other more violent gangs.

What Mar didn't realize was that, though he was in a somewhat privileged position for a time, he was not invulnerable. It turned out that Mar, too, could be subject to investigation, especially after some of his associates attempted to corrupt certain police officers. Bill Mar, who had obviously outlived his usefulness to the police, and his colleagues didn't know that one of the police officers they were targeting, Inspector Julian Fantino (now the police chief of London, Ontario, Fantino was for years considered by many to be in serious contention to become the next chief of police in Toronto), was working undercover in early 1985 in an attempt to close the gambling houses. In October 1988 Mar was charged with conspiracy to keep a common gaming house along with Wilson Wong, Wing Keung Wong, and David Kwow Wing To, the owner of David's Cameras and a gambling house at 139 Dundas Street. The two

Wongs, both owners of the Chinese Gourmet Restaurant on Dundas Street, and To were also charged with bribery of a police officer. According to Fantino, he was made an offer by which he and three other officers would receive "an additional salary" of $200 a week plus an additional $800 for all other officers at 52 Division. Fantino was given $250 cash in a men's room "as a sign of good faith." Wilson Wong, who had admitted to Fantino that he had once been in the prostitution business, even offered to bribe officers by providing young Korean women through Wing Wong's contacts. When Wilson Wong was charged with being an accessory to an attempted murder, Wilson Wong offered Fantino $2,000 to have the charges dropped.

Police used audio and videotape in the long operation. At one point, on April 9, 1985, they videotaped Wing Wong carefully counting out $1,000 in cash and handing it to Fantino while saying, "They count the money like this in a gaming house." Testimony at the trial revealed that seven businessmen, including Mar, the two Wongs and To, were prepared to pay police up to $40,000 a year to keep a *fan tan* house in Chinatown from being raided. Fantino also testified that Wilson Wong "was anxious to get into prostitution" by buying a downtown hotel where the Korean prostitutes would be based.

Fantino testified that the sixty-six-year-old Mar was the wiliest of the syndicate: "I always had the feeling that he was one step ahead of me. . . . He was right on top of things all the time." When discussing the establishment of a gambling house at To's place on 139 Dundas Street West, Mar "always appeared to be [speaking] in riddles," according to the veteran policeman. But there was nothing ambiguous about his weekly collection of $400 a week from three *fan tan* houses and $100 a week from hotels for prostitutes, which Mar allegedly received from his partners to pay for police protection. The gambling houses were said to clear up to $30,000 on a good night.

The entire scheme is very reminiscent of the 1920s evidence at the Vancouver Lennie Inquiry, except that the money figures had gone up slightly in the sixty year interim. The system also exactly duplicated what Dave Fu had reported in 1982 in his "Fifth Estate" interview.*

The trial ended abruptly on November 9, 1988, when the judge declared a mistrial after the *Globe and Mail* published *voir dire* proceedings, including excerpts from police wiretaps. The *Globe* later apologized, explaining that their lawyer at the time had advised that they could report on part of the *voir dire* proceedings. In a later trial in 1989, Wilson Wong was found guilty of five counts and David To of one count; three others of the seven businessmen pleaded guilty. The one man to be totally exonerated, ironically enough, was Bill Mar, who was acquitted on all charges.

Even while they were going after the gaming-house owners, the special police unit didn't let up on Danny Mo. One of the most serious charges ever brought against Danny Mo, and one of the most convoluted court cases to be brought by the police against alleged leaders of organized crime in Toronto's Chinatowns, was the 1983 immigration scam case. Charged with fraud along with Kung Lok leaders Mo and Charlie Kwan (Kwan Yee Man), were an Immigration official, Sean Herbert Pollock and a Toronto Lawyer, Oscar Wong, who had recently run unsuccessfully for the Ward Six City Council seats won by Jack Layton and John Sewell. Charges, which were later dropped, were also brought against Wai Hing Chan and Yuk Tak Li, the owners of Chinese Media, a Dundas Street West printing company. According to the charges, the investigation "showed that people living outside Canada were paying fees to get 'preferential treatment' while applying for immigration status." Counterfeit immigration forms were also allegedly being printed and distributed in the phoney immigration racket. Pollock, a senior member of the personnel department of

* Also it confirmed what I had earlier heard in a meeting I had with another former top gambling organizer, who had named Bill Mar as one of the "partners with the police" in a number of gambling houses. What my source didn't know was that the police involvement was almost certainly part of an undercover operation.

THE TEFLON DRAGON HEAD

Canada's Employment and Immigration Department, also
faced charges of breach of trust and accepting a secret commission. Mo, who was described in the newspapers at the time as
"an employee of Chinese Media printing," was, in addition to
fraud, charged with possession of a counterfeit mark used on
federal immigration documents. Lawyer Oscar Wong was
charged with conspiracy to commit fraud on the government
and offering a secret commission. These charges were later
dropped. Alleged gunrunning from Hong Kong by Mo and the
Kung Lok was also part of the original police probe, though no
charges were brought on this part of the investigation, just the
alleged immigration scam charges.

Though there had been a one-year-long joint RCMP/Metro
police undercover investigation, the case was built almost
entirely on wiretaps of Danny Mo, Sean Pollock, and others.
And these turned out to be one of the most problematic parts
of the Crown case, because ultimately some of the wiretaps,
particularly those on Pollock's phones, were deemed to have
been improperly obtained by the police. Pollock's "legal night-
mare," as the Judge called it, ended when charges against him
were stayed in 1987. Pollock, in turn, laid charges with the
public complaints commissioner, who investigates allegations
of police wrongdoing in Ontario, against Inspector Barry Hill
and Detective-Sergeant George Cowley, two of the police investigators and both former heads of the special police unit on
Asian gangs, for illegally wiretapping his home and office.
Pollock, still working with Immigration in Toronto after being
cleared by an internal investigation, alleged that the two thousand hours of wiretaps on him went beyond the court order. At
the inquiry, which began in January 1992, Hill and Cowley
maintained that a junior officer made the wiretap decisions in
question. A judgement by the Public Complaints Commission
will be made after the hearing is completed later in 1992.

But Mo's luck eventually appeared to run out. In June 1985
he was convicted of a March 21, 1985, armed robbery, involving
a shakedown of his ex-partner. The Teflon dragon head had
"coerced" (according to Crown attorney Mike Engel) and coun-

selled two masked "soldiers" of the Kung Lok, Walter Ip and Tom Leung, to rob at knifepoint a Vancouver-based promoter in his Toronto office at 434 Dundas Street West of $10,000 worth of tickets for a concert at the O'Keefe Centre and the master seating plan. In sentencing Mo, Judge Sydney Harris called him a "dangerous individual with many gangland connections" and noted that Mo had "used his position as one of the leaders of the Kung Lok gang to prey on the Chinese community for personal gain." Earlier, Inspector Barry Hill had testified at the trial that Mo was "the most dangerous member of the Kung Lok triad in Toronto," and the prosecutor had added in his summation that "the spectre of gangland violence had poisoned other prosecutions in which Mo was involved." Judge Harris gave Mo four and a half years for robbery.

The verdict was appealed and Mo was freed on bail. Through a legal technicality, the appeal overturned the original guilty verdict and a re-trial was ordered. But a key witness suddenly refused to testify and left Toronto. As in so many other cases involving Mo and the Kung Lok leadership, the victim/complainants were nowhere to be found. The prosecution against Mo was stayed. Inspector Barry Hill, who had handled the security for the witnesses, wryly quipped, "We made arrangements for the key witness to disappear — and we were too successful."

In 1987 Revenue Canada decided to go after Kung Lok gangsters for tax fraud, but Danny Mo was lucky once again. The Department of National Revenue and police selected Kung Lok president, Raven Tsoi (Tsoi Ip Shun), an old Danny Mo follower and friend, to be audited in a first effort to combat Asian organized crime in the tax courts. (Generally, the tax department goes after everyday Canadians rather than organized criminals, for it is far easier and less dangerous for them.) Raven Tsoi had been publicly identified as a Kung Lok leader in a 1987 trial of a Vietnamese enforcer who worked for him in shaking down Chinatown restaurant owners. On September 15, 1987, Revenue Canada served Tsoi with a notice that he had to justify his income for 1985, 1986, and 1987. He eventually had to pay significant back taxes. But, once again, Mo was off the hook, as Revenue Canada, for some unknown reason, did not go after him.

Danny Mo is now in his third decade of leadership in Toronto's Asian underworld. He has not merely survived — he has prospered, particularly in legitimate businesses which include restaurants and the Oriental entertainment industry. According to well-informed gangsters in Toronto's Oriental underworld, even in the 1990s, "few entertainers from the Orient can play in Toronto without Danny Mo having a piece of the action." Danny Mo is still the Teflon dragon head, but he no longer reigns alone.

Chapter Twelve

YEAR OF THE DRAGON
Eddie Chan and the Gangs of New York City

As the Kung Lok were expanding and developing in Canada in the 1970s and early 1980s, extraordinary developments were taking place in the United States, many connected in one way or another to what was happening in Canada. As we have seen, under Nickie Louie's leadership, the Ghost Shadows Chinese gang in New York, with its close ties to the On Leong tong, protected the gambling houses in New York City and fought vicious turf wars on the city streets in the mid- to late 1970s with the Hip Sing tong-connected youth gang, the Flying Dragons. Dozens of innocent people were shot down in the cross-fire.

The 1970s and 1980s also saw a new violence in Asian gangs. A series of brutal massacres in Chinatowns across North America horrified the general public. In 1977 five people were killed and eleven wounded during a shootout between Hop Sing gang members and gangsters of the rival Wah Ching gang run by Michael Louie in the crowded Golden Dragon Restaurant in San Francisco. In Seattle 13 people were butchered in the brutal robbery of a gambling house by a youth gang in February 1983. One of the killers, Wai Chu Ng, was placed on the FBI's Most Wanted list and later found while hiding out in Calgary's Chinatown. In New York City, on December 24, 1982, three innocent people were shot dead in a Chinatown bar in runaway gang violence. In the following year, also in New York City, eleven people were shot at the Golden Star bar by members of the Flying Dragons gang as a part of their continuing war with the Ghost Shadows gang.

Although the United States had experienced such violence in the past from Chinese organized crime, most notably in the tong wars from the turn of the century until the late 1920s, the massacres of the 1970s and 1980s signalled the presence and growth in Chinatowns across the Continent of a new force — violent youth gangs, connected to both tongs and triads, who were willing to use all the firepower available to realize their goals. By the middle of the 1980s, the Flying Dragons and the Ghost Shadows were killing each other in the streets of New York almost on a daily basis. New gangs, like the Flaming Eagles led by Johnny Kon (Kon Yu-leung) and specializing in heroin importation, were springing up.

At the same time as the rise in the level of violence, there was the parallel rise of Eddie Chan (Chan Tse-Chiu), a triad-connected former Royal Hong Kong police sergeant, who had become the President of the powerful On Leong tong in the 1970s and early 1980s and the Chairman of the National Chinese Welfare Council in the United States. In the mid-1970s Chan had brought the Ghost Shadows youth gang under his direction to act as enforcers for the On Leong and to protect their gambling houses in Chinatown. Chan, who was also the owner of a major restaurant and funeral parlour in New York City, was one of the major targets of President Reagan's Commission on Organized Crime (1983–1986), whose 1984 hearings, Organized Crime of Asian Origin, focused on the triads and the Chinese youth gangs (which were euphemistically called "an emerging crime group" even though Chinese gangs had been around for well over one hundred years), with a particular emphasis on Eddie Chan's control of the On Leong tong and the Ghost Shadows gang.* In their final report, the

---

* The report of President Reagan's Commission on Organized Crime also cited the growing power of the Kung Lok and Lau Wing Kui and listed a number of connections between the Kung Lok and American gang

Presidential Commission called Chan "the chief of organized crime in New York's Chinatown." Eddie Chan was also the figure upon which Robert Daly based one of the major characters in his novel, *The Year of the Dragon*, and the subsequent popular film of the same name starring Mickey Rourke.* Chan even figured in the mudslinging surrounding the 1984 Presidential election campaign when it was revealed that Democratic vice presidential nominee Geraldine Ferraro had received a major contribution from him during her congressional campaign. And Chan is featured heavily in *Warlords of Crime*, Gerald Posner's 1988 exposé on the triads in Hong Kong and their impact on the United States; in the book, he is depicted as "Fast Eddie," one of the major kingpins of heroin smuggling in Asia and the head of the largest tong in the United States, locked in a battle to the finish with Hip Sing tong overlord Benny Ong. After Chan's disappearance from New York City in 1984, Posner through his DEA sources, declared that the Hip

---

leaders through people like Lau himself, Danny Mo, Paul Kwok (now in a U.S. jail after a RICO conviction), Kit Jai, Bill Yuko, Vincent Jew (now ensconced as a gang leader in San Francisco), and other prominent Kung Lok members and associates. Toronto Police Sergeant Barry Hill testified before the Commission in New York City in October 1984 and is quoted at length in the final report. According to his testimony, the main Chinese criminal group in Toronto was the Kung Lok triad founded by Lau Wing Kui, which had a membership base of about three hundred members. Hill also testified to the Lau meetings in Hong Kong with Danny Mo, Stephen Tse (leader of the Ping On gang in Boston), William Tse and Tony Young (leaders of the Wah Ching of Los Angeles), as well as the entertainment activities of Danny Mo through his company Oriental Arts and Promotion, with American-based gang members Tony Young, Stephen Tse, and Kit Jai and Vincent Jew, two gang members by now in New York and San Francisco respectively. They brought Chinese singers and other entertainers into Canada and the U.S. from Hong Kong. Hill also testified that some 14 K triad leaders were emerging both in Toronto and in the United States. He described a swindle scheme called Lo Chin run by the 14 K by which people in Los Angeles and Toronto were defrauded of over $100,000 each.

* The central Chinese gang character is a composite figure of Chan, Nickie Louie, and others; like Chan, he is an ex-Hong Kong policeman who runs a funeral parlour.

Sing tong leader, then eighty-seven years old, had taken over "the pre-eminent position in the Chinese American community" from Chan. According to one reliable source, Eddie Chan is now in the Dominican Republic, helping to run Lau Wing Kui's old casino at the Ambassador, but this has not been confirmed. We have already seen the well-established connections between Chan and Lau Wing Kui, and Chan's attempt to expand his empire to Toronto in the statements of Nickie Louie's godfather, Dave Fu, and of Lau Wing Kui himself. One police report even indicated that Lau had moved considerable sums of money from Hong Kong to Canada through the Oriental Bank of New York. This was Eddie Chan's bank.

There was also an incursion into Toronto in the mid-seventies by factions of Chan's youth gang, the Ghost Shadows. Just around the time Lau arrived, Nicky Louie tried to establish a similar gang in Toronto. Although there were a number of contacts and interconnections between Lau's Kung Lok and the gangs and tongs in New York City, it is not certain that Louie was operating under Lau's instructions or even with his approval. But the attempt to set up a group by Nickie Louie was nipped in the bud. The Ghost Shadows didn't take off in Toronto because the police and the Immigration department went right after Nickie Louie as an undesirable visitor. Significantly, Nickie Louie was neither a landed immigrant nor a citizen. Moreover, Nickie had been running a very high-profile operation in New York protecting the On Leong gambling houses on Mott Street in New York's Chinatown. Nicky Louie came to Toronto more for a respite from all of the violence in New York City than for imperial ambitions, though Toronto (and Canada) certainly looked like friendly and lucrative territory.

When Nickie Louie first came to Toronto with his brother Eddie, he was already a criminal legend, though he was still only in his mid-twenties. New York police had a huge file on him and his operations, and Canadian Immigration was able to deport Nicky Louie under section 39 of the Immigration Act, which allowed for the deportation of visitors to Canada based on criminal intelligence information. When Nicky left to take on the major gangs in Chinatown in "the Big Apple," his brother remained in Toronto. But rather than continue the Ghost Shadows branch here, Eddie Louie, a less sinister figure than his brother, started a restaurant in downtown Toronto.*

All of these events in North America were watched with bemused detachment by the Royal Hong Kong Police force's Triad Bureau. A mid-1980s RHKP report, entitled *"The Evolution of Gangs in Chinatown during the Past Decade,"* on the gang developments in North America, was quite revealing. It showed that what in the United States and Canada seemed like isolated local phenomena in fact had international connections. It also demonstrated a knowledgeable historical and cultural perspective all too rare in similar police reports by American and Canadian authorities:

> In the past decade, triad gangs such as "Fu Tau Chai Wua" (The Small Axe Association), "Pai Ying Gang" (The gang of White Eagle), "Fei Lung Tong" (The Flying Dragon) emerged. Members of these gangs usually were young and strong. Gradually their powers increased. They demanded a protection fee, or the so-called "Donation" from shop owners. They even set aside some places inside the gang premises for gambling purposes and claimed that [the proceeds] would subsidize organization funds. To avoid trouble and any possible disturbances, most of the shop owners in Chinatown would pay their protection fee. As a result, the shop owners in Chinatown could do their business only when they were protected by the triad gangs.

The RHKP report described the importance of the sudden emergence of the Ghost Shadows in New York City in the mid-seventies.

---

* Lau attempted to recruit Eddie Louie for the Kung Lok, but Louie would have nothing to do with it. Though Eddie Louie kept his hand in small-time gambling in floating games in Toronto, he has never become a serious criminal force.

It often fought with other gangs so as to seize power and establish their base. At that time the means used by the "Ghost Shadows" grew more and more influential, no shop owners dare disobey them and paid them a huge amount of protection money every month. The "Ghost Shadow" developed rather rapidly. . . . Later, New York Police noticed that the "Ghost Shadow" with its headquarters in New York was co-operating with other gangs in an attempt to enter the international narcotic market by trafficking drugs from Golden Triangle to Hong Kong, and from Northern America to Europe. In the past, the "Ghost Shadow" was just an organization of some young people. Later, some young Hong Kong immigrants, some of whom were ex-triad elements in Hong Kong, participated in the gang. During the past eight years, "Ghost Shadow" shot people and committed various kinds of crime in Chinatown . . . . Later, the "Ghost Shadow" did business and set up night clubs, etc. to hide their drug trafficking activities.

A 1989 U.S. government report compiled by U.S. law enforcement for the General Accounting Office, entitled "Non-Traditional Organized Crime," also described the Ghost Shadows acting "as mid level heroin carriers traveling frequently between Toronto, Boston, Chicago, New Orleans, and Miami." The RHKP report in addition focused on Nickie Louie, the charismatic young "ring-leader" whom it described as a "brave and resourceful person." It went on to suggest that Nickie Louie and the Ghost Shadows were behind the mid-seventies assassination of Lee Man-Pan, the Chairman of the Chinese Association and the unofficial mayor of New York's Chinatown (a hit which featured prominently in the film "The Year of the Dragon"). This killing added to the growing stature of the gang:

In the year 1975, the power of "Ghost Shadow" kept rising. In order to consolidate its position and to get the whole benefits, "Ghost Shadow" decided to destroy other gangs. At that time, the "Ghost Shadow" was supported by several gangs. They wanted to destroy the "Pai Ying" (The Gang of White Eagle) and the "Fei Lung" (The Gang of Flying Dragon). From that time onwards, gun shooting and murder cases kept occurring. Once Nickie Louie nearly died. The insufficient Police manpower could not control triad elements. Thus, the triad influence in Chinatown was increasingly deep.

Shop owners in New York City were intimidated and didn't report extortions by the gangs to the police, on pain of a beating or even death. Chinese associations which were supposed to help maintain law and order didn't dare do anything against the growing gang and triad activity. Shop windows were broken if payments were late. As more and more immigrants from Hong Kong and Taiwan came into the States in the late 1970s and early 1980s, the "competition among triad gangs became more keen." Soon the Flying Dragons, who had recruited younger members from Taiwan, were openly challenging the authority and the turf of the Ghost Shadows. The ongoing fight between the Flying Dragons and the Ghost Shadows was described in detail, in the report, including the early 1980s "cold-blooded" killing of three people by the Flying Dragons "in an attempt to get the upper hand."

Another important element of the RHKP report on the New York gangs is their connection with groups and activities in Hong Kong itself. The report detailed an incident in which Jackie Chan, a famous Hong Kong actor and kung fu star, was approached in June 1983 in Hong Kong by Vincent Jew, the head of the Wah Ching in the United States. Jew attempted to get Chan, who was under contract to Golden Harvest, to play a role in a movie financed by the Wah Ching. When Chan refused because of his contractual obligations, shots were fired into the Golden Harvest office in San Francisco while Chan was filming *Cannonball Run*. Jew later told Chan that he had to give him $4 million dollars "to save face." Chan was later approached in Hong Kong for some of the money "owed" the Wah Ching by a group of 14 K triad people affiliated with the San Francisco gang. This demonstrated for the RHKP "another link between groups in Hong Kong and the U.S."

The *Evolution of Gangs in Chinatown during the Past Decade"* astutely detailed what the RHKP called the "two different triad forces operating" in the Chinatowns of North America. These were the "street gangs," such as the Flying Dragons and the Ghost Shadows, organized by Americans and Canadians. They were involved in extortions and protection rackets and had few connections in Hong Kong. The second, more sinister group, according to their report, were the triad groups "directly imported from Hong Kong," which came into North America in the early seventies and allied themselves with "various active triad tongs headed by established citizens who are also of Hong Kong/Chinese origin." The Kung Lok triad in Canada and the Wah Ching in the United States are listed as examples of these imported triads:

It is believed that the second group mentioned have now risen from street level criminal activities to sophisticated organised crime activities ranging from illegal gambling/extortion, drug trafficking through to almost full control of the entertainment business of Asia origin and laundering money through legitimate banking/financial institutions controlled by the groups. Various street gangs are believed to have turned to affiliate themselves with these groups to survive.

The 1983 RHKP report then focused on ex-RHKP officer and On Leong tong president Eddie Chan, whom it described as an "entrepreneur," who owned a funeral parlour and "various properties and investment companies" and was the vice president of the Oriental Bank of New York. One of his achievements was "convincing" the Ghost Shadows "to come under his wing." Chan also invested money and fronted for other corrupt members of the RHKP and their associates who had made it to the United States and Canada. In its conclusion, the RHKP report offered this perceptive overview, which, though less hyperbolic and sensational than most American police and journalistic accounts, was nevertheless right on target:

> There are various well-organised groups of naturalized Chinese of Hong Kong origin operating in North America utilizing some form of the traditional Triad nomenclature. They maintain their bases in one of the major cities and have branches across the country. There is no doubt that they do maintain certain ties with Hong Kong. However, it is firmly believed that these ties do not represent the possibility of Hong Kong Triads having direct or indirect control over their activities in North America. It has been said often that certain Triad organizations in North America have "reciprocal rights" arrangements with their counterparts in Hong Kong but there has been no evidence to confirm such belief. It is assessed that these "reciprocal rights" merely extend to the provision of entertainment to visiting members than extending an open invitation to operate in each others territory . . . . [Nevertheless] [c]onnections with Hong Kong-based organised crime figures and those from Chinese syndicates in the United States, Canada and Taiwan are becoming increasingly common.

The American and Canadian triads and gangs are not run by one person or a group in Hong Kong that pulls all the strings. This simple point is missed by many otherwise knowledgeable American observers of Asian gang activity in North America, who often want to believe in a giant, hierarchical conspiracy directed by omnipotent triad bosses in Hong Kong influencing or determining most of the organized criminal activity in North America. Organized crime is not *that* well-organized.

The report ended with a postscript which looked ahead to 1997. Surprisingly, the RHKP did not foresee a mass exodus of triad members to North America and Europe, but rather expected that the "normal" flow of Hong Kong criminals to North America would continue: "There is no doubt that some of the well off Hong Kong criminals will leave between now and 1997. However, for the last 100 years, Hong Kong criminals have been going abroad to settle in various Chinatowns to start up rackets. Some also have gone abroad, not to settle but to forge links with resident organised crime groups." The report then detailed a case in point, the career of Lau Wing Kui in Canada and the Dominican Republic and his ties with key triad and gang figures from a number of American cities. But many will stay in Hong Kong, even after the takeover by the People's Republic. "Whilst there is still money to be made in Hong Kong a vast majority of criminals here will stay and take their chances. After all, many are already openly dealing with officials in China, particularly around Canton." This was referring to the partnership between drug and alien-smuggling triads in Hong Kong and corrupt mainland Chinese officials.

Enforcement efforts in relation to the known Chinese gangs began to actually improve in the United States in the middle 1980s. As a result of all the attention on Asian gangs and new violence, the U.S. authorities took on the gangs under the United States federal racketeering statutes (RICO), which make it a crime to be a member of an organized crime group if a pattern of criminal activity can be proven in court. There have been at least two RICO cases against Chinese gangs. The first, in 1985, against the Ghost Shadows in New York was against twenty-five members of the Ghost Shadows gang (about half the hard-core membership, including Nickie Louie, who was only twenty-nine at the time, and Danny Mo's ally and Kung Lok associate, Kit Jai). The case was successful; it not only broke the power of Nickie Louie (though before his conviction, he was nearly killed in Chicago's Chinatown by a breakaway group of the On Leong), it also sent other Ghost Shadows members to jail for up to thirty years. The second RICO case was against the United Bamboo. A Taiwanese-based triad involved in gambling, extortion, prostitution and associated with the KMT, the United Bamboo operated primarily on the West coast, where members murdered a prominent Chinese-American journalist in 1984 after he wrote a book critical of the Taiwanese President.

Two United Bamboo members were convicted of the murder in 1986.

  With the breakdown of the power of these Chinese gangs in New York, and the undermining of Eddie Chan's power base by the Presidential Commission on Organized Crime, however, has come the growth in power and stature of newer Vietnamese groups, such as the *Born To Kill* gang which has machine-gunned its way to the top of the Asian gang crime heap in New York City. In 1992 yet another successful RICO prosecution resulted in the long-term imprisonment of nine Born To Kill gang leaders.

PART THREE

The New Dragons of Crime

Chapter Thirteen

THE GANGS WARS
OF VANCOUVER

It's like a huge grey monster lurking in the back alleys of Chinatown. Everyone's afraid of it, but no one wants to talk about it.

— John Turvey, a social worker and Director of the Carnegie Centre, Vancouver, on the Chinatown gang scene as quoted in the *Vancouver Sun*, June 28, 1984.

During the 1970s and 1980s, while Chinese gang violence was exploding in New York City and Toronto, Vancouver also had its fair share of gang rivalry. Vancouver's long history of Asian organized crime activity included wide-open gambling and drug-trafficking syndicates as well as corruption and bribery of police and city officials. The Chinese organized crime gangs of the 1920s and 1930s, though their leadership had changed, continued to flourish throughout the post-war period in the fifties and sixties and were particularly active in illegal gambling houses, extortion/protection rackets, alien smuggling, and narcotics-trafficking activities. But by the 1970s and 1980s, new criminal elements were coming to prominence in Vancouver's Chinatown. Although not as centralized as Ontario's Chinese communities under the Kung Lok triad, long-established Vancouver Chinatown natives were certainly shaken by the vicious new gang element in their midst, made up mostly of new criminal immigrants from Hong Kong, Vietnam, and China. In addition, the Kung Lok and the Vietnamese gangs in Toronto, as well as other triads and gangs in Hong Kong and California, had associates who were players in the new gang scene in Vancouver.

Doug Sam worked in Immigration intelligence in Vancouver from the 1950s until his retirement in the 1980s. During that time, he became an expert on Chinese and Vietnamese criminal activity in Canada and was instrumental in uncovering the five dragons as well as other criminals coming to Canada for refuge or expansion. As an example of imported criminals, Sam told of the branch of a Hong Kong triad that started a martial arts club in Vancouver in 1975. But quick action by Sam and the Immigration department kept the Wah Ching ("one of the most murderous of the gangs") from San Francisco, allied with the Kung Lok in Toronto, from setting up a chapter in Vancouver. Sam deported the Wah Ching recruiters back to the United States. According to Sam, the founder of another triad in Canada, Lau Wing Kui, came to Vancouver for several visits. Lau had friends, a relative, and part interest in a nightclub in the Vancouver area in the late 1970s. But, according to a source who was a friend of Lau, "Lau never had a chance in Vancouver" as he "knew he was being closely watched" by Sam and his colleagues while he was there.

Sam, who felt that most of the professional criminals were coming from Hong Kong posing as entrepreneurs, appeared in court as early as 1977 to detail the make up of Chinese organized crime activity in British Columbia; he strongly felt this activity "should always be exposed" and never hushed up, as some in the community urged. Sam, who remained active in the Chinese community in Vancouver until his death in 1991, said that by 1997 "many more of the criminal element will get in Canada." As Sam put it in a 1988 interview, "Today there is unfortunately an open door to Canada for Hong Kong criminals."

Vancouver also played a major role in one of the biggest international narcotics trafficking cases of the 1970s. A massive, year-long DEA/RCMP worldwide undercover operation, much of it centred in Vancouver, revealed the shift that was taking place in heroin trafficking. In the 1960s the majority of heroin came to North America through the old Mafia-controlled French Connection route from Turkey to France, where it was processed and then sent on to New York City generally by way of Montreal. In the 1970s, the route heroin took was more frequently from Asia to Vancouver and then to the United States. This route, of course, was the same one taken by opium in the early part of the century, but now the triads in Hong Kong, with the help of some of the five dragons and other corrupt Hong Kong police, were the principal movers of this new quality heroin.

One of the main undercover operatives in this case was a triad-connected heroin importer named Stanley Wong who had turned and was working for the DEA. The elusive Wong was interviewed for the CBC's "Connections" series in 1977 in New York City (where most of the heroin had been destined) in silhouette and without being identified by name. At that time, he said that for the international drug-trafficking cartel for whom he worked, Vancouver was second in importance only to Amsterdam. The drug network, he explained, was controlled by the 14 K triad in Hong Kong, and it brought the heroin from the Golden Triangle area (Burma, Thailand, and Laos) through Hong Kong to Vancouver and then on to New York and other American cities. Each courier coming to Vancouver, usually by plane, brought in twenty to thirty pounds, and there were up to three shipments a week. Most of the heroin was for United States destinations, but there were also some Canadian buyers, including two local Chinese businessmen who bought more than ten pounds a month for Canadian consumption, mostly in Vancouver. One of Wong's Chinese buyers in Vancouver sold his heroin to a big-time "white Canadian buyer" who needed up to "forty pounds per time."

For the "Connections" program, Stanley Wong was also able to identify some of the investments in Vancouver of Lui Lok and Nam Kong, two of the five dragons. These consisted of several blocks of prime downtown real estate. Wong also suggested that certain Vancouver law enforcement officials were on the payroll of the five dragons and the drug trafficking network. But the "Connections" team was unable to corroborate these allegations, except to show some curious meetings between some of the five dragons and certain Canadian Immigration and RCMP officers.

Another undercover operative who successfully infiltrated several major Chinese-run heroin-trafficking rings in the mid-seventies was Dorothy Proctor, a woman of partly Chinese descent. As a result of her undercover work, the RCMP drug squad was able to charge and convict a number of Vancouver-area heroin traffickers, including David Wong, Jack Mar, and Fook Lay Tang, one of Stanley Wong's buyers who was later stabbed to death in October 1986 in continuing Vancouver gang warfare. Dorothy sees a major difference between the main Chinese mobs of the 1970s and the Asian gangs of today:

> I could compare the Asian gangs now with the Asians that I was working on in the 70s. You know their big downfall was crossing over into the Anglo Saxon community; when they were among themselves, it was pretty good. But as soon as they started to branch out, that's when they did it to themselves. The old school, the old guard, the old tongs, worked within a pretty tight group. But now you've got these Asian gangs who really don't give a damn about anyone. They have no culture or tradition or anything.

Dorothy, who also worked for years undercover on Mafia drug traffickers in Ontario (for example, Project Scorpion, a joint forces operation based in the Ottawa area from 1987–88), made a similar observation of the changes in the Mafia in Canada over the same period with the additional point that the older generation in the mob as a rule didn't use the drugs they sold, but the younger generation of *mafiosi* started taking the drugs as well as selling them.

In the fall of 1980, a special seventy-fifth Anniversary issue of the Canadian Association of Chiefs of Police report included an analysis of intelligence information on Chinese gang activity in British Columbia at the time. It listed seven criminal groups as active in the Vancouver area. (In each case an educated guess was given on the size of the gang. Though police numbers can be unreliable, and often exaggerated, it does give one a sense of the officially perceived threat.) The Red Eagles, or the Hung Ying, were named "the most dominant group" and were said to have more than one hundred members and associates, mostly recent Hong Kong immigrants, though only about thirty of them were "hard-core, active" members. They were involved, like the Kung Lok in Ontario, primarily in extortions of students and restaurant owners. The second major group, and the Red Eagle's major rival, was the Lotus Family, a slightly older gang founded by David So (Ling Yue Jai) in 1976 as a splinter group from the original Jung Ching. They were said to have about forty members who were recruited from high schools and were active in assaults and auto thefts. Of the other five gangs listed — the Star Wars and the Wild Animals, both with only twelve members, the Ching Tao (Justice Scale), the Yee Tong, and the Jung Ching — only the Jung Ching or Soccer Club was criminally significant. Founded in 1965 as an athletic club, it was one of the first of the modern youth gangs in Vancouver. In 1967 it became criminally active, and by 1973, "its peak year," more than fifty members were involved in extortions, armed robberies, assaults, loansharking, and drug trafficking. It eventually became closely allied to and absorbed by the Lotus Family.

The Canadian Police Chief's fall 1980 report on Chinese gangs also listed a number of specific incidents of criminal activity and trends involving Chinese gangs in Vancouver. Some of the serious incidents listed included twelve Red Eagles attacking three Star Wars members in May 1979 on Commercial Drive, causing a fractured skull and other serious injuries; a second serious assault in May 1979 by one of the gangs on two victims, one of whom suffered a fractured skull; an extortion and fight at a Chinese dance in September 1979 by twenty Red Eagles member — the victim of the extortion later withdrew his complaint against the gang members for fear of reprisals by the gang; the shooting of a Red Eagles member in the foot by a Jung Ching gang member over a dispute about which gang had the right to extort a Hong Kong entertainer in September 1979 — significantly, the Red Eagles had the support of the Hop Sing tong in Seattle in this jurisdictional dispute; and finally in April 1980, two hit men fired fourteen .22 calibre semi-automatic shots into the bedroom of the Lotus Family's leader. This assassination attempt resulted in the wounding of the brother of the Lotus gang's leader and, according to the report, "was the most recent development in an escalating dispute between the Hung Ying and the Lotus Family."

The report was an incisive account of where the police and the gangs stood at the beginning of the decade during which Asian youth gangs really took off in British Columbia. A special task force set up in September 1979 served only to "slow down the gang development and activity for several months."

The report also looked at developing Chinese gang activity in Alberta, where extortions by Edmonton- and Vancouver-based youth gangs had started in 1974. By 1976 there was a new element:

> Young men recently arriving from Hong Kong were being fronted money by gambling house operators and loan sharks and persuaded to gamble, with the wagering process requiring extremely high interest rates. These large pay backs were collected by gang members who used physical violence and threats to the victim's families. One such recipient stated that the gangs were not solicited for such purposes but volunteered their services for a portion of the outstanding debt.

There was also an Alberta connection to Operation Ying Yang, a major international police drug operation:

> During the investigation of Operation Ying Yang, members of a triad group surfaced who were acting as bodyguards for

Y.O. Tang, an international heroin trafficker recently sentenced to twenty years imprisonment for the importation of three pounds of heroin worth 6.4 million dollars at street value. . . . During this investigation a member of a Triad Society Chapter, that had been involved in a gang war shootout in San Francisco . . . was in Calgary lying low in fear of retaliation from a rival gang.

The 1980 report's sombre conclusions were that there were "many angry Chinese youths in Vancouver. Gang activity is unstable and any confrontations between rival gang members could have serious results."

By 1982 there were only three major youth gangs of importance in Vancouver's Chinatown: the two older and fractious Chinese gangs, both growing in power and prestige — the Lotus (now led by Park Shing Low, one of the original Jung Ching members) and the Red Eagles — and the still modest but rapidly growing Viet Ching, the first major Vietnamese gang in British Columbia, run by Hy Hang and Allan Law (Law Kin Keung). There were also some smaller youth gangs, including the new Gum Gong (Gum Wah), associated with the Red Eagles. All three major gangs were involved in the resurgence of a gang war that had started in the late seventies and was to last on and off throughout the 1980s. Even the venerable *Hong Kong South China Morning Post* reported anxiously about the new violence in Vancouver's increasingly turbulent gang scene in January 1982 under the headline *"Gang Wars shock a city: Hong Kong immigrants blamed in Vancouver."* The story by journalist Paul Baran reported:

Chinese youth gangs involved in drug, prostitution and extortion rackets in Vancouver are being watched closely by police as gang violence takes a sharp upswing. According to police officials, violence between rival gangs and extortion bids on merchants have spilled out of the Chinatown area to other parts of the city as the gangs set out to expand their turf. Police attempts to crack down on the gangs have not been easy. Made up mostly of recent immigrants from Hong Kong aged between 16 and 22, the gangs operate out of the social clubs and restaurants of Vancouver's Chinatown, an area home to about 90,000 Chinese which remains much of a mystery to outside observers. Gang members, who frequently fight openly to display strength and superiority, once operated only in Chinatown, but are now moving out of the area to meet in pool halls, restaurants and discos, where many fights break out between warring gangs. During the past year, fights between rival gangs and attacks on merchants refusing to knuckle under to extortion attempts have become a regular occurrence inside and outside of Chinatown.

The increasing incidence of extortion in Chinatown and the use of revolvers and knives instead of fists were noted with alarm. The major gangs described were the Red Eagles, by now the largest and most dangerous gang with about fifty members, and the Lotus Family and the Gum Gong gang, each with approximately forty members. The reluctance of owners being extorted to go to the police in Vancouver, at the time home of North America's second largest Chinatown, was one of the central problems. But the *South China Morning Post* exposé in 1982 ended on a positive note, citing possible solutions to the new gang activity:

Vancouver, however, is learning from the example of its sister city, San Francisco, where Chinese gang violence often erupts into full-scale wars between different factions. San Francisco police learned long ago that their presence on the streets of Chinatown is the best way to win the community's confidence in their ability to tackle the problem. Modelled after a project in San Francisco, police in Vancouver re-established a beat patrol in the Chinatown area manned by officers of Chinese origin or officers who speak Chinese, which paid off in tips leading to several convictions for gang members. Special detectives are also assigned to investigate crimes involving Chinese victims. Canadian immigration officials are also taking pains to make sure young Chinese immigrants to the country have steered clear of gang activity in Hong Kong. Although the immigration officials cannot deport on the basis of gang activity or refuse admission because they were involved back in Hong Kong, they let new arrivals know early in the game that there is no room in the country for criminals.

Canadian Immigration and the Vancouver police had also instituted a very aggressive policy of deportation. From 1980 to 1982 alone, twenty-five gang members had been deported back to Hong Kong "on grounds of illegal entry, working without permission, overstaying a visiting permit or criminal conviction." But this hard-line Immigration policy of deporting all known or suspected criminals on one technicality or another did not last and succeeded in providing only temporary relief.

Throughout the 1980s the ongoing battle between the Chinese gangs, instigated mostly by the aggressive Red Eagles, continued with varying levels of violence. By early 1984 the intensity of gang in-fighting reached new heights. The *Vancouver Province*, never at a loss for words when it comes to Asian gang violence, reported on the battle for the streets in a front page headline story, "*Gang Terror Soars: Cops Fear Fullscale War*." "There's trouble brewing in Chinatown, where police say tension among rival youth gangs has reached a fever pitch," was the opening salvo. Quoting experienced Asian gang investigator Constable Peter Ditchfield, the story outlined the bloody battle of the gangs who were using everything from guns and baseball bats to meat cleavers and machetes in their fight for control of the lucrative extortion market in Chinatown. "Pride and vengeance guide their actions," Ditchfield reported. A second piece accompanying this story was a sidebar itemizing the many acts of violence as reported by the police in just the previous year. It included incidents of knifings, shootings, assaults, kidnappings, extortions, robberies, and credit card fraud.

Not to be outdone, the *Vancouver Sun* followed suit on June

28, 1984, with its own full-page account of gang warfare. After listing the incidents of violence, *Sun* reporter Kim Bolan quoted one of the "elected" leaders of the Lotus gang, Park Lo, who said that he himself had received a threat of "execution" from a group that called itself the Chinatown Death Squad. But Lo was not worried. "It might have been another gang trying to intimidate us," said Lo, when he was interviewed sitting in a dim corner of an East Hastings beer parlour. "Maybe it was the police." Police said they knew who sent the letter. Another Chinatown resident, former street worker Stan Mah, was quoted as saying, "You can just feel the tension everywhere. Nobody knows just what's going to happen. I think we'll see the biggest gang fight ever in Chinatown. We'll end up having a mini-New York in Vancouver if someone doesn't do something."

Amazingly, even these melodramatic accounts understated the true situation, for it wasn't long after this story that things got very nasty in Vancouver's Chinatown. In November 1984 Steven Lok Man Wong, a member of the Red Eagles, was shot in front of a restaurant on West Broadway in Vancouver by a Lotus gang member. In the same month, a Red Eagles member and heroin trafficker named Wan Chiu Tsang was shot in the head outside the Blue Boy Hotel in South Vancouver. In both shootings, the victims survived, and police were unable to lay charges because, as with so many other cases, neither witnesses nor victims were willing to co-operate with the police investigations. Also in November, Hy Hang and two other members of the Viet Ching gang, Kenny Lam and another, armed with handguns, tried to extort a Jung Ching gang member at a Chinese gambling club at 147 East Pender Street in downtown Vancouver. The Viet Ching members chased the Chinese gang member, Ly Cong Pham, into the street where they placed a gun to his head. Unfortunately for the Viet Ching, the police had the whole incident under surveillance and arrested Hang and his colleagues before they could execute Pham in the street. Two of the Viet Ching were later charged and convicted of weapons offences, but because Pham refused to appear at the

trial, they were not convicted of attempted murder. Early in the
next year, Ricky Choi, a restaurant manager and reputed Red
Eagles associate, was ambushed and killed on the streets of
Chinatown by a rival who later fled to Hong Kong.*

But it was another event which got the attention of even the
most jaded Vancouverite, by now accustomed to gangland
killings, violent extortions, and drive-by shootings in and
around Chinatown. The brutality and callousness of the January 20, 1985, kidnapping of Taiwanese immigrants Jimmy and
Lily Ming from their Chinatown home at 272 Princess Street
by a "ruthless Chinatown gang" shocked all of British Columbia. The victims had run the Yangtze Kitchen restaurant on
Robson Street. A ransom note to the Ming family, left at the
scene of the kidnapping demanded $700,000 for their return and
warned Jim Ming's father, Ping Chang Ming, not to go to the
police. But the senior Ming did contact the police immediately,
though he also tried to raise the cash. Somehow the kidnappers
found out that Ping had gone to the police. Their demand for
an apology was answered in a plaintive ad in the two community papers, the *Chinese Voice* and *Chinese Times*. "Last time
I was wrong please forgive me" wrote the senior Ming. A second
ransom note boasted that the kidnappers' "organization"
extended into the United States, and warned that the abductors
would strike again.

Because of the way the ransom notes were written, Vancouver
police were certain that one of the Vancouver-based Asian
gangs was involved. By this time, police estimated that there
were about two hundred hard-core youth gang members in the
Oriental community in the Vancouver area (including the Red
Eagles, the Viet Ching, and the Lotus, which by now was in
serious decline).

The bodies were not discovered until March 10, 1985, when
hikers spotted them in dense brush below the Squamish High-

---

* Constable Bob Cooper of the Vancouver Police, a veteran Asian gang
police specialist, detailed some of the intense gang rivalry and increased
activity in this period in testimony in a 1987 attempted murder case.

way. The couple had been strangled and partially dismembered. Jimmy Ming's legs had been severed. Weeks of fruitless negotiations had taken place between the Ming family and the kidnappers, who by then had delivered six ransom notes throughout the fifty day ordeal. Some of these had been answered once again in ads in the two local community papers.

The choice of the Mings as the victims baffled their family. "If they were looking to get a lot of money, they picked the wrong family," said Harry Ming, Jimmy's younger brother. "We could have sold everything we had and still not raised enough money." The two young children (six and seven years old) of the murdered Mings were sent by the family back to Taiwan, for fear the kidnappers would return for them.

Chinese police officers later combed Chinatown searching for information about the kidnapping and murders but came up with very little of substance. In addition, they offered a $12,000 reward, which was significantly boosted by a separate trust fund set up by the Chinese Benevolent Association of Canada. Still, no one has talked, not even to the "Crimestoppers" hotline, which guarantees anonymity. Homicide Sergeant Bob Desmarais speculated in one interview with the *Vancouver Sun* on May 17, 1985 "possibly [community members] don't have all the confidence in [the police] that they should have." Desmarais confirmed the police still suspected one of the Chinese or Vietnamese youth gangs in Vancouver had been responsible for the kidnap-murders, but more than seven years after the shocking crime, the case remains officially unsolved.

After the Ming killings came a serious proliferation of gang activity. In 1986 and early 1987, there was a spate of violent gang-related activities — several shootings, including a shoot-out at a popular Vancouver restaurant and another at a theatre, as well as several highly publicized drive-by shootings in Vancouver's Chinatown, not to mention countless extortions, robberies, and assaults throughout the Vancouver area. In October 1986 the well known drug trafficker and criminal Fook Lay Tang was murdered in his home on Parker Street in Vancouver. In December of that year, a group of Viet Ching were attacked by a Chinese gang in the Metrotown Mall in Burnaby. Two of the Viet Ching leaders, Kenny Lam and Allan Law were stabbed during the attack, Law losing several tendons in his right hand. The same month, members of the Red Eagles were attacked by members of the Lotus gang in another mall attack, resulting in injuries to several Red Eagles. Not long afterwards, a member of the Lotus gang, Ming Trin, was stabbed through the lung and severely beaten in a savage attack outside a Vancouver poolhall. Also during December 1986 and January 1987, at least eight armed robberies of restaurants in Chinatown were orchestrated by members of the Lotus gang. During one of the robberies, the manager of the Excelsior Restaurant was shot.

In the escalating violence, on February 28, 1987, three members of the Viet Ching — Khai Chi Truong, Chi Ton, and Hy Hang, one of its original leaders — were charged with shooting at and trying to wound and/or murder Brian To and Kim Tam, two members of the Red Eagles gang, at the Akasaka Restaurant, a second-floor after-hours club on Richards Street in downtown Vancouver catering to Hong Kong immigrants. Six shots were fired and one of the Red Eagles was wounded. Police suspected that the Viet Ching gangsters had come to the restaurant looking for revenge against the Red Eagles because one of their gang members had been beaten up the night before in the Akasaka. As usual in these incidents, virtually no one co-operated with the police investigation. Chi Ton escaped to Seattle and remained on the lam, and charges against him were eventually stayed. At the trial of Hy Hang and Khai Chi Truong in June 1987, several court officials received anonymous death threats. Both Hy Hang and Khai Chi Truong were found guilty and sentenced to four years in jail for weapons offences.

In September 1987 there was the gangland-style killing of a sixteen-year-old Iranian high school student and martial arts enthusiast who was thought to have been associated with one of the Oriental youth gangs. Babbak "Bob" Moieni was found bound and gagged at his family's Vancouver home on East 49th Street. He had been shot in the head. No one has been charged with the Moieni murder, though it was widely rumoured to have been done by a Lotus gang hit team.

Finally, in October 1987, Attorney General Brian Smith had had enough. His preferred course of action — deporting all convicted gang members to their country of origin — would have taken too long, as he said, because of the long appeals procedure in Canada. Instead, he decided to prosecute the gangsters and "try and put them in jail for many years." With this in mind, in the fall of 1987, Smith appointed a special provincial prosecutor, James T. McBride, a natty Ivy League dresser with a workaholic's zeal, to work full-time on gang-related cases. McBride, whose official title was Special Prosecutor, Asian Gang Unit, found that Asian gangs ran "very sophisticated operations" and that the gangsters were "very complicated and intelligent people" whose gangs became "a breeding ground for organized crime."

As special prosecutor, the athletic, highly energetic, and self-confident McBride, decided to crack down particularly on youthful defendants. Under Canada's Young Offenders Act, juvenile offenders under eighteen can receive a maximum three-year sentence, no matter how heinous the crime. As a result, many older, more sophisticated criminals often use youths under eighteen as hit men and for other serious crimes. McBride's landmark case was a January 1987 shooting in the Golden Princess Theater, where he succeeded in having a youthful offender tried in adult court. William Yeung, a sixteen-year-old high school dropout and member of the Viet Ching, along with a gang colleague, had boldly walked up to a fourteen-year-old gang associate named Tony Hong and shot him point-blank with a .38 calibre pistol. The boy survived, but lost his right eye. Yeung was found guilty and was given a lengthy prison term in an adult facility.

The Judge in the case, Mr. Justice Hinds, said at sentencing that the Golden Princess shooting was an attempt by the Viet Ching to kill a member of the rival Lotus / Jung gang "in a public place where the intended execution would be observed by members of the Vancouver Chinese community." Despite observing that the courts have a duty to rehabilitate juvenile offenders, Hinds concluded that public safety demands that gang members be dealt with "in ordinary court where the proceedings can be observed and reported. Full disclosure accompanied by publication," might, he felt, encourage members of the Chinese community "in reporting unlawful acts perpetrated against them and in testifying in court." The judgement sent a potent message to the gangs, and the police and members of the Chinese community hailed the decision. McBride has since retired as the Special Asian Gang prosecutor, and he has been replaced by Bob Wright, who recommends the tightening of Immigration screening of both immigrants and refugees and more deportations of convicted criminals, especially to Vietnam and China.

The Asian gangs of Vancouver have received a great deal of press coverage in British Columbia, and it is often extremely difficult to separate the truth from the sensationalism since many of the reports are based solely on police accounts, rather than carefully checked independent research. In some cases the gangster himself is cocky enough to try and present his side of the story. In one recent article, "Leader of the Pack," in the September 1990 issue of *Vancouver Magazine*, the traditional Chinese triads surfaced in the unlikely person of twenty-six-year-old leader of the Red Eagle associated-gang, the Gum Wah gang. When interviewed for the article, Steven Wong proudly proclaimed that he was a member of the 14 K triad and that he was in the international heroin-importation business with triad colleagues in Hong Kong. The overconfident Wong even bragged to journalist Terry Gould that he had access through "friends" in Hong Kong to most secret Royal Hong Kong Police reports on the triads as well as the "top secret" internal memos of Vancouver's Co-ordinated Law Enforcement Unit (CLEU). Wong, who is described as having a "magnificent dragon tattoo on his hairless chest," gave a highly exaggerated picture of life in Vancouver's Chinatown. "Most of Chinatown is run by the gangs. The massage parlours, the *pai gow* (gambling) casinos, and a lot of nightclubs and restaurants. Even if the owners don't belong to the gangs, they still pay someone to do business."

While the Vancouver RCMP's most articulate Asian crime specialist, Bill Chu, admitted that Wong was "certainly in the heroin trade," and "certainly has ties to Asian organized crime" in Hong Kong and elsewhere, he also stated that Steven Wong's Gum Wah was just one of many groups operating in Vancouver's crowded Chinatown organized crime scene.

Gould also interviewed a nineteen-year-old Lotus gang member nicknamed "Goat Head," who made a very important point. He said he shared one thing in common with his enemy Steve Wong — a total contempt for the Vietnamese gangs emerging in Vancouver. This attitude explains one of the causes of the endless violence in Chinatowns across North America — a deadly ongoing rivalry between the Chinese and Vietnamese gangs.

Even the staid, self-proclaimed "national" newspaper of Canada, the *Globe and Mail*, has occasionally sensationalized the problem by not putting the story in a proper historical and criminal context. In October 1986 there were front page headlines about triads and Asian gangs massively moving into Canada and "terrorizing" whole cities and school systems. In a front-page story about the Asian gangs of Vancouver under the dramatic headline "Police cannot stop B.C. Gangs," reporter Robert Matas, on April 17, 1992, stated that not only are the Asian gangs in British Columbia "out of control," but that the police "cannot do much about it." Staff Sergeant Andy Nimmo, who had been on the gang squad for a mere three years, added that the police will "probably never cure the problem." The story went on to maintain that twelve hundred or more gang members and associates roam freely in an Asian population estimated to be now more than 250,000 in the greater Vancouver area, extorting restaurants and high schools, running sophisticated credit card frauds, and operating whorehouses that "open at new locations every month." This in spite of the fact that today the Vancouver police and the RCMP through CLEU maintain two special crime units with more than forty policemen continually targeting and monitoring the activities and movements of all the Asian gangs, and despite the fact that a senior British Columbia special prosecutor's sole job is targeting Asian gang members for prosecution. In fact, in Vancouver the police and the Crown attorneys are more on top of the Asian gang situation, which has been evolving now for almost one hundred years, than Toronto police are in Toronto. However, as in Toronto and other major North American cities, the Asian gang menace in Vancouver has been growing at an alarming rate, and obviously, it is not something the government and police alone can stop. It's the Asian community itself, by coming forward as problems arise, that must work to rid itself of the increasing organized crime activity. As Staff Sergeant Nimmo told a community group of social workers, school administrators, and other police officers, to date there has not been enough community trust of the police and the criminal justice system "to control the youth gangs," which were described as being "co-ordinated by sophisticated adult criminals." Police Chief Bill Marshall warned the gangs in May, 1992, that the police were not going to allow them to "control" Chinatown.

In Vancouver, the Chinese and Vietnamese gangs have a higher profile than other crime groups, including the Mafia, because of their *lack* of organization and structure.* Vancouver no longer has the distinction of having the second largest Chinese population in North America. Toronto now has that ranking. It wasn't until the early 1990s, though, that Toronto clearly passed Vancouver by achieving the dubious distinction of becoming the capital of Asian gang violence in Canada.

---

* This does not mean that even in Vancouver the Mafia is not, silently, a major player, though the traditional mob is certainly less a factor in Vancouver than in Southern Ontario, Montreal, and most northeastern American cities. CLEU still keeps a watchful eye on Mafia activity.

Chapter Fourteen

TIGERS OF CRIME
The Rise and Fall of a Vietnamese Ganglord

One of the most significant criminal developments in the Chinatowns in North America in the early and mid-1980s was the arrival and establishment of violent new Vietnamese gangs. In Vancouver, as we have seen, the Vietnamese gangs have seriously challenged the Chinese gangs. In Ontario, the Vietnamese gangs helped to displace the Kung Lok from its supreme position in the various Chinatowns.

In retrospect, perhaps the most ominous event of the mid-eighties for Danny Mo and the Kung Lok occurred in the fall of 1983. Danny Mo had had a bit of a falling-out with Big John Yue. Of course, for years, many of the leaders of the Kung Lok ran their own autonomous groups outside the triad itself. Yue, like some of the other original Kung Lok leaders, had had his own loosely knit gang in Toronto before Lau brought everyone together. And there was some friction between some of the leaders — the Kung Lok was not always a co-operative, cohesive unit. Yue had some gambling interests as well as some other freelance operations ongoing. He had recently lowered payments due for protection from his people. (The illegal gambling business, like mainstream businesses, was suffering from the recession.) Other leaders had their own interests, such as Victor Cheng and his boys, who were running some freelance extortions of Hong Kong students at the time, according to Yue.

From time to time, Big John Yue, like most intelligent organized criminals, has assisted the police and even, occasionally, an informed reporter. In September 1983 I was researching material for the upcoming "Fifth Estate" program on the Kung Lok and needed some additional first-hand insights from one of the leaders of the triad. Surprisingly, Yue agreed to a formal meeting with me. We talked for more than five hours over dinner and drinks at a trendy Chinese restaurant safely away from Chinatown. The hulking thirty-year-old Yue filled me in on his participation in the Kung Lok over the years, what extortions were going down at the time, who was who in the triad, and how the entertainment business worked with protection rackets as an inherent part of its operation. Yue was expansive and regal. He kept referring to "my boys," and which of his associates treated him with due "respect." He said that the original Kung Lok group with Lau were Jimmy Kan, Danny Mo, and himself, a group he described as pledging to be "brothers forever." Yue said that the normal Kung Lok rate for *lomo*, or protection, of a gambling house would be about $350 to $400 a night.

Yue spoke ambivalently about Mo, whom he described variously as an ex-partner, a brother, and finally as a "second-level" official. Although admitting that at least four Kung Lok initiation ceremonies had taken place at his home (and at least three at Mo's residence), Yue seemed strangely negative about the triad. Several times he stated firmly that "the Kung Lok does no good." He constantly appeared to distance himself from the triad and Mo, though he seemed proud of his role in establishing the gang and of what it had achieved.

Everyone connected with the elegant Chinese restaurant treated Yue with the greatest respect throughout the long banquet. Waiters stood attentively throughout, catering to our every need; excellent wine and drinks were sent out of respect, and there was no bill at the end of the evening — another sign of respect. It seemed from my five-hour tête-à-tête with Yue that the respected warlord was at the peak of his personal power.

Yet within four weeks of the dinner Big John Yue was a spent force in Toronto. It wasn't his sometime ally, sometime rival,

Danny Mo, who finished him off, but a severe beating by members of Asau Tran's nascent, but rapidly growing Vietnamese gang that got him. During the attack, Yue was badly beaten about the head, resulting in some permanent damage. But the greatest damage was psychological, as Big John lost a lot of face in the streets of Chinatown. He didn't or couldn't retaliate and left town almost immediately after recovering from his wounds.

This was at a time of a massive concerted effort by the police — called "saturation coverage" by the cops who work organized crime — to target the leadership of the Kung Lok for around-the-clock surveillance. This effort resulted in a number of charges being laid against Kung Lok members, and it gave the Vietnamese gangs a window of opportunity for exploitation in Chinatown. The gangs had also been moving aggressively on Kung Lok protected gambling houses, boldly robbing three or four of them a week.

By the end of 1983, Yue was ensconced somewhere in Saskatchewan. In the early 1990s, Yue returned to Toronto to run a restaurant, but he no longer has any real power in the criminal underworld. Now the Vietnamese gangs and other Chinese gangs maintain almost total dominance in Toronto's Chinatowns. During the years Yue was away licking his wounds, the once all-powerful Kung Lok went from a powerful triad with more than four hundred members to an almost non-existent, dispersed group of only fifty members.*

---

* This is according to the official 1991 report on organized crime of the Criminal Intelligence Service of Canada (CISC), presented in a glossy one-hundred page booklet in early September 1991 at the annual convention of police chiefs of Canada. In meetings with the author during the summer of 1991, senior members of the Asian Investigative Unit stated that the Kung Lok was "just about gone" and that the unit did not have anyone of their forty-plus people working on the Kung Lok on a regular basis any more. The Kung Lok seemed to have unravelled faster than the Soviet Union. The 1990 report had evidence of a full complement of a four-hundred-man strong Kung Lok triad, while just a year later there were only fifty. Three hundred and fifty people disappeared without a trace. Actually, when pushed, senior police intelligence people informed me that many of the original four hundred figure were "inactive" mem-

There were several waves of Vietnamese immigrants and refugees to North America in the 1970s and 1980s. The first wave settled mostly in Montreal in Canada and in California in the United States. These immigrants were predominantly rich, middle-class, and well-connected — Vietnamese professionals, ex-military officers, and politicians. One former prominent Vietnamese general (and many colonels) came to Montreal, while former prime minister General Ky and some of his colleagues set up in California. Many of these former top military officers were suspected of criminal activity even back in Vietnam, where they had held positions of power and trust for years. A very small number of these were involved in the drug trade, and they were the first ones to leave Vietnam in the first wave in the early to mid-seventies as South Vietnam totally collapsed.

The next wave of Vietnamese immigrants were the boat people, who unfortunately included a lot of the criminals now making up the majority of the street gangs in Toronto, Vancouver, Montreal, New York City, Arlington, Virginia, Dallas,

---

bers, and that there was a major lag between the reality — the decline in power, influence, and numbers of the Kung Lok from the mid-1980s on; the rise of the new leaner, more violent Vietnamese gangs; and the arrival and ascent of the mainland Chinese gangs in Canada — and the old perception of Kung Lok power reported in the annual CISC reports until 1991.

Significantly, the official police view covers only criminal activities that are highly visible, such as robberies, extortions, street violence, etc., where the newer gangs have definitely taken over. The multi-billion dollar drug trade, though, with the exception of busts of some mainland Chinese Big Circle Boys drug rings, is not really in the equation. That is, the Kung Lok, according to RCMP drug intelligence, is currently running a major international drug-trafficking ring from Ottawa and Toronto to the States, but everyday crime statistics don't count this intelligence information. Even if it did, and some of the Kung Lok were arrested for drug trafficking, it would be statistically insignificant compared to the massive numbers of violent robberies, extortions, assaults, and other street crimes occurring weekly in Ontario as the result of the newer, more violent Vietnamese and mainland Chinese groups currently running amok in Toronto's six Chinatowns.

Philadelphia, Boston, Seattle, San Francisco, and other California cities. The boat people came because of economic desperation. When those who made it to a new country finally settled, whether in Canada or the United States, they took advantage of family reunification schemes to bring what remained of their families. These people made up the third wave of Vietnamese refugees.

One of the most prominent Vietnamese gangsters to establish himself in Canada was Asau Tran (a.k.a. A Sau Tran and Johnny Tran). As a youth, he had been in the South Vietnamese army. But like thousands of other poor inhabitants of that war-ravaged country, he had left Vietnam after the Communist victory in the mid-1970s. Tran had huddled with hundreds of others in a boat that sailed the treacherous South China Sea in search of freedom. He made it to Hong Kong where the authorities, rather than welcoming the boat people and helping to integrate them into society, put the refugees in prison-like refugee camps. Having survived the horrors of Vietnam, the American bombers, and the napalm, Tran now had to adjust to a new hell — a very tough capitalistic world where he was at the bottom of the bottom. As a Chinese Canadian Immigration intelligence agent explained it in 1991, "Vietnamese gangsters are more ruthless than the Chinese. Their country was at war all the time. Life to them was nothing."

In a hidden camera/hidden mike television interview shortly before his murder in July 1991, Tran described life in those camps to CFTO producer/reporter Isabel Bassett. Members of his own gang "family" were often unmanageable and ruthless. While in the detention camp in Hong Kong, he used to scale the walls at night and slip into Hong Kong, where he bought or stole things he could later turn around in the camps for a lot of money. It was in the tough, cramped Hong Kong refugee camps that Tran honed his criminal skills. He was a natural leader, with both organizational and political talents. In the Hong Kong camps, he soon had his own gang of criminals. Many of these people had suffered terribly, both in Vietnam and in the camps, and life itself had little value for them. The more hardened and brutal of this lot later came to Canada as refugees, just like Tran, and became the core of his Toronto-based gang in the early 1980s.

Tran didn't start at the top of the Asian underworld in Toronto, which he reached in 1979 via Hong Kong along with other refugees seeking a new life in Canada. When he arrived, the Kung Lok were close to their prime. Though Vietnamese, Asau Tran was an ethnic Chinese, and soon he started to work as an enforcer with the Kung Lok, offering protection services for some of the gambling houses. He first came to real prominence in the Oriental gang world in 1983. In September 1983, just days after holding up three Chinese gaming houses protected by the Kung Lok, Tran ruthlessly killed a man in the Kensington Market area of Toronto, near a small but fast-growing Vietnamese community. Three youths had just left a teenagers' dance party at St. Stephen's Community House on Bellevue Avenue near College Street and Spadina Avenue, when Tran and two gang colleagues mowed them down.

One of the youths, nineteen-year-old Hong Trieu Thai, was shot in the neck as he tried to escape and died almost instantly. Two other victims, one twenty-eight and another only seventeen-years-old, survived their serious gunshot wounds. The attack was apparently part of a continuing battle between Tran's gang and another Vietnamese gang.*

Within hours of the shootings, police issued murder warrants for two men described as "armed and extremely dangerous." They were Asau Tran and Sang-Minh Nguyen, 28, identified as fleeing the scene of the crime in a speeding red car. Tran himself was identified by at least one witness as the man who fired many of the fifteen shots aimed at the Vietnamese victims.

---

* The *Toronto Star* and other media outlets suggested, no doubt hearing it from police intelligence sources, that the shootings were part of "a gang war between Chinese and Vietnamese in Toronto's Chinatown." But in fact they were the result of internal Vietnamese gang feuding. Blood had already been spilled in the battle between the Kung Lok and the various Vietnamese gangs, and this ongoing rivalry continued throughout the 1980s. But this was not part of that gang war.

Though charged, arrested and tried for the shootings and murder, Tran and his colleague eventually got off, for, as the police put it, the key witness "went south." Getting acquitted for the audacious shooting in the middle of a quiet residential section of Toronto was a major coup for Tran, winning him tremendous face in both Vietnamese and Chinese gang circles.

Soon Tran was the undisputed leader of his own street gang, no longer just working for the Kung Lok. With close ties to Vietnamese gangs in Boston, New York, and California, Tran developed his own gambling, fraud, protection, and prostitution rackets in Toronto. Tran's gang extorted the Vietnamese and Chinese businesses in Chinatown, especially restaurants, with a vengeance. His methods were brutal. If a restaurant owner didn't pay, the place was shot up or fire-bombed. Savage beatings were not uncommon. Many in the community got the message, and by the late 1980s most of the Vietnamese restaurants as well as some Chinese restaurants were paying tribute or protection to Tran's gang. Tran's group also took over protection of the gambling houses from the Kung Lok; as well Tran organized a major armed robbery ring in Toronto that specialized in knocking off jewellery stores.

Tran was the boss in his gang, but controlling "his boys," as he always called them, could be problematic. These were tough and cynical young men who had come through the horrors of life in Vietnam, Communist re-education camps, then the bleak refugee camps in Hong Kong. But as Tran explained, there was a very good reason for recruiting such brutal young thugs: "They are teenagers. . . . so they get nothing." Like gang bosses in Vancouver, Tran brilliantly exploited Canada's Young Offenders Act.

In early 1986, Tran and his gang were heavily involved in extorting concert promoters in Toronto. In February 1986 two of Tran's gang members, Quay Truong and Dieu Tan Quach, tried to extort a Chinese promoter, who was so terrified that he went to the police. An undercover operation was mounted that tied into other ongoing police investigations into Tran's growing criminal empire.

Although Tran may be the best-known member of Toronto's Vietnamese criminal community, he never reigned alone in the Asian underworld. There were always other up-and-coming Vietnamese gangs. In the mid-1980s, Tran was charged, along with a number of other Vietnamese gangsters including rival gang boss A Cuu, with a series of offences, most notably a number of brutal extortions. In a massive police crackdown on the Vietnamese gangs, eighty-eight charges were laid against twenty-eight suspected gang members, Tran among them. The eleven-month-long investigation had been a special joint forces operation involving police from the OPP, Metro Toronto police, Waterloo Regional Police, and the London police force. The details of the charges and the history of the unprecedented operation were laid out in an unusually long sixteen-page police press release on May 29, 1986. Phase one of the operation had begun in July, 1985 and centred on a juvenile prostitution ring run by a Vietnamese gang. The investigation resulted in abduction, procuring, and narcotics charges against nineteen Vietnamese gang members. The second phase of the operation began in January, 1986 and concentrated solely on two Vietnamese gangs, one run by Asau Tran and the other by A Cuu.

The charges against Tran included a number of extortions and a protection racket similar to Danny Mo's, though more overtly violent, that Tran ran in connection with concerts by Chinese entertainers playing at Massey Hall and Roy Thomson Hall between November 1985 and February 1986. Tran was also charged with threatening a loanshark victim (and his six-months' pregnant wife) "with serious bodily harm or death" if he failed to repay a loan of several thousand dollars. In addition to these serious charges, there were a number of counts of conspiracy to keep a common gaming house (these floating games were run from several hotels between 1985 and 1986 and a house that operated behind a restaurant at Gerrard and Broadview in the new Riverdale-area Chinatown).

A Cuu had also been charged with a number of offences, including living off the avails of prostitution, procurement, and conspiracy to administer drugs. Some of the young women working for A Cuu in his whorehouses in 1985 were girls as young as thirteen and fourteen years old, runaways from a London, Ontario, group home, many of them forced into lives as prostitutes. A Cuu was found guilty of the charges and, after serving a prison term, was deported from Canada as he was not a Canadian citizen nor even a landed immigrant.

Tran was more fortunate, at least for the short term. He had jumped bail in June, 1987 and fled to Los Angeles, California. But in September 1988, the American authorities deported him as an undesirable, and he was re-arrested when he arrived in Vancouver. Sergeant Benny Eng well remembers accompanying Tran back to Toronto on a plane from Vancouver. When they hit some turbulence in the air, Tran panicked and told Eng that it was absurd that he should die because of "that ridiculous extortion." According to Benny Eng, Tran was not a brave man, in spite of his bravado and reputation for brutality and ruthlessness on the street.

Tran was tried, convicted, and sentenced to nine months in jail for extortion in October 1988, but since he had been a Canadian citizen since 1984, there was no move to have the one-time refugee claimant deported from Canada after his sentence was served.* In sentencing one of the younger Vietnamese gangsters, a landed immigrant, to thirty-four months in jail, the colourful and often controversial Toronto provincial court judge Robert Dneiper made headlines in the Toronto press by stating that the "vicious youth," a sixteen-

---

* The policy of External Affairs was not to deport people to Vietnam, because of the fear that those repatriated might be executed or "re-educated" by a Communist government not known for its gentleness to returning boat people: some criminals returning are known to have been summarily executed. Recently, the Government of Vietnam has softened its stance towards expatriates because the Socialist Republic of Vietnam now desperately needs hard foreign currency and even encourages them to return, claiming that they will not be harmed. Only in 1992, did the Canadian government allow for the deportation of some convicted criminals to Vietnam. Tran could have been stripped of his citizenship and deported to Hong Kong from whence he came.

year-old member of Tran's gang who had been convicted of extortion, was beyond rehabilitation and that "the only answer for him is deportation and the suggestion that he try his gang activities in Ho Chi Minh City." In the ensuing controversy, a spokesman for Canadian Immigration differed with Judge Dneiper, stating that a landed immigrant could only be deported for "fairly serious" crimes — "I don't think extortion of $500 would be considered serious enough to send someone back to Vietnam, especially if the family were refugees." No one that young had ever been deported by Immigration, except to rejoin parents, and it is very unlikely that the young up-and-coming enforcer for Tran would have been deported, but Dneiper's remarks were generally well-received by the law-and-order crowd in Toronto and badly received by civil libertarians and those concerned with a possible racist backlash.

While Tran was on the lam in California and Vancouver, and then in jail, a sinister new force emerged in Toronto's China-town in the form of Trung Chi Truong (a.k.a. Ah Sing and Sing Gow), a highly mobile Vietnamese gang leader who had already made a name for himself in both Montreal's and Boston's Chinatowns. Like Tran, Truong was an ethnically Chinese Vietnamese criminal who made his start by working with Chinese triads. Truong had left Saigon (Ho Chi Minh City) in 1979 at the age of nineteen with his younger brother. The brothers made their way to a refugee camp in Malaysia and the following year came to the United States as refugees. Truong first lived in Texas, but his brother soon opened up a hair salon in the Boston area, where Truong joined him and, for a while, even worked as a hairdresser in his brother's salon.

But the five-foot-six-inch-tall Trung Chi Truong soon found more stimulating work. In his mid-twenties, he became an enforcer for the Ping On triad in Boston, run by Danny Mo's associate, Stephen Tse (a.k.a. Tin Lung). As early as the mid-1980s Truong was known to Boston police as a protector for some of the Ping On gambling houses in Boston's small but teeming Chinatown.

Truong came to police attention in a big way as the result of a 1986 murder in Oakland, California. Twenty-eight-year-old Son Van Vu, a former Vietnamese gang member in Boston, had left that city because he owed a great deal of money in gambling and drug debts to the Ping On triad. After Ping On triad sources located Vu in California, Truong and another enforcer were sent in to take care of him. In December 1986 Vu was murdered in his Hollywood motel room. When questioned by police about the murder, Truong simply said that he had met with Vu, but knew nothing about his death. Neither Truong nor his colleagues were ever charged with the murder.

Back in Boston, Truong quickly set up his own Vietnamese gang, specializing in armed robbery. But Truong, based in Malden, Massachusetts, just outside Boston, introduced an interesting new wrinkle into his gang — mobility. He decided there was no reason he had to confine his lucrative jewellery store robberies to just Massachusetts or, for that matter, the United States. As early as 1986, he came to Toronto, where two jewellery store robberies in Chinatown in December 1986 (one on December 1 at 560 Dundas Street and the other on Christmas Eve at 310 Spadina Avenue) netted close to a quarter of a million dollars for him, his twenty-seven-year-old wife, Joanne Loan Thai, and seven other gang colleagues from Boston. Both robberies were captured by store videocameras, and in one of them, Truong's group fired on store staff.

Boston police helped out Toronto police in the investigation. But before he could be arrested for the Toronto heists, Truong was arrested in Massachusetts for more local crimes. Toronto police Staff Sergeant Bert Novis, who first linked the Toronto robberies with Truong and his gang in Boston in early 1987, described the Truong gang as "Oriental gypsies." He said that "they just go from city to city and rob. They lie, they change their names around. You don't know who you are dealing with."

In January 1987 Truong was charged with a particularly nasty armed robbery in Lowell, Massachusetts, a small city twenty-five miles from Boston. During the robbery, members of Truong's gang physically assaulted the wife of the store's owner, pistol-whipping and nearly killing her. For his role in organizing the Lowell robbery, Truong was sentenced in June 1988 to eighteen years in jail. But Truong didn't stay in Massachusetts prisons for very long. After only five months, he escaped from a minimum security jail in Shirley, Massachusetts.

For twenty-eight months, from November 1988, when the thirty-year-old Truong escaped from the Massachusetts jail, to his arrest as an accessory to a murder and for weapons offences in Toronto in March 1991, Trung Chi Truong operated with Vietnamese gangs in Montreal and Toronto. In Montreal, a city where some of the first wave of Vietnamese immigrants had arrived in the 1970s, Truong had a gang of about sixty youths, creating a wave of extortions, armed robberies, and shootings in Montreal's generally quiet Chinatown. According to a well researched account of Truong's career in *Maclean's* magazine by Montreal reporter Dan Burke, Truong took control of the Oriental underworld there for about a year:

> Police in Montreal told *Maclean's* that [Truong's] headquarters for operations in that city were provided by two natives of Hong Kong — one of them recently arrested for carrying an unregistered handgun — who operate a downtown restaurant. At the same time, Truong also recruited an expanding cadre of criminal foot soldiers. . . . Meanwhile, police estimated that by the beginning of this year [1991], Truong's syndicate was extorting up to $10,000 a week from Montreal Chinatown businesses. Said one restaurant owner, who complained that Asian Montrealers now avoid Chinatown at night: "The whole thing is like a bad Hollywood movie."

After his escape from jail, Truong was also in and out of Toronto, once again organizing jewellery store robberies. Writing about Truong's criminal career from 1986 until 1990, journalist Dan Burke called his meteoric rise in Boston, Montreal, and Toronto a "reign of terror" by a "rising kingpin of the underworld." Truong was only thirty-one years old when he was last deported from Canada, and he didn't become a kingpin of anything in Toronto, though he did make his mark because of his boldness and ruthlessness. What is clear about Truong's chequered career is that he was one of the most mobile and vicious of Vietnamese gangsters now operating with relative ease in Chinatowns across North America. Arrested in Toronto, Montreal, California, and Massachusetts, Truong nonetheless carried on a viable criminal career in several locations. He was never in Canada legally, though he managed to operate gangs in two major Canadian cities; even during the period when he was wanted by Massachusetts prison authorities, Truong seemed to be able to operate quite freely from a number of Canadian locations.

Like Truong, Tran also got out of jail in 1989. With A Cuu out of the picture, Tran emerged from prison criminally stronger than he had ever been. But there was the dark shadow of the ambitious, vicious, and ubiquitous Trung Chi Truong hanging over him as well as other emerging smaller gangs in Toronto's Chinatowns.

Although Tran tolerated Truong for a short time, by February, when a Truong associate was shot on a Toronto Chinatown sidewalk, open and violent warfare erupted between the two Vietnamese gang leaders. Truong was eventually arrested on an anonymous tip the police got regarding his whereabouts after a series of killings in Chinatown in March 1991. Truong was deported a couple of months later and sent back to his Massachusetts prison. It was a convenient way for Tran to get rid of a serious rival. But for Truong it really had just been a question of time, since he was wanted in the States and had had to live in Toronto incognito as an undesirable, illegal alien.

Tran also had reason to be wary of Danny Mo, despite his apparently strong alliance with the Kung Lok leader. Although outwardly friendly with Tran, Danny Mo "played it many ways," according to veteran police Asian crime investigator Benny Eng. For example, Eng explained, Mo would give Tran and his "boys" free tickets to his concerts at Roy Thomson Hall, but then he would quietly let the Asian Investigative Unit officers know where the block of seats was so that they could more efficiently keep an eye on Tran.

Nevertheless, Tran and Mo continued to do business together, sometimes even co-sponsoring a concert tour. According to Tran, Mo was "not a terrible person. He is a nice guy, too. . . . Cops don't like him, but it doesn't mean I don't like him. We are just friends." Tran also admitted that he and Mo were partners in the Pot of Gold restaurant, where he frequently met with Mo and other associates in the late night and early morning hours. "If you don't trust a partner, how can you make money?" was his rhetorical question. Yet on paper, the nightclub, on the second floor of 393 Dundas Street West, was principally owned by a Chinese gentleman with no known gang affiliation, Conrad Kwai Chuen Leung, who signed the registration papers in January 1990 as president.

The events in Toronto's Chinatown through 1991 were nightmarish for the city's Oriental community. The Born To Kill, a very serious Vietnamese gang from the New York area operating in Canada, was involved in some of the killings in Toronto as well as a number of violent robberies and extortions. The Born To Kill — ironically named after an insignia worn by some U.S. Marines in Vietnam and carried on some American Air Force jets as they tried to bomb Vietnam back into the Stone Age — were involved in an ongoing turf fight with the Chinese Ghost Shadows gang as well as with other Vietnamese gangs in New York's small but crowded Chinatown. During a funeral for a Born To Kill gang member named Vinh "Amigo" Vu, in July 1990 in Linden, New Jersey, members of a rival gang opened up on the mourners with Uzi sub-machine guns at the burial ground seriously wounding nine gang members.

Bloodshed in Toronto started in earnest when members of the Born To Kill gang committed a cold-blooded murder in a downtown Toronto restaurant. On December 27, 1990, Vietnamese gunmen opened fire in broad daylight at the Kim Bo restaurant on Dundas Street West, resulting in the public execution of a thirty-one-year-old New York City-based Vietnamese gang member named Dan Vi Tran. Two bystanders, Mau Luy Quach and Hoan Thanh Luu, were seriously wounded as the gunmen sprayed the restaurant with bullets. The following February,

Son Long, a member of New York City's Born To Kill gang, was arrested in New York City for Dan Vi Tran's murder. Also charged with first-degree murder was Thanh Tat (a.k.a. Buc Sing), a Winnipeg-based Vietnamese gang member with close ties to the Born To Kill; he was arrested in Vancouver on a gun charge along with some Vancouver-based Viet Ching gang members who were in a car packed with an arsenal of weapons. During a six-week trial in 1992, eyewitnesses were scarce, though one Winnipeg teenager testified against the pair. The jury ended up hearing nothing about the Born To Kill gang connections of the two accused. In May 1992, both Vietnamese gangsters were found guilty and sentenced to a mandatory twenty-five-year prison term.

On January 4, a few days after Dan Vi Tran's murder, a Vietnamese man got into an argument with a Vietnamese gang member in a downtown Toronto restaurant. The gang member fired four shots at him at point-blank range, miraculously only grazing his forehead. Just a week later in Boston, five people were brutally murdered in the robbery of the Vietnamese gambling house in that city's Chinatown. In Vancouver on January 26, 1991, two Vietnamese men were killed and another was seriously injured in a downtown restaurant in an incident police believe to be related to the ongoing battle between the Viet Ching and the Red Eagles.

Back in Toronto, on Sunday night, February 3, 1991, gunmen in Toronto opened up on a twenty-nine-year-old small-time Vietnamese gang leader originally from New York City, Vinh Duc Tat. Horrified passersby looked on as the corner of Dundas Street and Kensington Avenue, just a few doors away from the earlier killing at the Kim Bo restaurant, was peppered with .38 calibre revolver slugs. Tat was killed, and three men with him were wounded. Tat had been associated with Trung Chi Truong and was now running a gaming house and a protection racket in Chinatown. Some officers in the Toronto police's Asian Investigative Unit felt that the murder had been a potent message from Asau Tran to Truong to back off his territory in Toronto's Chinatown.

On February 15, 1991, a twenty-nine year old man, Thien Ngo, was stabbed to death after an argument in the Chieu Tiem Cafe, a Vietnamese restaurant/karaoke club on Dundas Street West, and a hangout frequented by Asau Tran and members of his gang. A Vietnamese man was arrested two days later in Ottawa and charged with the killing.

Then, on March 3, 1991, the worst atrocity in the Chinatown bloodbath leading up to Tran's own assassination occurred: at least four gunmen with automatic weapons opened up on a group of Vietnamese men, at the A Dong Restaurant at Spadina and College. Three people were killed; a fourth was seriously wounded — all four were innocent bystanders. The gunmen were Vietnamese gang members associated with Trung Chi Truong, who was still hiding out and operating in Toronto. The apparent reason for the killings was a perceived insult to the gang members coming from the victims' table. The Oriental community in Toronto recoiled in shock and horror as the body count mounted in Chinatown.

Then, on Friday, August 16, 1991 at 3:20 a.m., a couple of months after rival Vietnamese gang leader Trung Chi Truong had been finally extradited back to his jail cell in Massachusetts, two well-dressed hit men struck down Tran and two associates in a hail of bullets. Killed along with Tran were Amy Lui (Lui Tin Wah), a twenty-seven-year-old hostess, and Tony Keung Pun, thirty-three, an assistant manager and business associate of Tran's.

Tony Pun and Amy Lui were presented in most newspaper accounts as relatively innocent bystanders, which was true enough for Amy Lui. But Tony Pun had been in the concert and entertainment business with Tran and as recently as late April 1991 he had been seen publicly with Danny Mo at a concert for the celebrated Hong Kong singer, Anita Mui. Pun even snapped a photograph for journalist Yves Lavigne of Mo, Mui, and Lavigne standing outside the theatre. Although Pun was not, as reported in several media outlets, a former member of the Royal Hong Kong Police Force, he was Assistant Manager of the Pot of Gold, and a partner of Tran and Mo in the entertainment business — hardly a total innocent.

The bold execution of Tran and two others on the street in the heart of Toronto brought the heaviest media coverage of the recent Chinatown carnage. This was, after all, the tenth murder involving gangsters in Chinatown in the nine months since the killing of Dan Vi Tran, at the Kim Bo Restaurant. After the A Dong massacre, the *Toronto Sun* ran a cartoon by artist Andy Donato showing a typical Canadian couple having dinner in a Chinese restaurant, decked out in army helmets and bullet-proof vests as they casually ordered their eggrolls. It had been a grim period for those in Chinatown. The killings had caused the murder rate in Toronto to climb to its worst ever, even edging out the more violence-prone Montreal as the murder capital of Canada for 1991. Alexis Yam, the President of the Chinese Business Association dismissed the shootings as iso-lated acts: "The nature of the shootings appears to be gang-related and targeted some particular people, so the ordinary Chinese person need not be overly concerned." But this state-ment overlooked the cold-blooded murders of several non-gang members, and the fear was real in the streets of Chinatown. Yam went on to urge the Police Services Board to urgently provide the Chinese community with "special police attention now."

Stories abounded in the Toronto newspapers about extortion as a way of life in Chinatown. One courageous soul, Quy Bui, who owned a karaoke restaurant bar in Kensington Market, detailed in the press and on television how the Vietnamese gangs were systematically shaking down the businessmen. Just a few days after Tran's murder, Bui had already received a visit from members of Tran's gang, collecting money for his funeral. It was a new extortion wrinkle, one that gang members and associates claimed was a cultural phenomenon, namely the Vietnamese community giving money to help out the victim's family. But those who paid the money to the gang did so out of fear, not respect.

Television journalist Isabel Bassett had been videotaping a documentary on Asian gangs since the Spring of 1991. Originally scheduled to run in November, it was quickly packaged and moved up to air in September to take full advantage of the extensive media coverage of the Tran murder. Entitled "The Dark Society," a Chinese designation for the triads,* the centre-piece of the program was Bassett's exclusive interview with Asau Tran. The glamourous socialite reporter and the upwardly mobile gangster seemed to have hit it off. In all, Tran and Bassett had five meetings, several of them filmed and recorded by hidden cameras and mikes, in preparation for her fifty-min-ute documentary.

The program, completed just days before he was killed, was a media coup. The handsome, youthful, well-dressed, and well-groomed gangster wore his best white dinner jacket. His long black hair was carefully styled for his meetings with Mrs. Bassett. The interviews offered a unique glimpse into the Vietnamese criminal world in Toronto. Bassett introduced Tran as "one of the most feared Asian gangsters" and "one of the most powerful gang leaders in Canada." Tran talked about many things in his interviews, including, according to Bassett "his marriage break-up, his kids, his love of dogs, and his desire to break into the criminal world of Vancouver and Montreal." Tran also provided Bassett with some colourful quotes, many of them particularly meaningful after his assassination:

> Maybe they will try and kill me. . . . Maybe they heard my name a lot and they don't like it. . . . But now TV comes to me and make a lot hate me . . . . These guys — one of these groups may not let me stay alive. . . . Why let this guy stay alive?"

His words were of course prophetic. It was another old cliché come true: those who live by the sword die by the sword (or

---

* This title was not original with CFTO. It was also the title (with a slight variation, "The Dark Societies") of a very successful two-part documentary on the triads in Europe produced in the mid-1970s by Gavin McFaydden for Grenada Television's investigative team.

rather, in this case, the gun). Tran knew his days were numbered; he mentioned it a number of times during the interviews. But while his strength was his ruthlessness, he also attained power because of his skilful use of diplomacy and politics. He didn't try to eliminate Danny Mo, but instead worked out an arrangement with him. He also made deals with other Vietnamese gangs and the Big Circle Boys gangs. At his funeral, some workers at the funeral home were amazed by the number of Italian and Chinese mourners who came to view the body over the weekend — away from the glare of the cameras at the actual funeral service.

The funeral itself was quiet. It was held at a Buddhist funeral home on Spadina Avenue near the University of Toronto on August 26, ten days after the murder, to allow many days for people to pay their respects privately. The crowd consisted mostly of journalists and police.* But attending also were Tran's two young sons and distraught daughter, his wife, and senior members of his gang, along with other friends and associates, including the elegantly dressed mourner, Lam Canh, who was described in the Bassett documentary as "parti-

---

* When I ran into Isabel Bassett with her crew and bodyguards at Tran's funeral on a sweltering August day, she was standing outside the Buddhist funeral home with other reporters including "The Fifth Estate's" Victor Malarek. I suggested to Mrs. Bassett that we go into the funeral home for a better look, especially since we were both wired for sound and had film crews there. We got as far as the last pew when we were stopped by several of Tran's bodyguards, who protected him even in death. We were asked why we were there. I said I was with CITY-TV. Mrs. Bassett and I were then firmly asked to leave the funeral home as the funeral was "closed" to the media. That night, on her report on CFTO's newscast, the lead was that "journalists were turned away" at Asau Tran's funeral. She then used some exclusive clips from her interview with Tran for the forthcoming documentary, which made the CFTO item stand out as the best coverage of the event. While several of the senior members of Tran's gang were conspicuously present, either at the funeral or at the burial later, Danny Mo was nowhere to be seen on the day of Tran's funeral. He was lying low, though sources maintain that Mo had paid his respects earlier, during viewings of the body at the funeral home over the weekend.

cularly close to Tran."* The funeral procession stopped in busy traffic at Dundas Street at the scene of the killing, where priests ritualistically burned play money for the peace of Tran's soul.

The Tran murder remains officially unsolved, although there are many theories. Some maintain a rival Vietnamese gang rubbed him out, while others, including senior police investigators, contend that some of Tran's own ambitious gang members orchestrated his demise. The most plausible theory to date for Tran's assassination is that the peripatetic Trung Chi Truong, working through ambitious gang members, was behind the classic "payback," gangland-style murder. Truong, who saw Tran "as a rich lazy despot who had other people doing the dirty work while he wore the fancy clothes and swaggered around, had become a direct challenge to the already well-established Tran."** It is said in the street that while police were looking for the murderers in the A Dong shootings in March, Asau Tran tipped police off to his rival's whereabouts. Truong was arrested and deported back to Massachusetts where he is back in prison. The killing of Tran, sources say, was Truong striking back through his Toronto gang members. As of late spring 1992, investigators reported that they saw the light at the end of the tunnel. "It's a long tunnel," stated veteran Asian crime investigator Detective Ken Yates, "and we see the light ever so faintly."

Whoever was actually behind the Tran murder, it was typical of the underworld that gang leadership changed hands violently at the end of a gun. It's an age-old tradition, from the turn of the century to today, in the Italian Mafia, in the Chinese tongs and triads, and in many other organized crime groups.

The Vietnamese gangs in Toronto continued to be a major

---

* On February 20, 1992, just six months after Tran's murder, Lam Canh was charged along with thirty-three other people, with being a found-in at an illegal Chinese gaming house on Gerrard Street East near Logan Avenue.

** This was revealed in the *Toronto Sun* in an excellent article by crime reporter Lee Lamothe, who was quoting an American police source.

problem long after Trung Chi Truong's deportation and Asau Tran's murder. The new Tran gang leader was identified by police after he was charged in February 1992 in a gambling raid. There are also several new, meaner Vietnamese gangs on the Toronto Chinatown crime scene, including elements of the infamous Born To Kill gang of New York and New Jersey. They are involved in extortion of local businesses and recent immigrants in the Chinese and Vietnamese communities, and in muggings by armed thugs in broad daylight. In one recent case, a Chinese-Canadian doctor and his patients were robbed in his downtown Toronto office during the middle of the day. These Vietnamese criminals generally have little regard for the Kung Lok or, for that matter, the police; in the robbery of a Chinese gambling house in Scarborough, Vietnamese gangsters sadistically beat up Constable Peter Yuen, a known undercover policeman, nearly killing him. On July 14, 1992, a young Vietnamese man, Quoc Toan Chung, was shot to death by Vietnamese gangsters in front of the Pearl Theatre in downtown Toronto.

Former Constable Mike King today feels that Vietnamese gangs represent one of the major threats to peace in the Chinese community. Although less organized and structured than the triads, they are, according to King, "organized thugs who have the community by the throat, prowling and extorting where and when they can." Many residents of Toronto's Chinatown are now living in fear as "gang mayhem," as many in the community refer to the violence, often rules the streets.

Recently the police and the courts in both the United States and Canada have been getting even more tough with the Vietnamese gangs. In March 1992 nine senior members of the Born To Kill gang in New York City were convicted of murder, extortion, and racketeering in a U.S. Justice Department RICO action against the gang. The Born To Kill had been responsible for more than thirty-five murders in just a few years.

In April 1992 Tuan Quoc Tran, a New Jersey Born To Kill lieutenant, was convicted of a number of violent jewellery store robberies in Metro after Toronto police successfully arrested gang members in Operation Old Ham. The judge sentenced Tuan Tran to nine years stating that "the courts will not allow the Vietnamese community to be intimidated" by Vietnamese gangsters. Tran, known on the street as Danny Whiteboy, had also been seen at the Born to Kill funeral in the summer of 1990 when rival gangsters opened up with sub-machine guns on the funeral party.

One of the reasons the Vietnamese gangs are so difficult to break up is that they are extremely mobile and "are always in a state of flux," according to Detective Ken Yates. "In one week they will be loyal to one boss, and perhaps the next week will shift their allegiance to another group — they don't have the discipline to keep to a structure." This perhaps helps explain how Asau Tran was so easily taken out, and how the vacuums created by the deportation of Trung Chi Truong and the murder of Tran were so quickly and easily filled.

Chapter Fifteen

SNAKEHEADS
The Big Circles of Crime from Hong Kong to Vancouver and Toronto

After the proliferation of Vietnamese gangs in the 1980s, the most significant new development in the Asian underworld in Canada in the last decade has been the arrival and establishment in major Chinatowns across the country of the many Big Circle Boys gangs. Made up of immigrants or mainly bogus refugees to North America from the People's Republic of China, but most arriving by way of Hong Kong, the Big Circle Boys have been one of the fastest growing threats to Canadian and American Chinatowns, especially in Vancouver, Toronto, and New York City, since the late 1980s.

The Dai Huen Jai (as they are known in China and Hong Kong) or the Big Circle Boys got their name from law enforcement agencies that wanted to distinguish them from Vietnamese and Hong Kong or native Canadian gangs. Dai Huen Jai originally emerged in mainland China after the Cultural Revolution in the late sixties. The original gang members were mostly ex-Red Guards or Chinese military who were purged and sent to detention camps around the city of Canton (Guangzhou). Their name, the Big Circle Boys gangs, comes from the mainland Chinese military camps from which they originally came and which "appeared as a big circle on the few rough maps allowed by the Communist government. . . . The older generation in

Hong Kong . . . still know the provincial capital of Canton as the Big City."*

According to A.P. "Tony" Lee, a veteran triad specialist and former superintendent with the Royal Hong Kong Police who did a study of the Big Circle Boys (BCBs) for the RHKP and, more recently in 1991, for the Metropolitan Toronto Police's Asian Investigative Unit, these ex-Red Guards detained around Canton "were treated like hardened criminals and were constantly abused by the People's Liberation Army guards." Lee explained that between 1969 and 1975, a number of these Red Guard prisoners were either released or escaped and made it to Hong Kong as illegal immigrants. In Hong Kong more than one hundred of the original Big Circle Boys were granted resident status and got involved in criminal activity, specializing in violent armed robberies. A new crime wave hit Hong Kong in the mid- to late seventies, and eighty per cent of all robberies "involving cash in transit or high value property," according to Superintendent Lee, "were committed by the BCBs."

Many journalists and even some police in North America frequently make the mistake of referring to the Big Circle Boys as one unified gang.** They are anything but unified. Their name is used to refer to all Chinese gangs in Canada and the United States made up of essentially recent mainland Chinese refugees or immigrants, many of whom are now so-called "second generation" and have never been in the Red Guards or the mainland Chinese military. In Canada there are well over one hundred hard-core members of the BCBs, mostly located in Vancouver and Toronto. Though still relatively small in numbers (compared to the Vietnamese gangs, for example), the Big

---

* Lynn Pan, *Sons of the Yellow Emperor*, p. 344.

** One recent example was Jan Wong in the *Globe and Mail*, April 11, 1992, in a feature article "How China's Snakeheads Ship Their Human Cargo." Not only does Wong mistakenly refer to the Big Circle Boys as a single gang, but she states that they were a "Fujian ring," coming from the Fujian or Fukien province in southeastern China. Most of the Big Circle Boys gangs originally came from the area around Canton (Guangzhou) in the neighbouring Guangdong province.

Circle Boys are a powerful presence, feared by many in the Chinese community. Most are men in their thirties, many with military training, and almost all speak Cantonese. Police believe the majority are bogus refugees, coming to Canada and the United States through various alien-smuggling networks via Hong Kong, although their origins in mainland China allow many to claim refugee status as student protesters from Tiananmen Square at the time of the Spring 1989 uprising and subsequent massacre. The BCBS were quick to exploit the Canadian government's reluctance to return refugees from mainland China because of China's appalling human rights record. Despite their claims, many of them were already safely ensconced in Hong Kong pursuing their criminal activities at the time of the student-led revolt.

The Big Circle Boys gangs specialize primarily in running alien smuggling rings, bringing people — including their own members — illegally from Hong Kong and mainland China into North America. This is achieved through "snakeheads," a slang term for gangsters specializing in alien smuggling, who operate, in conjunction with elaborate international criminal networks, with people in China, Hong Kong, and North America. The BCBS themselves have also referred to their own alien smugglers as "sewer rats." (The BCBS use a lot of colourful language — in several police wiretaps in Toronto, the BCBS referred to the police investigating them as "cunt dogs.") The BCBS are also adept at smuggling heroin, usually from Hong Kong or direct from China to the U.S. through Vancouver and Toronto. They are also heavily involved in assaults, arms trafficking, robberies, and kidnappings. They have also innovated, with colleagues in Hong Kong, some fairly sophisticated new credit card scams, including forging the magnetic strips on the back of cards. Although Big Circle Boys members only surfaced in Vancouver and Toronto in the late 1980s, they are associated with other similar groups in Hong Kong, Montreal, Amsterdam, and New York City and have already carved a large niche in all the prime criminal areas dominated by other gangs, including protection rackets and extortions.

Surprisingly, in the macho world of Asian gangs, women have risen to prominence in the Big Circle Boys gangs, particularly in the smuggling of aliens. One woman, King Fong Yue, a thirty-nine-year-old mother of four who resided in Toronto, was one of the masterminds of the 1990 alien-smuggling scam uncovered by the massive police Operation Overflight. In Buffalo, a lengthy U.S. Immigration Service investigation in 1990 revealed that the leader of a major ring smuggling Chinese into the United States via the Niagara border points was Cheng Chui-Ping, dubbed by the American press "the Empress" of alien-smugglers.

The Big Circle Boys gangs didn't become noticeable to police in Canada until the winter of 1986/87. Between November 1986 and February 1987, there was a string of ten violent armed robberies of a number of Oriental businesses in Vancouver. Some of the robberies were on territory controlled by the Lotus and the Red Eagles, but these gangs were not behind the new crime wave. Even a Chinese gang-protected gambling house was knocked off, and police realized that the new gang was a Cantonese-speaking group from mainland China — a Big Circle Boys gang. By the March 1989 annual meeting of North American police specialists in Asian organized crime, held in Vancouver, the problems with the Big Circle Boys gangs had accelerated to the point that Constable Bill Chu delivered a well-researched paper on the new problem at the conference; Chu was one of the most knowledgeable and dedicated officers on British Columbia's Co-ordinated Law Enforcement Unit's special joint forces operation on Asian gangs.

Chu wrote that there were at least thirty hard core members of the gang in Vancouver by 1988, but that the numbers were steadily increasing. Most of the gang members were in their twenties or thirties, and almost all of them had come to Canada as bogus refugees, many using false or altered passports that they conveniently disposed of before claiming refugee status in Canada. Even in early 1989, Chu described the Dai Huen Jai as ruthless and professional gangsters involved in a wide variety of crimes in Vancouver and elsewhere in Canada. These included documented cases in Vancouver of "thefts (pick-pocketing), commercial break and enterings, frauds (cheques/credit cards), armed robberies (both residential and commercial), murders and drug importation (Heroin)." Chu also attributed the spree of robberies in 1987 to a joint Lotus gang/Big Circle Boys gang crime wave. Sources indicated that the Dai Huen Jai were being assisted by senior members of the long-established Lotus Gang. The Lotus gang picked the victims and put up the firearms. The robberies were of video stores, restaurants, and theatres, as well as of the owners of these places while they were leaving the businesses or their homes. In at least one case, an employee of a store was shot in the arm during the robbery.

In another 1987 incident recounted by Chu, two Big Circle Boys members, Mok Siu Hung and Leung Kwok Hung, were fleeing the scene after a robbery of the Fisherman's Gambling Club on Gore Street in Vancouver, which had been under police surveillance. One officer chased and apprehended one of the men a block away, while the other officer was threatened with a loaded .357 magnum at the club entrance. Although in this case the officer was able to disarm the robber safely, Chu chillingly stated, "Information was received following this incident that in any future confrontations there would be no hesitation to kill a police officer." Mok and Leung, who had been in Canada for less than a year before the incident, received seven- and five-year jail terms respectively and were deported after they finished their time in jail.

In October 1987 there was a murder that police believed to be the first Big Circle Boys gang hit in Canada, and typical of many Big Circle Boys gangs' criminal activities, it involved gang members operating in several countries. The subsequent massive police investigation revealed "the strong international connections the Dai Huen Jai have established, particularly between the cities of Hong Kong, Vancouver and Toronto." A senior Hong Kong member of the Dai Huen Jai, Li Siu Ming, had arranged to have a shipment of diamonds smuggled into Canada through gang members in Vancouver, including one

named Wong King Hung. Wong worked out a cold-blooded
scheme to murder the couriers and steal the diamonds for
himself. Two couriers from Hong Kong, Lin Hoi Chau and Man
Chiu Tai, arrived at Vancouver Airport on October 21, 1987 at
10 p.m., were met by Wong King Hung, and were taken to the
East Hotel in Vancouver's Chinatown. A few days later, on the
twenty-sixth, Wong invited both couriers to a house he had
rented on Windsor Street in Vancouver. Once in the house,
Wong sent Man to the basement to find something and then
calmly took out a .22 calibre gun and shot Lin in the back of
the head, severing the brain stem. Lin died instantly. Wong then
shot Man, who collapsed to the floor, pretending to be dead,
though he was only shot in the arm. Wong then left the house
with two accomplices. Man escaped to a neighbours house
across the street and provided enough information to the police
to enable them to arrest Wong, who was captured near his home
after he attempted to flee. Man also agreed to testify against
Wong, who was convicted of first degree murder, receiving the
mandatory twenty-five-year jail term in February 1989. But
Wong's two unidentified Vancouver associates escaped without
any charges ever being laid.

Meanwhile, in Hong Kong, police arrested Li Siu Ming and
charged him with the armed robbery of the diamonds from a
Hong Kong firm and illegal possession of ten guns. With the
crucial help of testimony from Vancouver police in Hong Kong,
Li was later convicted and received a twenty-two-year sentence. Further work by the police in Hong Kong and Vancouver
uncovered the existence of a safety deposit box in the name of
Lam Shuk Fong, Li's girlfriend. In it they found more than a
million dollars (Hong Kong) and a cache of jewellery. Police
believed that the money and the jewels were from robberies in
Vancouver. Most of the money, it turned out, had been directly
transferred from Vancouver. Lam has since immigrated to
Canada, married a Canadian citizen, and resides in the Toronto
area.

Former Hong Kong Superintendent Tony Lee, now living in
Toronto and working on contract for the police's Asian

Investigative Unit, has studied the gangs both in Hong Kong and Toronto, and wrote perceptively about the Big Circle Boys gangs' structure in a 1991 analysis prepared for the Toronto police. Lee maintained that although the Big Circle Boys gangs can be ruthless and have solid international connections, they do not use triad rituals or structures and remain very loosely organized. Lee also separated the first-generation Big Circle Boys gang members, those who are now in their late thirties and forties, as senior organized crime leaders "mainly engaged in international heroin trafficking based in Hong Kong, Taiwan and Thailand," from the younger and more violent second-generation of BCBS, the ones who prevail in Chinatowns in Toronto and Vancouver today. These more recent immigrants/refugees from Canton (Guangzhou) or Hong Kong are involved in many types of crime. Having survived battles against Vietnamese gangs for control of Chinatowns, they were primarily involved in armed robberies and home invasions "where the victims are of Chinese origin." A new, potentially explosive activity of this hardened second generation of gangs, according to Lee, is the armed robbery of heavily guarded illegal gambling houses.

The second generation of BCBS, like the first, generally arrived through Hong Kong, but many went back and forth from mainland China into Hong Kong. They financed their trips to North America by first entering Hong Kong as illegal aliens and pulling a number of armed robberies. From Hong Kong they "then sneak back into China with the money to begin their long journey into Canada." According to Lee and other Asian crime investigators, the BCBS generally take very circuitous routes to get to North America because of their forged travel documents. Often they first go to some Southeast Asian or South American country where, according to Lee, "they can buy their way in and out." According to Lee, the second generation of the BCBS use the Big Circle Boys designation mainly for the status. Violent as they are, "they lack in one important quality: they have not been to Hell and Back!" But while they lack the background of imprisonment and torture by the zealous leaders of the cultural revolution, they have established contacts worldwide, which are invaluable for heroin and alien smuggling. And there has emerged a leadership in the second generation of BCBs whom analyst Lee has called the "Smart Ones."

> The "smart ones," and there are plenty, are involved in organized alien-smuggling operations and importation of heroin. They are extremely successful in these activities because of their established links with China and Hong Kong. Their relatives in China and in Hong Kong can provide potential "clients" to be smuggled into North America and export links for heroin importation. Within three years of their arrival, some can and have risen to be heads of Organized Crime syndicates.[*]

In Toronto recently, the Big Circle Boys gangs have begun to extort wealthy Chinese living in the Bayview area. Their operations are executed with a characteristic military precision. Violence is not used; a gang member simply asks for gifts, or a friendly helping hand. Often, though, the victim, who has been carefully selected because of his apparent vulnerability, will be told that there could be consequences should he consider going to the police. Children might have "some problems." But if these methods fail, the gang moves from subtlety to violent home invasions, a crime which has become more frequent in Toronto and Vancouver in the 1990s. In these robberies, the

---

[*] Yet another Chinese crime group looms on the horizon for Canada according to Tony Lee's recent report. It is the gangs from Fujian or Fukien province that are already established in the States, especially in New York City and Los Angeles. The Fuk Ching (Fujianese youth) gang surfaced in New York City in the late 1980s. They speak a different dialect than the Hong Kong and BCB gangs. It is the Fujianese dialect, not understood by most Chinese in North America. In addition, there are Mandarin-speaking gangs of Taiwanese and Shanghainese emerging in Los Angeles and Texas. But the Fukien gangs have worked closely in joint alien- and drug-smuggling projects with the Cantonese Big Circle Boys gangs, both in North America and in China.

gang enters a selected victim's house and extorts him. Police are having a difficult time having victims come forward, as there is great fear of retaliation from the gangs.

In late February 1992, a sensational kidnapping took place in Vancouver; it strongly resembled the *modus operandi* of a Big Circle Boys gang operation. International in its organization and execution, it was a bold, violent, and outrageous crime. The victim, a twenty-six-year-old Vancouver businessman, was kidnapped in Vancouver on February 9 and taken to an East Vancouver house while criminal colleagues in Hong Kong contacted the man's father in Taiwan and demanded a $1 million ransom. A quarter of a million dollars was paid by the Taiwanese businessman on Valentine's Day to the associates in Hong Kong, and the victim was released unharmed on February 15. An international investigation involving police in Vancouver, Hong Kong, Los Angeles, Taiwan, and San Francisco quickly resulted in the arrests of five men in Vancouver and two men in Hong Kong.

In Ontario, the rise of the triad-like Big Circle Boys gangs, along with the establishment of the new Vietnamese gangs, has helped in the displacement of the Kung Lok from its pre-eminent position in Toronto's Chinatowns. But as they did with the Vietnamese gangs, Kung Lok members have made their accommodations. The Kung Lok has formed new partnerships with certain Big Circle Boys gang leaders. Together they are involved in the smuggling of aliens and other immigration scams, as well as in the restaurant business, the entertainment business, and the extortion and protection rackets. One Big Circle Boys gang leader has become the liaison with the Kung Lok, and in addition, has been the go-between for immigration brokers supplying the aliens and refugees here. Another Big Circle Boys gang member acts as liaison with the Vietnamese gangs for joint ventures and to prevent turf battles. What has helped Danny Mo and the Kung Lok to survive into the 1990s has been their uncanny business sense. They know when to give up territory and know how to do business with both of the new forces that now prevail in Toronto Asian communities.

The Kung Lok's ability to adapt to the superior power of these two new organized crime phenomena, the Vietnamese gangs in the 1980s and the "Big Circle Boy" gangs in the late 1980s and early 1990s, was key to the survival of the triad and individual Chinese gang leaders like Mo.

Although violent robberies orchestrated by the BCBS in Toronto's Chinatowns has been steadily rising, it was a major alien-smuggling ring run by one of the estimated ten Big Circle Boys gangs now operating in Metro Toronto which first captured the police, media, and public 's attention in a big way in Ontario. Its exposure was the result of a highly publicized RCMP undercover operation on the alien-smuggling activities of one of the Big Circle Boys gangs in Canada, dubbed by the police "Project (Operation) Overflight." It was run by a crack team in the RCMP's Immigration and Passport Section under a colourful and resourceful Mountie veteran, named Staff Sergeant A.F. (Andy) Rayne, working closely with the Metro Toronto's Joint Forces Asian Investigative Unit and the Royal Hong Kong Police.

The Big Circle Boys gang alien-smuggling ring that came to be known by "Overflight" was a highly sophisticated and well-organized operation according to Rayne. It was controlled by two people whom Tony Lee would almost certainly designate "smart ones," Chiu Sing Tsang, 39, and his wife, King Fong Yue, 37. Tsang, who came into Canada himself with false papers in 1988, was described in court as the chief executive officer of the ring. Tsang, who was working closely with Fukien gangsters in New York City and China, was planning to bring many of the aliens into the United States where they would be "indentured," as one investigator put it, into the Fukien and Cantonese Big Circle Boys gangs there. His "lieutenant general" — his wife — lived in luxury in a plush Queen's Quay condo while drawing welfare* and was responsible, along with her husband,

---

* King Fong Yue was heavily subsidized by the taxpayers while pursuing her criminal fortune — she received welfare (as all refugee claimants waiting for final determination of their status do) and free Ontario Health

for bringing in between one and two thousand illegal aliens and bogus refugees, although to date only 263 of these illegal entries could be proved in court. The couple and their gang made millions of dollars. The judge in the case in Toronto, Hugh Porter, called the smuggling scheme a "diabolical program," made even worse because Yue and Tsang were themselves refugees and thus abusing Canada's compassionate refugee system in more ways than one.

The illegal aliens, some of whom were Big Circle Boys gang members, paid an average of $15,000 each, $10,000 of which was profit for the organization. For an additional $4,500, the aliens would be smuggled into the United States. The profit was conservatively estimated at about $10 to $15 million dollars for the two-year period of its operations. Many of the Overflight customers were first smuggled from mainland China to Hong Kong. About ten percent of the bogus refugees (anywhere from 150 to 400 people, according to the RCMP) were hard-core members of one of the Big Circle Boys gangs coming to Canada or the United States to get involved in a more lucrative criminal territory. The aliens were given fraudulent passports (generally from Hong Kong or Singapore), which they used to gain admission to Canada, usually through Toronto's Pearson Airport, though sometimes through Montreal or Vancouver. They took a circuitous route to Canada, via Thailand, Germany, Romania, England, Finland, Switzerland, and Sweden, sometimes even from the former Soviet Union. The aliens almost always travelled in the company of escorts, whose duties included getting rid of or re-cycling the phoney documents. For their work, they were paid $1,000 plus expenses.

In all, nine people in Hong Kong and six people, including

Insurance (OHIP) and even legal aid. Canada is indeed generous to her refugee claimants, costing the taxpayers about $50,000 per person according to veteran immigration lawyer Mendel Green and over a billion dollars a year according to some estimates. Many countries, such as Germany and Hong Kong, intern or tightly regulate refugees until their claims are more closely examined.

Tsang and Yue in Toronto were charged in August 1990 after a
four-month investigation. All but one were convicted. Tsang
was convicted in 1990 of illegally bringing in ten aliens and was
sentenced to two and half years in jail. Others convicted in
Canada included two Singapore men, Hock Peng Teng and
Thiam Seng Sim. Some of the gang, including Yue, are already
out of jail, still awaiting final determination of their refugee
status, like many of the "refugees" whom they illegally brought
in.

Clearly, alien smuggling is a growth industry for organized
crime in the 1990s. For $15,000 to $20,000, virtually anyone
can buy his or her way into Canada. One of the main problems
seems to be Canada's relatively lax refugee rules. According to
a longtime undercover agent for Immigration intelligence, people come to Toronto claiming to be refugees and wearing mink
coats and jewels. "It's become really bad in the last four or five
years. All they have to do to get into Canada is say the magic
word — 'Refugee.'" With approximately forty thousand people
a year relocating to Canada as refugees, it's become a major
problem sifting out the criminals from the legitimate refugees.
And while many of these aliens being smuggled in are criminals, the vast majority of them are innocent people trying to
jump the lineup to get into Canada.

The problem is an expensive one as well. As of January 1992,
there were twenty-four thousand refugee claimants receiving
welfare in Metro Toronto alone, costing the Ontario taxpayers
tens of millions of dollars. In a January 1992 report on "W5"
entitled "Jumping the Queue," Eric Malling said that Canada
"has the most generous refugee policy in the Western world."
While many countries such as the United States, England, and
Germany eventually allow ten to twenty-five percent of refugee
claimants to remain in their country, Canada, in 1991, generously allowed sixty-five percent of all refugee claimants to
settle here. Even the well known and experienced immigration
lawyer Mendel Green has concluded that the refugee system is
now seriously out of control.

There is so much money to be made through immigration,

both legal and illegal, that many are tempted to bend the laws to get their clients into Canada. Immigration lawyer Martin Pilzmaker, while a partner in the prestigious Ontario law firm of Lang, Michener, Lash & Johnston, created phoney addresses, telephone numbers, and even businesses for many of his clients, who then obtained Canadian landed immigrant status at a cost of up to $40,000 each. Passport and mortgage fraud, even the creation of phantom clients, became part of his everyday immigration counselling business. Although Pilzmaker's crooked schemes were exposed in a series of front-page stories by Victor Malarek in the *Globe and Mail* in 1988, it was only after the RCMP laid forty-three charges of fraud and conspiracy against him in January 1990 that the Law Society finally took action. Disbarred and faced with going to jail, the thirty-nine-year-old Pilzmaker committed suicide in April 1991. Others, including corrupt Immigration court judges in Newfoundland and Manitoba, have also committed suicide in the last couple of years rather than face public humiliation and jail. According to the RCMP there are many unscrupulous consultants and Immigration officials who will prey on people's vulnerabilities.

Alien-smuggling has today become almost as lucrative as heroin smuggling. According to RCMP Immigration and Passport officer Fred Bowen, who worked on Project Overflight, "Drug dealers are getting out of the drug business and devoting all their time and resources strictly to smuggle people into Canada." The more illegal aliens entering the country, the more new body-smuggling networks bringing in other illegal aliens will develop. The penalties, if a person is caught, are minimal, compared to the more severe sentences for drug trafficking, and the profit margins can now be just as large as those in heroin trafficking. Unless there is some severe tightening up of Canadian refugee requirements, for the foreseeable future there will be increasing numbers of criminals among the immigrants and refugees coming illegally to Canada from mainland China and Hong Kong.

Chapter Sixteen

CHASING THE DRAGON TODAY
Of Ginseng, Ice Buckets, and Umbrellas

The RCMP and the DEA have revealed over the last two years that the majority of quality heroin coming into North America since the late 1980s is no longer routed by the famed French Connection and controlled by the Mafia. Today the majority of heroin sold in North America comes via Oriental drug-trafficking networks direct from the Far East or via Amsterdam and other European cities to Toronto, Montreal, or Vancouver and then on to the lucrative American markets. In the late 1980s and early 1990s, seizures of more than a billion dollars' worth of heroin at a time were becoming routine in Boston, New York, Toronto, and other entry points in North America. Despite the highly touted show trials of senior Mafia leaders in the United States and Italy, the American and Sicilian Mafia still maintain their heroin routes, including the old French Connection from Turkey to Marseille (for processing) and on to New York City via Montreal. There has been a restructuring of the international Mafia. New leaders have emerged, and younger men are rising to the top more quickly. But as it did in the 1920s and 1930s, the Mafia is still making deals with Chinese triads and using the Oriental routes. Rocco Perri in Canada and Charles "Lucky" Luciano in New York City are only two of the prominent Mafiosi of an earlier period who regularly got quality opium and heroin from the Orient through Chinese traffickers. In the thirties, the opium was processed in Europe or North America; nowadays triad chemists often process the opium into heroin in the Orient itself.

The DEA's Operation Seahorse in the late 1980s revealed the extent to which Chinese gangs and triads in North America were involved in the importation of heroin from Southeast Asia. Seahorse began accidentally, with the arrest in June 1985 at the Seattle airport of two heroin couriers, Fang Han Sheng and Tommy Chen, who had a massive 216 pounds of heroin stashed in metal ice buckets. Fang Han Sheng escaped and was later murdered in Bangkok, Thailand. Not surprisingly, Chen refused to talk and was sentenced to a long prison term.

The DEA soon discovered that Fang Han Sheng and Tommy Chen worked for Johnny Kon (Kon Yu-leung), the New York City-based, Big Circle Boys gang leader. Since the early 1980s, Kon had run a street gang in New York called the Flaming Eagles, specializing in armed robbery and drug trafficking and composed of mostly former mainland Chinese gangsters as well as some Hong Kong and American Chinese. Kon was born in Shanghai and had made his fortune during the Vietnam War by selling smuggled fur coats to U.S. troops. He owned a movie theatre in New York City, a million-dollar home in Panama, a factory in Paraguay, and real estate in San Francisco. According to the DEA, he also had corrupt officials all over the world on his payroll.

In 1986 Antonio Ronnie Vacas, a Eurasian Hong Kong businessman and associate of Kon, was arrested by the DEA in Seattle with a passport which had been tampered with. Vacas agreed to operate undercover and eventually to testify for the government. Other key witnesses had been murdered, committed suicide, or simply were not talking. But Vacas, who had operated undercover for the DEA for more than a year, provided crucial evidence that resulted finally in Kon's arrest in New York City. The DEA estimates that Kon's organization from 1984 until his arrest brought into the United States more than seventeen hundred pounds of heroin, worth close to $2 billion dollars on the street. Sentenced to twenty-seven years in jail, Kon had threatened the life of Catherine Palmer, an assistant U.S. Attorney on the case; "Others will die, then you." Although Ms Palmer later did receive a booby-trapped package with a loaded rifle, she escaped unharmed.

Kon is still in jail, and his international organization is finished. According to a key DEA agent who worked on the case, "Kon was the first one who woke us up to the fact that Southeast Asian heroin had become a major factor in the United States." But this was only an early glimpse of the new heroin pipeline that ran into North America from Southeast Asia.

The 14 K triad had been established by Nationalists from China who fled to Hong Kong after World War 11 and later emerged in Hong Kong, Taiwan, and Amsterdam as one of the most important international triads. Today it still has control of one of the major heroin trafficking routes into Europe and North America. It was the legendary drug baron "White Powder" Ma (Ma Sik-yu), one of Hong Kong's most successful and wealthiest heroin traffickers from the 1960s through the 1980s, who with his brother and nephew had made a deal with the 14 K for supplying heroin throughout Hong Kong. Limpy Ho (Ng Shek-ho), the other major drug kingpin in Hong Kong in the 1960s and 1970s, was an honorary member of the 14 K and an associate of the Kung Lok's Lau Wing Kui, and the five dragons' Lui Lok. He, along with Ma and the corrupt RHKP police, for many years supplied the heroin to Hong Kong and the rest of the world.*

Operation White Mare began in October 1987, when sixty-nine-year-old New York City-based businessman Peter Woo (Woo Kok-Leung), the respected, low-key owner of a liquor store on Mott Street in New York's Chinatown and co-founder of the Chinatown Democratic Club in New York, was identi-

---

* Limpy Ho died shortly after a lengthy jail term in 1991, but Ma had escaped to Taiwan when things got too hot for him in Hong Kong in the mid-seventies. White Powder Ma and the 14 K still have their hand in heroin smuggling through Hong Kong by way of various underlings.

fied by a credible FBI informant as an official of the 14 K triad and operating an international heroin smuggling-ring. In December of that same year, Simon Au Yeung, an FBI undercover agent of Chinese descent, pretending to be a major international drug dealer, insinuated himself into Woo's extensive organization. After making a number of smaller buys from Woo from December until March, 1988 in New York, the FBI agent struck paydirt when in March 1988, he was invited to go to Hong Kong for a bigger buy and to meet some of Woo's heroin sources in the Crown colony.

Police wiretaps and videotapes of Woo and his Hong Kong associates revealed the existence of an elaborate code used to talk about the heroin. The Cantonese word for ginseng referred to heroin and "pieces" referred to eight-hundred-gram bags of heroin. In March 1988 Woo was heard discussing a shipment of fifty pieces into New York City via Canada, and the RCMP were brought into the undercover operation. On March 21 Woo came to Vancouver. The next day he was shadowed by Mounties when he took a plane to Calgary and met his contacts at the airport. He then flew on to Hong Kong. One of Woo's criminal colleagues was Calgary resident, Kenny "Baby Face" Wong (Wong Cheung Wa), an unassuming thirty-year-old living with his mother and, so he said, working as a cook. But Wong, who had lived in Calgary for more than ten years, was the Canadian connection for the worldwide, multibillion-dollar heroin ring. Carrying both Hong Kong and Canadian passports, he generally operated from hotels and restaurants in Toronto and Calgary. The drugs would be stored in Calgary until buyers were lined up in New York City. Then the couriers arranged to have the heroin delivered to New York City via Toronto. Woo had referred to Wong in his discussions with the FBI undercover operative only as "the Canadian" who was his "Hong Kong connection."

Also working with Woo in a separate but related heroin-trafficking ring was Chan Hok Pang, a citizen of Hong Kong and a personal friend of famed Burmese warlord General Khun Sa (Chang Chi Fu), who had been indicted for heroin trafficking by a grand jury in the United States but lived safely with his private army in the wilds of Burma. Police found a picture of Pang with Khun Sa when they raided his Hong Kong residence. It was Pang who had arranged with Woo for the final massive shipment of heroin to be sent to North America.

On February 21, 1989, more than one hundred policemen from the RCMP, FBI, DEA, and RHKP moved in nine cities — Toronto, Calgary, Vancouver, New York City, Detroit, Los Angeles, San Francisco, Hong Kong, and Singapore — to arrest fifty-four members of this huge international drug-trafficking network. They seized more than eight hundred pounds of heroin — worth more than a billion dollars on the street — and $3 million in American cash. It was enough heroin, according to assistant FBI director James Fox, to supply "half of all the heroin used by two hundred thousand addicts in New York City for a year." The high-grade, China White heroin had been concealed inside hundreds of hollowed-out rubber tires, designed for small carts. More than 260 boxes of tires had been smuggled into Los Angeles and then driven to New York, where they were discovered by police in rented trucks outside two homes in Queens. U.S. Attorney Andrew Maloney said at the time that Chinese criminals were now "responsible for seventy to eighty percent of the heroin that is smuggled into New York City" and that "Asian drug rings had now supplanted heroin operations run by traditional American organized crime families." In total, more than fifty people were arrested, including Woo in New York City, Wong in Calgary, and Pang in Hong Kong. Woo, who was seventy two years old when he came to trial in 1990, pleaded guilty and received a lengthy prison term.

The White Mare investigation uncovered other Chinese organized crime heroin rings in addition to the 14 K triad one run by Woo. One of these also brought their heroin from Hong Kong via Europe through the airports at Toronto or Vancouver, where new couriers picked up the heroin shipments for New York City or San Francisco. "They find Toronto to be very convenient," an assistant U.S. attorney in New York said of the drug trafficking gang's use of Pearson Airport as a meeting and trans-shipment place. In October 1988, four months before the main White Mare arrests, the RCMP arrested six people in a hotel room in Agincourt, a suburb in northeastern Toronto, with more than two and a half kilograms of heroin. Four of the traffickers were Hong Kong citizens, the other two were landed immigrants in Canada. The same day, two New York City natives were arrested by U.S. Customs as they tried to cross the Rainbow Bridge at Niagara Falls with body packs of heroin. In two cases, police wiretaps revealed that Hong Kong couriers phoned contacts in Hong Kong when they arrived in Toronto to transmit a code to tell the bosses they had made it through Canadian customs, and subsequently also phoned gang members in New York for final arrangements for the pick-up in Toronto. More than $25 million worth of heroin was seized in this second network, which was closely tied to Hong Kong triads.

Another direct spin-off of the hugely successful White Mare project was a worldwide joint forces operation code-named Red Star. During this operation, the RCMP worked for the first time directly with the police of The People's Republic of China to bust a major Big Circle Boys drug ring operating in China, Canada, and the United States. The growing power of Big Circle Boys gangs in international heroin trafficking as well as other crime groups in China makes the continued co-operation of the Chinese authorities essential to the police's ability to keep a lid on the heroin flow from Asia.*

Red Star began on St. Patrick's Day, 1989, when a "confidential" DEA source in Hong Kong detailed a plan to import heroin from China via Hong Kong and Toronto to New York City. The source told the DEA that in September of 1988 he had been introduced in Hong Kong to a Canadian calling himself

---

* Until recently the Canadian government has not allowed extraditions to mainland China, even of bogus refugees convicted in Canada of serious crimes, because of the totalitarian nature of the Communist government and its abysmal human rights record. China is now working to change that image, and by working with the RCMP and the FBI on Red Star they hoped to break out of their isolation.

"Ah Chiu," but who was later identified as Peter Lau (Lau Veng-Tat) of Brampton, Ontario, a small city west of Toronto, where he owned the Oriental Regency Restaurant and Tavern. Lau needed a consignee company in Toronto for handling a container shipment from Canton (Guangzhou). The DEA informant was told that Lau's organization was seeking a new method of shipping heroin to the United States by way of Canada, and the DEA provided Lau with a company called Asian Source Ltd., in Ajax, just east of Toronto on Lake Ontario.

Lau visited Asian Source's offices in Ajax in January 1989, met with the informant, and confirmed that the shipment would be coming through the company. In March 1989 the informant met with Lau in Canton and was shown five boxes of umbrellas (from a shipment of three hundred), which were to contain ninety pounds of heroin, worth close to $200 million on the street. When the DEA and the RCMP informed the Chinese police of the details of the trafficking scheme, the Chinese authorities agreed to take part in the worldwide operation.*

On March 21, 1989 the Interpol office in Canton along with the Customs officials of the People's Republic, seized eighty seven pounds of heroin in five umbrella boxes, leaving only six pounds in the boxes so that the DEA and RCMP could follow the shipment. In Hong Kong on April 15, Lau met with the informant and promised him a payment of $350,000 in Toronto for making all the arrangements, including the rental of a specially equipped truck to ship the umbrellas from Toronto to New York City. A massive surveillance operation was mounted by Canada Customs, the RCMP, and Canadian Pacific security. The shipment arrived on the Chinese ship *Jian He*, in Vancouver on April 24, was delivered by freight train to the company in Ajax, Ontario, and from there was forwarded to New York City. On April 25, 1989, two mainland Chinese police officials turned

---

* This was the second time the Chinese government has assisted American law enforcement officials in a drug bust — the first being in 1988 when they helped the DEA make arrests of heroin traffickers who were shipping heroin from China to San Francisco.

over some of the seized heroin to the RCMP so that they would have a sample of the drug for the American end of the operation.

On May 6 Peter Lau, who had followed the heroin's route from Hong Kong to Vancouver and Toronto to New York City, was arrested in Times Square in New York City. Ka Yiu Mak, one of Lau's New York colleagues, was arrested in Queens. He was carrying the six pounds of heroin on his person as well as two illegal handguns. Another member of the gang, Christopher Hong Chau, of Whitestone, New York, was also arrested. All of the defendants were tried and convicted in the southern district court of New York City.

In yet another recent international heroin-smuggling case involving Toronto, eight members of a Big Circle Boys drug-smuggling gang were arrested on November 8, 1990, in New York City, Hong Kong, and Toronto as the result of two police operations code-named Project Dragon and Dragon IV. On February 5, 1991, police in Toronto and New York arrested 12 members of what they alleged was a major heroin smuggling ring run by a syndicate based in Hong Kong and operating in Metro Toronto and New York City. Police seized more than $8 million in U.S. cash in New York, and about $70 million worth of quality heroin in Toronto and the United States. These arrests were quickly followed on February 21, 1991, with the arrest of Ernest Liu, a New York City banker originally from Hong Kong, who was charged in a 113-count indictment by the U.S. attorney of Brooklyn, Arthur Maloney, with laundering millions of dollars for what he called "a Chinese crime organization."

As for the role of Ontario's Kung Lok in international drug trafficking, DEA and RCMP intelligence have believed for some time that the triad has been actively involved in the heroin trade over the past decade, but there is no evidence that Danny Mo is in the heroin business, and Lau Wing Kui, though suspected by Hong Kong police and the DEA of involvement in the drug trade particularly because of his closeness to Limpy Ho and some of the five dragons, has never been convicted of drug trafficking. But members of the Kung Lok have, however, been arrested and convicted of drug trafficking over the years.

Paul Kwok, who had fled Canada because of the heat from the police in Toronto, was convicted in the United States of importing ten pounds of heroin in the early 1980s after the DEA targeted him in New York City. He is now serving time in Millhaven Penitentiary in Kingston, having successfully applied for the prison exchange program between the United States and Canada. Police fear that he will once again be criminally active in the drug business in Canada.

Also, the RCMP national intelligence division reported in a detailed, confidential intelligence report in November 1990 that the leaders and members of the Ottawa branch of the Kung Lok, along with associates in Toronto, Calgary, and Hong Kong, are suspected of being heavily involved in the international heroin-trafficking business. For the trafficking, the Kung Lok group allegedly employs Big Circle Boys gang members and a female associate in Ottawa known as "the Shanghai lady." An Ottawa-based trading company is suspected of being used for the two major deliveries a year of the heroin that the RCMP suspect are coming in. The street value of this heroin would be worth about a billion dollars. Some key former Kung Lok leaders in Toronto are suspected of being involved in this trafficking. Unfortunately, according to a senior police source, at the moment, the Asian Investigative Unit in Toronto has neither the time nor money to pursue this lead in depth. The violent and very visible Vietnamese and Big Circle Boys gang activity in the streets of Toronto has been getting most of the police and media attention for the last couple of years. Meanwhile the heroin keeps pouring in to Toronto.

Chapter Seventeen

SLAYING THE DRAGONS
OF CRIME

Across North America, Asian gang activity is a growth industry for the 1990s. The fourteenth annual international police conference on Asian gangs held in Calgary in mid-July 1992 grimly concluded that Asian organized crime was going to be "the major crime problem of the next century." As the 1997 takeover of Hong Kong by the People's Republic of China approaches, more and more of the approximately fifty thousand triad members resident in the Crown colony are making their way to the West. Even Lau Wing Kui, now living in Hong Kong and working at Stanley Ho's casino in Macao, may yet try to get back into Canada, though he does still have his Dominican Republic citizenship. The Chinese government certainly has not guaranteed the safety of triad leaders after it takes control, and their previous record of re-education camps or, even worse, execution, will not inspire Lau and his triad colleagues.

Much has changed on the Asian crime scene in Canada since I first began research for this book in 1988. Just a little more than three years ago Detective-Sergeant George Cowley, the head of the Asian crime unit from 1986 until 1990, emphatically declared that Toronto was different than other cities in North America with large oriental populations: "You cannot compare Toronto to any other city; we have greater numbers here, yet we don't have the level of violence as in Vancouver and New York. We don't have open shootouts in the street as

in Vancouver or gang wars." This view seems hopelessly out-
dated after the killings in Chinatown in 1991 and 1992.

Cowley had also stated that, unlike New York City, the turf
is not carved up by the gangs. "We [in Toronto] are split section
wise — Broadview, Chinatown, Scarborough, Mississauga; but
gang members can freely go to all the Chinatown areas. But in
New York City it is different with different streets run by
different gangs." This too is changing as more and more gangs
(several Vietnamese and several Chinese) compete for territory.
There are now six Chinatowns: the main one downtown, now
greatly expanded; one in Scarborough, including parts of Agincourt (now dubbed "Asiancourt" by some residents as about
150,000 Asian Canadians now live in the suburbs far from the
overcrowded downtown Chinatowns); one in Riverdale alongside the Greek community at Broadview and Gerrard; and
others have emerged in North York, Mississauga, and Markham.

In the Greater Metropolitan Toronto area today, a region now
with well over four hundred thousand Chinese and sixty thousand Vietnamese residents, there are up to ten Big Circle Boys
gangs, at least three major Vietnamese gangs, the core of the
original Kung Lok (now with fewer than a hundred members),
as well as some representation from other major Hong Kong-
based triads, such as the Sun Yee On and the 14 K. Kung Lok
boss Danny Mo is still bringing in Asian entertainers, mostly
to Roy Thomson Hall, and is involved in a number of other
businesses. Although the forty-five year old Mo has kept an
extremely low profile since Asau Tran's untimely demise, his
influence in Toronto's Chinatowns is still strong and far out of
proportion to the diminished muscle now at his command.

In Greater Vancouver, whose Asian population is now approximately two hundred thousand (now only a little more than half
of that of the Greater Toronto area), there are, according to
British Columbia law enforcement authorities, approximately
thirty gangs with more than 1,100 members. In 1992, a wave
of home invasions by Asian gangs hit Vancouver, and even
Chinese-Canadians living in the fashionable Shaughnessy area

were targeted for attack. Police Chief Bill Marshall declared in May 1992 that he would do whatever it takes to control the gangs and that he was not going to "allow thugs and gangs to control Chinatown and the people in it."

Calgary today has several triad groups and up to six Vietnamese gangs. In Winnipeg and Edmonton there are several new Asian youth gangs, and in Montreal there are Vietnamese gangs (some from the United States) as well as established Chinese criminals operating in the city's old Chinatown. Ottawa has both Vietnamese and Chinese gangs, including the Kung Lok branch, which is strongly suspected by RCMP intelligence of being involved in heroin trafficking. There is also Asian gang activity in Windsor, Saskatoon, Hamilton, and other Canadian cities in Ontario and the Maritimes. The Vietnamese gangs in all the Canadian cities are hard to pinpoint, highly mobile, and always in a state of flux. Allegiances change daily. According to Ken Yates, a veteran Toronto police intelligence officer, "One day a gang member will be loyal to his boss, but then in the next week he will belong to another gang."

In New York City today, there are many emerging Big Circle Boys gangs as well as well-established gangs such as the Ghost Shadows, the criminally connected tongs, the Born To Kill and other Vietnamese gangs, and a new gang from the Fukien province of China, the Fuk Ching, which has been working with the Big Circle Boys gangs in Canada in alien smuggling. From Virginia to New Jersey to Texas to California, there is growing violence among the Vietnamese gangs. According to Robert Mueller, the assistant U.S. attorney general in charge of the criminal division of the Justice Department, the Sun Yee On triad of Hong Kong has also recently established a base in New York City using the Tung On tong as its front. Triads and tongs are now criminally active in Los Angeles, San Francisco, Chicago, Philadelphia, Boston, New York City, Atlantic City, and other American cities. The Wop Ho To triad has recently been gaining strength in California. San Francisco police say Peter Chong is the triad's leader. Triad numbers and violence have also been increasing in Britain and Australia.

F.B.I. Director William Sessions told the U.S. Senate Committee on Government Affairs' Permanent Subcommittee of Investigations in November 1991 that "Chinese criminal organizations currently pose the most serious threat . . . . Only a few years ago, Chinese criminal groups operating in the United States were small and disorganized. Now they are the most developed of the Asian groups and are rapidly expanding their operations outside the Asian community." Permanent Subcommittee of Investigations member Senator William Roth agreed, stating that "crime perpetrated by Chinese criminal groups is now being committed at previously unheard of levels." Senator Sam Nunn, the subcommittee's chairman, added that the tongs operating in various Chinatowns across America were the "backbone of the Chinese underworld" in illegal gambling and heroin-smuggling operations. In July 1992 two veteran Toronto police Asian crime specialists were scheduled to testify before the committee about the close ties between Asian criminal networks in Canada and similar groups in the United States.

In addition, there are now other Asian criminal groups on the horizon. In Hawaii and California, elements of the Japanese Mafia, the Yakuza, are active. These are the gangsters famous worldwide for their elaborately tattooed bodies. Although the Yakuza has not yet penetrated Canada in a major way, there were Japanese organized criminals operating as early as the 1930s in British Columbia. In 1992 the government in Japan launched a crackdown against the Yakuza, urging citizens to turn in members and further criminalizing membership in the popular criminal fraternity that now has hundreds of thousands of members. This new anti-Yakuza movement in Japan may precipitate an exodus to North America.

Filipino gangs are also now active in New York City and Vancouver. And in the United States, Korean organized crime is increasingly evident across the country in the prostitution and smuggling businesses. In addition, there are also Mandarin-speaking Chinese gangs of Taiwanese and Shanghai immigrants emerging in Los Angeles and Texas.

It is important to remember that to date the main victims of the Asian gangs and triads in Canada are citizens living in the country's large and growing Oriental communities. Although there has been some spillover recently, with Vietnamese gangs robbing jewellery stores outside Chinatowns and Big Circle Boys gangs robbing warehouses just outside of Toronto, the targets of most organized crime activity by the gangs are still inside the Chinatowns. But it is a major problem for all Canadians that so many innocent people in one of our largest ethnic communities in Canada are victimized from within. Combating the proliferation of Asian gangs in Canada has not been easy. There is still too much distrust of the authorities and a reluctance by the Asian communities to organize effective opposition to the gangsters.

What is the best way to effectively fight the growing power of Chinese triads and Vietnamese gangs? First of all, Canadian Immigration needs much better screening procedures. We have enough indigenous criminals here without importing them. Cutting back on immigrants from Hong Kong, China, and Vietnam is not the answer, but today too many known criminals are getting in without proper security checks. Once immigrants and refugees are in Canada, the rules also are lax. When immigrants or refugees who are not yet citizens of Canada are convicted of major criminal offences, they should be automatically deported to their country of origin after finishing their prison sentences. The sections of the Immigration Act under which Lau Wing Kui and Nickie Louie were deported from Canada, based solely on *criminal intelligence* information that the person is a threat to Canadian society, have since been combined and made much harder for Immigration intelligence to use. These changes should be reversed. In some cases drastic action is called for. Particularly dangerous criminals who have already obtained Canadian citizenship could be stripped of their citizenship by an aggressive government policy, if, for instance, it could be proved that they lied on their entry forms or citizenship papers about their background.

In criticizing those in his own ministry who would shrink

from their duty, Toronto Immigration officer George Best, wrote in a 1986 memo that Canadian Immigration had an essential role to play in combating Asian organized crime:

> Every effort should be made to neutralize these gangs. Immigration has an active role to play. Our interest cannot and should not be confined simply to what happens after a visitor or immigrant arrives in Canada. . . . It should not be forgotten that two of Parliament's objectives with respect to the present Immigration Act are: "to maintain and protect the health, safety and good order of Canadian society"; and "to promote international order and justice by denying the use of Canadian territory to persons who are likely to engage in criminal activity." . . . Not too many years ago an Attorney General for Ontario denied the existence of Italian organized crime in this province. Possibly it was politic to do so at the time. We doubt if any Attorney General would make that statement today. Immigration cannot bury its head in the sand and pretend that a similar situation does not exist in Canada today with respect to the Asian community — a situation which has the potential for serious consequences as 1997 approaches and Hong Kong enters the 50-year transitional period prior to complete assimilation by China.

In the Mulroney government's massive new Immigration Bill (C-86), are provisions for deporting permanent residents in Canada and denying entry to others on the basis of allegations by the government of involvement in organized crime. This is a step in the right direction, though it is unclear what process would determine whether someone were involved in organized crime.

In addition, there should certainly be a major tightening and re-thinking of Canada's overly generous refugee policy as suggested by Bill C-86. Today, while many legitimate refugees particularly from Africa and South America, are denied entry, hundreds of bogus refugees are living here at taxpayers' expense while pursuing criminal careers. At the same time, Great Britain is turning over its Crown colony to Communist China without offering any sanctuary to most endangered Hong Kong citizens. It is imperative that Canada and other western nations help Hong Kong natives by taking as many immigrants and legitimate refugees as is feasible. But there is no reason to accept criminals.

In spite of its horrendous human rights record, the People's Republic of China is now working with the RCMP and Western police agencies to curb international drug traffickers operating out of China, and Vietnam is inviting refugees to return without fear of punishment in an effort to moderate its image. The Canadian government has recently taken a few hesitant steps to confront this issue. In April 1992 seven convicted violent Vietnamese extortionists and armed robbers were deported by Canadian Immigration from the Toronto area to Vietnam, and two convicted Big Circle Boys gang members were sent back to China. These deportations, especially of refugees and immigrants convicted in Canada of serious criminal offences, should become the routine, not the exception.

What we need is an open immigration policy that allows for entrance to Canada of legitimate immigrants but denies entry to those whom police and Immigration intelligence have identified as professional criminals or corrupt individuals. When recently asked what the solution was to the growing Asian gang violence in Canada, a long-serving Chinese undercover agent for Canadian Immigration said that it was very simple: "Arrest them. Prosecute them. And then deport them."

Veteran Asian crime fighter former Sergeant Benny Eng flatly stated before the Toronto Crime Inquiry on July 24, 1991, that "Most of the serious crime in our community is the result of the actions of a significant number of refugee criminals, who while they comprise a small percentage of the overall Asian community, commit high-profile and numerous offences." Sergeant Eng, who has worked on scores of major Asian gang investigations in the last decade, concluded his frank lecture by suggesting some solutions. These included, among others, the following specific recommendations: a review of refugee determination guidelines, improved background checks on refugee applicants, a tightening up of the regulations governing immigration consultants, the deportation of refugee claimants who are convicted of criminal offences, the rooting out of "bogus refugee claimants," and the removal of the "stay" on deportations to China and Vietnam.* The Chinatown Merchants Association in Vancouver has agreed, and in a statement released in May 1992 it blamed a new wave of gang violence and home invasions on what it called "lax immigration and deportation laws" in Canada.

The new Canadian government Immigration and Refugee policy (Bill C-86) answers some of these concerns by allowing for fingerprinting of all new refugees and by providing for stiffer sentences for smuggling of people into Canada. Also, under the proposed changes, airlines will be required to make security deposits to ensure that their passengers have valid travel docu-

---

* Predictably, Benny Eng's sensible proposals and his use of statistics based on country of origin created an uproar in the media. As a result, the suggestions were soundly dismissed by many liberal and politically correct observers, including the chair of the Metropolitan Toronto Police Services Board, Susan Eng, as intolerant and even racist. This in spite of the fact that Sergeant Eng never mentioned race se and merely observed that the "vast majority of the criminals" — meaning criminals who were highly visible because of the nature of their crime — mostly violent robberies or assaults — in the Asian community in Metro Toronto were originally from two countries, mainland China and Vietnam. Many in leadership positions in the Chinese community in Toronto supported Benny Eng's observations as an accurate reflection of what was going on in Chinatown, because many of them feel that "outsiders" are now the major source of the crime problem. Significantly, Sergeant Eng excluded immigrants from Hong Kong, currently the largest source of new immigrants to Canada (at around thirty thousand per year) from his list of where potentially dangerous criminals were coming from. Eng should also have emphasized a statistic that he knows painfully well, that a disproportionate number (to use the unfortunate expression that Toronto mayor June Rowlands applied to black criminals in Toronto) of Chinese and Vietnamese citizens in Metro Toronto are the *victims* of Chinese and Vietnamese gang activity. This is the other side of the equation, which is often left out in debates about the use of ethnic crime statistics.

ments, and refugees who have yet to become citizens may be deported if the government determines that they are members of an organized crime or terrorist group.

An unofficial code of silence has long enveloped the Chinatowns in Canada. When faced with criminal activity, Chinese in Canada have not tended to go to the authorities. Instead, they have dealt with the problems within the community, even if that meant paying extortionists or allowing illegal gambling houses and other criminal enterprises to flourish. The many violent robberies and murders in the Chinatowns of Canada over the past two years have made it all the more imperative that things are no longer swept under the rug.

Today there is a real fear growing in these communities. The new Asian gangs, particularly the Vietnamese and the mainland Chinese gangs, do not hesitate to use any available fire power, including semi-automatic weapons and machine guns. There has been an alarming increase of violent shootings and killings in the Chinatowns over the past several years. Dr. Gordon Chong, a dentist who used to be a Metro Councillor in Toronto, speaks for many in Chinatowns across the country when he states that Chinese and Vietnamese Canadians fear reprisals from the new gangs of Vietnamese and mainland Chinese criminals. When criminals are caught, they generally receive only a year or two in jail. Chong asserts that people who have come forward after an extortion genuinely fear that the criminals "will come back and get even" after serving their time. Since many of the criminals who prey on the Asian communities are originally from Vietnam, Hong Kong, or mainland China, Chong feels, like Benny Eng, that most in the Chinese communities in Canada would like to see these criminals deported after they serve their jail time. This change, Chong maintains, would break the code of silence and apathy in the community and encourage people to co-operate with the police.

Dorothy Proctor, the veteran undercover operative who has worked extensively in Vancouver with Asian drug-trafficking gangs and is herself part Chinese, blames poorly thought-out Canadian Immigration and refugee policy for many of the current problems with Asian gangs. Her comments echo a theme heard from some of the older members of the Chinese community in Vancouver like retired Immigration intelligence officer Doug Sam:

> I'm sure you can remember when Chinese were our best citizens. . . . There was a time when it was unheard of for an Oriental to be in any of our prisons. And now we have Asian gangs walking the streets, terrorizing the older, established Chinese. How did they get here?

But Dorothy also believes strongly that we should offer social programs to reach out to the shattered youth in the Asian gangs:

> Within the Asian community, the Vietnamese youth gangs that are prominent in this country now, came to us broken. We should have offered some kind of counselling and some kind of recovery program for them before we allowed them out in the community. . . . They came to us hurt and broken and angry. . . . And now we are faced with all the problems that they brought with them manifesting themselves in a very violent way. No one is safe. . . . Why should the good citizens that came over here years ago and established themselves and their grandchildren — why should every-thing they built be destroyed by these Asian youth gangs?

The social programs offered to Asian youth are few and far between. We require a national program similar to the innova-tive Winnipeg Youth Entry Program and the Calgary Associa-tion of Immigrants program. These deal not just with English as a second language, but the very real and different problems of young Asian immigrants to Canada — particularly of the Vietnamese boat people who have come from broken families in a war-ravaged background. The Winnipeg Outreach Program, which started in 1989, brought in more than a dozen Asian dropouts from ages sixteen to twenty. As its founder Inger Howse said in a recent interview with *Maclean's*, "We try to give them an option, so they feel they can survive in Canada without choosing crime." As to why so many Vietnamese and Asian youths join gangs or triads, project co-ordinator Ying Hoh put it this way: "The underworld spots student talent fast. Adolescents are so vulnerable. They do anything for recognition." Programs that reach out to Asian youth in high risk for gang recruitment are essential in the fight against the growing power of the Asian gangs and triads in Canada.

Some new laws might help. In Hong Kong it is illegal to be a member of a triad, and in the United States, under the RICO Act, it is against the law to belong to an organized crime gang. In the past decades, many Mafia families and even Asian gangs have been seriously undermined by effective RICO prosecutions. In the Ghost Shadow RICO action in the mid-1980s, twenty-five members of the gang, including Kit Jai, Nickie Louie, and others with ties to Toronto's Kung Lok, went to jail for up to thirty years. Perhaps Canada should make it illegal to belong to a triad, youth gang, or organized crime grouping. As former Constable Mike King put it," Triad societies should be proscribed in Canada as they are in Hong Kong, Malaysia, and Singapore. It would be a tough and controversial law, but in the interest of society at large it must be done. The triads are a cancer that must be stopped." Of course there would have to be civil liberties' protections built in to see that the law is not abused. In the States, under the RICO laws, prosecutors must prove a criminal pattern of activity over a long period of time in order to obtain a conviction, as they have in several recent Asian gang cases including a RICO case against the very murderous New York/New Jersey Born To Kill gang. But when they do prove such a pattern of criminal acts in court the sentences are severe — some Mafia leaders in New York were given more than one hundred years in jail and Ghost Shadows gang leaders received sentences of more than thirty years. Add to that the knock-out blow of the RICO statutes — the seizure by the government of the criminally obtained assets of organized crime leaders — and one has a potent weapon against the mobs. In Canada, a more aggressive use of Revenue Canada, especially its auditors, in the war against the Asian gangs, is the very least that is necessary.

Canada should also adopt a national, unified Witness Protection Program to encourage people both in and out of the gangs to come forward. At the moment we have nothing more than a patchwork quilt of dozens of programs — one run by the RCMP, one by the Ontario Provincial Police, one by each of just about every major city and provincial police force in the country. Even former RCMP Assistant Commissioner Rod Stamler has recently admitted that the RCMP witness protection program is seriously flawed and needs to be revamped into a unified, national program. To avoid conflict of interest, the police force running the agent/informer should not be the one administering his or her protection. A new independent, national agency should be set up to care for protected witnesses, providing them with the psychological counselling desperately needed by many defectors from crime, and with job re-training and help with all the bureaucratic red tape required to establish a new identity.

Canada's overly generous Young Offenders Act should be altered so that teenage hit men and gangsters can be tried in adult court and given longer sentences.

Legalizing popular gambling activities is another possible solution to the rising crime rates in Chinatowns. In Ontario today, most gambling is illegal, except, of course, for government-run and promoted lotteries. Ontario does have important exceptions, such as allowing church-sponsored bingo games and gambling on the Indian reserves. Premier Bob Rae has recently proposed government-run casinos in six areas of the province as well as legalized off-track betting, but this will probably not have much impact on gambling in Chinatowns.

In British Columbia under the Societies Act, there are legal, licensed gambling houses, though many illegal houses still operate in Chinatown. Perhaps it is time to allow for legal gambling in areas across the country, like Chinatowns, where there is high demand for such services. As Chinese-born social scientist Lynn Pan has said of the Chinese overseas, "The man who emigrates, who goes abroad to seek his fortune, will be a gambler at heart, a seeker after quick money. . . ." This, plus the cultural reality that Pan called "the native enthusiasm for gambling" among the Chinese, necessitates that a legal means to gamble be allowed in our Chinatowns. As we have learned time and time again over many years, people are going to gamble anyway, whether it's legal or not. "It's there, so you have to deal with it," is how one policeman has put it. The government might as well make some revenue out of it, as well as provide a safety net for those involved in the gambling activities across the country. If the gambling houses were legal, the police, not the triads or gangs, would be invited to protect people — if protection were indeed still needed.

Putting community-based policing back into cities across North America like Toronto, Montreal and Vancouver would definitely assist in the battle against the gangs. Cops on the beat get to know the good guys and the bad guys; they can also recruit informers. There should also be a concerted effort to recruit more Vietnamese and Chinese cops and to send them on the beat in the Chinatowns across the country. Toronto and Vancouver have pitifully few Vietnamese and Chinese on their police forces. Relying just on informers, especially since most are criminals who are often allowed to continue their criminal activities, can be dangerous and counter-productive.

Just as important, the police involved in undercover work need better training. In a 1991 case, a police undercover officer was nearly killed during the robbery by a Vietnamese gang of an illegal gambling house in Scarborough's Chinatown. The undercover policeman did not have a gun, but, absurdly, did have his police badge on him, providing instant identification to the ruthless Vietnamese gangsters, who beat him up and tried to kill him, while his cover team watched from outside, their guns locked in the trunk of their car.

Police work should also be more pro-active rather then simply reactive. With all the criminal activity and violence, the Asian crime units in our major cities, particularly in Toronto and Vancouver, are hard pressed to do more than react to one crisis situation after another. Today the Metropolitan Toronto

Police's growing Asian Investigative Unit has just thirty offi-cers (including Metropolitan Toronto police, OPP, RCMP and Peel, Halton, York, and other regional force representation) for an Asian population rapidly approaching half a millon in the Greater Toronto area.

As a former police intelligence officer told me, "While the police keep the worst excesses of the gangs in check, the more skillful, sophisticated criminals are today going about their business unhindered." There is little time left for in-depth intelligence analysis of all of the criminal groups.

The Asian gangs have today become a national problem, from British Columbia to the Maritimes. But fighting the problem cannot just be left to the local police forces and governments. Many of the provinces and cities do not have the financial resources or the power to deal effectively with the gangs, many of whom have strong international connections. It is incum-bent on the federal government and its institutions, especially the Department of Justice, Employment and Immigration, the Solicitor General's office, and Revenue Canada, to launch an all-out, co-ordinated offensive against the dragons of crime operating in our midst.

POSTSCRIPT TO THE
PAPERBACK EDITION

The Conservative government's Bill C-86 came into effect on January 1, 1993 but Immigration officials have been slow to implement the bill's draconian measures for keeping out suspected criminals. In March 1993 *The Globe and Mail* published an internal Immigration memorandum prepared by Brian McAdam, a senior Canadian Immigration officer based in Hong Kong. The memo claimed that up to seventeen senior triad officers and enforcers were applying to get into Canada under various programs. Among the applicants was an enforcer in the Sun Yee On triad with convictions for theft and gambling who wanted to join his daughter in British Columbia. McAdam noted that several former Royal Hong Kong policemen with substantiated connections to triads were seeking to enter Ontario and Quebec to start businesses. Other requests were coming from drug traffickers, money launderers, even murderers. According to McAdam, Canada was viewed as a prime re-location site for triad members. Indeed, "Canadian society could be under assault by a human iceberg of which these cases represent only the tip."

The reluctance so far of the Conservative government to deny entry to suspected triad members probably stems from its concern that some of the broader provisions of Bill C-86 are likely to face Charter of Rights challenges. Still, Bill C-86 was devised in large part to stem the flow of criminal immigrants and refugees into Canada. With the People's Republic of China slated to take over Hong Kong in less that four years, Canadian immigration officials should intensify their efforts in investigating the backgrounds of Chinese and Hong Kong applicants.

Certainly there are already justifications for action. Just a few months before McAdam's memo was leaked, Chung Wan Chun, dragon head of the British Wo On Lok triad, was arrested in Toronto. He had been living in the Ontario capital for close to a year, even though Scotland Yard had a warrant for his arrest in a triad shooting in London in September 1991. In March 1993 Toronto police arrested forty-four individuals in an international heroin-trafficking ring allegedly run by Vietnamese gangs. According to the police, the drugs were coming in through connections with triad gangs in Hong Kong.

Clearly if a co-ordinated stemming of criminal immigration into this country is not forthcoming, Canada could enter the twenty-first century with even more dragons of crime controlling illegal operations and brutally imposing their will in Canada's many Chinatowns.

HOW TO ENFORCE THE OPIUM AND NARCOTIC DRUG ACT, HOW TO HANDLE INFORMERS, AND HOW TO PROPERLY RAID AN OPIUM DEN

The following are excerpts from unpublished RCMP lecture notes prepared by Inspector F.J. "Freddie" Mead for training Mounties in 1932.*

[Mead, who rose to be the deputy commissioner, began his lecture with a quick history of opium use in Hong Kong and China as well as a look at its use in Canada until the Opium and Narcotic-Drug Act was first passed in 1908.]

... Regarding the handling of informers, this is an art in itself, and the wise investigator can sometimes obtain remarkable results in the handling of these people. In the first place, it must be borne in mind that informers do not attempt to ingratiate themselves into the good graces of the Police except for some reason which may be: (1) They expect to obtain money for their work; (2) They may have something to cover up themselves. If the latter is the case, try to get to the bottom of it, as if you do

---

* I found these lecture notes in the closet at the Vancouver Police Museum in 1988. I want to thank the museum's curator, Joe Swan, for letting me look through the thousands of pages of documents there.

not, some serious trouble may result. There are a few cases, of course, where men of integrity and of high standing in the community will communicate to you certain suspicious movements that they have observed, and any investigator of common sense will recognize the class of people he is dealing with and act accordingly.

Informers in drug cases are always entitled to some remuneration for their time and efforts in assisting you in the investigation of a drug case. In handling these informers generally never bully them or cross-examine them too much; let them think you can trust them, but at the same time try to converse with them in such a way that they will know you understand your business and the drug traffic and that they cannot throw the lie to you or double-cross you.

A good investigator will make it a point to try and get on friendly terms with likely informers, and there is no class of people in the community that have a better knowledge of the underworld than taxi-drivers. Local druggists are people from whom an investigator of Narcotics can obtain useful information. These types detest the idea of being "stool-pigeons," and it is necessary that in order that their confidence be retained they be treated like men. Another class of informer is the drug addict and men of the underworld, but these people require the closest watching by an investigator or when attempting to secure evidence.

When observing or covering the work of an informer, try to appear as natural as possible; by that is meant dress the part, and if you are playing a role, keep in with your surroundings by your speech, etc. A very important thing to remember by an investigator is that he must at all times keep in touch with his Officer Commanding, so that he may be informed as to what line of investigation it is proposed to adopt when purchasing drugs. The reason for this is because the enforcement of the Drug Act is a line of police work that some people, even local police, have no knowledge of. Up-to-date methods used by a trained investigator in attempting to secure evidence may seem strange to them, and they commence to suspect that something may be wrong. Therefore, as a protection to yourself you should keep in touch with your Officer Commanding, verbally or by submission of detailed crime reports as to how the investigation is proceeding.

If working away from Headquarters, get a crime report in on the case as soon as possible after you come into possession of drugs. When drugs have been purchased or found, mark them at once, and always remember that your case commences from the very time you receive the information. Therefore, notes of every possible thing or happening in connection with time and places, that might possibly turn out to be evidence or corroborative evidence of your informer, should be taken down.

Owing to the great number of Confidence Men and Tricksters operating in the drug traffic it is imperative for the investigator to always bear in mind the maxim, "Be wary of the man who wants his money first." In other words, it is better to lose a case altogether than be "jipped" out of your money by trusting it to a man posing as a peddler and promising delivery later. This, of course, expresses the conservative idea of investigation. Circumstances may arise where the rules just quoted would not apply, but generally speaking, the rule is the correct one.

Take the case of a Chinese Drug Peddler, who would have a customer in a small town, lumber camp, or camp of that nature; the peddler will receive a letter with an order for Opium; it will not be referred to as Opium, but more likely as "medicine," "goods," "black stuff," and if the amount is more than one deck it will be referred to as "pieces" or "goods." On receipt of this order the peddler will make up the required amount in decks, which vary in size but are usually slightly larger than a postage stamp. (The paper used in decking drugs, especially opium, is always in oiled paper, something similar to that for wrapping butter and like fats.) He will then take some newspapers, place them end to end, and put the decks inside so that they will not slip out. Then he will address the parcel to a customer or to a Post Office Box, or if a Chinese store or café is located nearby, they will be addressed there. If to a Construction Camp, they will likely be addressed care of the Chinese Foreman.

In searching the premises of a Chinaman suspected of dealing in drugs, the finding of Scales in his possession is very good evidence. If your chances of arresting the person to whom the packet of newspapers is destined are not very good, due to the fact that a large number of Chinese receive their mail at that point and the particular individual is unknown, seize the newspapers in question with the Opium, and return same to the point of mailing, and if you have reasonable information as to the sender, invariably obtain a Search Warrant. "White Stuff" is morphine. Cocaine or Heroin is usually sent by letter, and the clients of the dealer are generally White people and will be known by him before he will enter into correspondence with them. If information of this kind reaches an investigator, it is invariably the best policy (if other means of detection are lacking) to shadow the suspect to ascertain if he places his mail in a Post Office or in a Post Office Box. With the cooperation of the Postmaster, get possession of the letters, and the search of a suspected person's premises will likely disclose connecting links in the chain of evidence in the way of handwriting, similar notepaper, envelopes, etc.

Drugs have sometimes been found in magazines with a hole cut in the centre, and when decks of Opium have been sent through the mail in letters it has been discovered that the individual decks are retained in place by the use of adhesive tape stuck on the inside of the envelope. . . .

. . . . As there is nearly always a suggestion of a "frame-up" in cases of prosecution where drugs are shipped by mail, it is suggested in C.I.B. Circular Memorandum No. 407–37, dated August 31st, 1928, that upon a package containing opium being found in the mail, such package should be used merely as a ground work upon which corroborative evidence can be obtained, as it can be safely assumed that within a reasonable period correspondence would ensue between the sender and the receiver, which with the cooperation of Post Office officials, would soon lead to satisfactory results and remove any doubt in the mind of the investigator that a "frame-up" existed.

It must not be forgotten that drug addicts and peddlers know the law and realize the danger they are placing themselves in when handling drugs. Various methods are used by the peddler and the addict in passing drugs from one place to the other, and, if you are shadowing a suspected peddler with the idea of finding him in possession of the drug, quick action must be taken so that he may not dispose of the drug on account of the investigator being too slow in his work. In many cases, the peddler will be holding the drug tightly in his hand in a pocket, ready to throw the drug away or "ditch" it, as it is called, if he finds he is trapped.

In a case tried in Vancouver in 1930, where the peddler was found in possession of Morphine, it was disclosed in the evidence that on the approach of the Police he swallowed the drug, which was in deck form, and the Police rushed him to the hospital, and by the use of a stomach pump, the deck of morphine was recovered. This was the only Morphine found on the peddler, and he was convicted of being in possession, although the Defence put up the ingenious plea that the drug being in the stomach of the accused, was part of his person and he was, therefore, lawfully in possession and the Police had no right to use force in securing possession of the drug.

. . . In attempting to secure evidence against drug peddlers, the common method is the use of "marked" money. That is, the numbers, denominations and other particulars of certain bills are taken; for instance —

One Five Dollar Bank of Toronto Note No. 5569890, which is then handed to the informant. Before this is done, however, he should be thoroughly searched in the presence of a witness to see that he has no other money or drugs on his person. He is then sent to make his connection, being covered by the investigator, who keeps him in sight at all times, if possible, without arousing the suspicions of the dealer. The reason for this being to witness, if possible, the entire transaction, and failing that, corroborate as much as possible the evidence of the informant. It should be reiterated here that the evidence of a drug addict acting as informant has very little weight before most Judges and Juries. Consequently, the most corroborative evidence is needed, as cases have been known where these addict-informers would not hesitate to "frame" anyone if it would suit their purpose.

The time and place that the so-called marked money is handed to the informant should be noted on the face of the receipt, and the same witnessed by one or two members of the Force working with the investigator. No writing or marking should be made on a Bank Note.

It often happens that the dealer makes the informant hand over the money, and tells him to be at a certain place later on where he will make delivery of the drugs. This gives him a chance to change the money before the delivery of the drugs, and in cases such as these, very close observation of the informant's movements is necessary. It often happens that the drugs will be left in certain spots such as near a certain post, behind a public telephone booth and cases have been known where it was thrown from a car in motion. If the dealer has been successful in changing the money, and you have an idea where the change was made, immediate action should be taken to cause the surrender of the bill to the investigator interested by its replacement with another, and the person receiving the marked bill should be subpoenaed as a witness against the dealer.

Immediately after the dealer is arrested, he should be carefully searched for marked money and other evidence, and this also applies to the premises in which he is living.

In attempting to make a contact the prospective buyer is quite often put to a severe test. Various methods are employed, one of the most common being to make an appointment and then disregard it, as they know that if a man wishes to purchase drugs in a bad way, he will always return at some other time.

The Chinese are very suspicious, and in questioning one regarding his connection with the drug traffic, it is very dangerous to attempt to speak to him in his own language, as he immediately suspects that you know too much about him and his people. Another thing to guard against in dealing with Chinese is not to appear too insistent, as if this fact is noted, their suspicion is immediately aroused. In approaching them, it is a good policy to convey the impression that you are a bit stupid and at the same time create an atmosphere of honesty. When attempting to buy drugs never boast of past transactions, or being a "big man" in the game, as it is better to have this information conveyed indirectly through a third party. Do not try to talk to Chinese in Pidgin English, and do not use familiar names, as he resents being addressed by such terms which he looks upon as vulgar. If the party to whom you are talking does not understand English, use the simplest language possible. If you do not know the Chinese by his correct name, it is always the best policy not to use any name at all. The Chinese as a rule are stoical and, incidentally, revengeful, and in dealing with them kindness and patience will go a long way in obtaining their confidence. When you have a Chinese informant assisting you in getting the evidence to convict a drug peddler, you on your part, should do everything possible for him in the way of affording protection, which is sometimes necessary.

NOTES ON SEARCHING OPIUM JOINTS

On starting to search a place for drugs or marked money, thoroughness is of most importance. First collect any smoking paraphernalia that may be lying on the bunk, especially any decks or partly used decks of Opium or Yen Shee, as the inmates may try to swallow them. Search every inmate of the room and place a guard over them.

Prevent persons from moving from one room to another, until you are satisfied it is all right for them to do so. As a smoke-joint generally contains a bunk to smoke on, tables, stools or benches — search the table and everything on it, take out any drawers and look for secret hiding places, especially if the table is a home-made one, as cases are known in which the table had slits in the side in which to drop money.

On searching a bunk or a bed strip everything off, including the rattan cover; sometimes things are hidden there. Opium pipes have often been found hidden on rails along the inner side of bench stands. Do not overlook the stove, as pipes have often been found suspended by wires on the bottom part of stoves, while narcotics have actually been discovered inside the stove. Boots or slippers are hiding places for drugs or pipe bowls, and all benches should be turned up as they may have false seats. When searching any clothes hanging in a room, if drugs are found in them, do not take them if you have not enough evidence, as the owner may be present, and on being taken to the Police Station will put the boot on which gives you the necessary proof of Possession.

Look inside of books that are lying around, as sometimes they are hollowed out and drugs concealed there.

Look around for trap-doors or secret panels in the woodwork, as sometimes a new nail or cracked wood will indicate a hidden cache. Take possession of all keys and pay particular attention to the locks on the doors of the premises on which drugs have been found, and if you are leaving the premises with a prisoner whom you suspect may be the owner, give him the opportunity of locking his own door, which furnishes evidence of Possession. In the Law Yipp case in Vancouver, members of the Force noticed a corner of the base-board in one of the rooms was not dusty like the rest, and on searching carefully the base-board was found to come out, and on the inside was a piece of string which led to a cache of 97 cans of Opium.

In a North Vancouver case, members of the Force observed a Chinaman place his hand down a hole in the garden. A search of all the rat holes disclosed twelve ounces of Cube Morphine.

A member of the Force searching a house in Vancouver found the Morphine hidden in some dirty wet wash, tied up in a dirty waterproof silk bag.

When making a purchase of Narcotics in Ladysmith, Vancouver Island, a Chinese was observed by members of the Force to go into the garden. A raid followed, and in digging up the garden 74 cans of Opium were found.

In a Vancouver case a Chinese woman was seen placing something under a baby in a baby-carriage. On searching the house nothing was discovered. The woman was asked to lift up the baby, and five envelopes containing Cocaine were found underneath the child.

In the WONG FOOK KAN case, which was closed out by members of the Force in Vancouver, 13 loads of wood were stacked up to the ceiling in the cellar. A search was commenced of this wood, and, working on the theory that narcotics would be some place handy of access, a search was made where the wood had been taken for fires. In the same case, marked money used for the purchase of narcotics was found hidden in a big pile of kindling wood, while upstairs in a laundry a large carton containing Ginger had one box containing Opium instead.

You will never find two places the same to search, and the foregoing should indicate to the investigator the absolute necessity of taking pains. . . .

ACKNOWLEDGEMENTS

First I would like to thank the Canada Council for a research grant in 1988–89 to pursue sources in Vancouver, Ottawa, New York City, Boston, and Washington, D.C.

A special thanks to my sister, Bev Lacey, and my aunt, Rita Lyons, for their love, support, and encouragement over the years.

Thanks to Sharron Budd, who first suggested that I write this book.

I also want to thank Trina McQueen, vice president of the CBC, for funding a research trip to Hong Kong and Macao for a proposed but never produced CBC documentary. Thanks also to Dick Nielsen of Under W Productions and Martyn Burke, my colleagues on that crime project.

The staffs of the Public Archives in Ottawa and National Archives in Washington, D.C., have, as usual, been most helpful, as have the archivists at the Ontario Archives in Toronto and the British Columbia Archives in Victoria.

I particularly want to express my profound gratitude to Mike King for all his invaluable assistance, above and beyond the call of duty, over the past decade.

I would also like to express my appreciation to Dave Fu, the former undercover operative, for his insights and information on the Asian underworld in North America.

Special thanks to Robin Rowland, my co-author in two previous books, who never left an archive without noting any new Oriental crime material I might need for my research.

My hearty thanks to New York City-based author and lawyer Gerry Posner, who generously shared with me some of his research material and knowledge.

There are many triad, gang, and police sources that cannot, for one reason or another, be publicly acknowledged. To them I express my profound gratitude.

Inspectors Barry Hill, Roy Teeft, and Sergeant George Cowley of the Metropolitan Toronto Police have been a tremendous assistance in researching this study, as well as Ken Yates, Tony Lee, Chuck Konkel, Benny Eng, Raymond Miu, Julian Fantino, Ron Sandelli, Inspector Mike Sale, Chief Bill McCormack, Inspector Roy Brenham, and the many current and former members of what is now called the Asian Investigative Unit in Toronto. Also, a special thanks to George Best and others at Canadian Immigration who have helped over the years; Corporal Fred Bowen, Inspector Wayne Blackburn, Staff Sergeant Andy Rayne, Staff Sergeant Tom Brown, Staff Sergeant Carl MacLeod, Corporal John Bothwell, former Corporal Mark Murphy, and former Assistant Commissioner Rodney Stamler, all of the RCMP; OPP Sergeant Carl Armstrong; Professor Bernard Hungkay Luk; Dr. Janet Rubinoff and her colleagues at the Canada and Hong Kong Research Project; Richard Yao, editor of *Sing Tao*; James R. Badey, former Arlington, Virginia, policeman and John Bean, Boston Police Department.

In Vancouver, Joe Swan, the resourceful (and colourful) curator of the Vancouver Police Museum, was most helpful, as were Stan Shillington and Helen Arnet of the Co-ordinated Law Enforcement Unit (CLEU); Corporal Bill Chu, Staff Sergeant Gord Spencer, Corporal Gordy Oke, Detective Peter Ditchfield, Sergeant Cam Scott, Special Crown attorney James MacBride, journalists Harry Phillips, Terry Gould, Hall Leiren, Adrian DuPlessis; Professor Graham Johnson of the University of British Columbia; and the late Doug Sam, Immigration Intelligence.

A special thanks to Staff Sergeant L.D. "Smokey" Stovern of the RCMP, who is that all-too-rare policeman who knows the importance of the historical material.

ACKNOWLEDGEMENTS

In Hong Kong and Macao a number of people were of invaluable assistance including Charles and Tom Lewis of the *South China Morning Post*; Kevin Sinclair of the *Hong Kong Standard*; Diana Wong and June Teng of Hong Kong's Television Broadcast Limited; James Mulvaney of *Newsday*, Chan Washek, the Hong Kong Commissioner of Correctional Services; David Tong (Tong Hin-yeung), Bureau Head, Hong Kong Customs Drug Investigation Branch; Theodore Ng (Ng Man-kim); Chief Inspector David J. Eaton and other courageous but anonymous souls on the Royal Hong Kong Police Force; Tony Godfrey, principal investigator, the Independent Commission Against Corruption; John Sham, film producer and friend; Dr. Antonio Manuel de P.B. Calaca, Assistant Director, and Superintendent Roberto "Bobby" Vadarraco, Macao Judiciary Police. For all the other people who worked in the shadows for me in Hong Kong and Macao, a special thanks.

I must also thank a number of friends and associates who have been of enormous help over the years. These include Jon Lidolt, Marnie Inskip, Rob Roy, Bill Macadam, David Skene-Melvin, Dorothy Proctor, Dr. Richard Wizansky, Professor Joe Wearing, John Grube, Professor Ian Chapman, Harry Petersen, Nedleigh Lynch, Joseph McGrath, Patricia Kennedy, Don Hutchison, Douglas Webb, Kit and Martha Vincent, Robert Chatelle, Ruth Matakas, Ed Hanson, Rick Malone, Dorothy Proctor, Tom Reeves, Richard Meyers, Jacques Viens, Doug Stewart, David Ostriker, Lee Lamothe, Peter Edwards, Peter Moon, and Howard Goldenthal.

Special thanks also to Ron Haggart, Marlene Perry, Gordon Stewart, Paul Lang, Eric Malling, Robin Taylor, Virginia Nelson, Claire Weissman-Wilks, and all my other former colleagues and friends at the *old* "Fifth Estate," and to Moses Znaimer, Mark Dailey, Gord Martineau, Steve Hurlbut, Clint Nickerson, Carrie Paupst, Dan Petkovsek, and all my other colleagues at CITY-TV on the gripping and timely ten-part news serial "Underworld: The Mobs of Metro," which we produced in the summer and fall of 1991, when Vietnamese gangsters were shooting it out on the streets of Toronto with alarming regularity.

Last, but not least, I want to thank my editor, Jennifer Glossop, for her painstaking work on the manuscript, my former publisher, Michael Murton, as well as Alexander Schultz, Liza Algar, Susan Bermingham, and Betty Quan of Octopus (now Reed Books Canada) for their enthusiastic support.

SELECTED BIBLIOGRAPHY

These are the major source books. Much of the historical material came from original documents available in the public archives in Ottawa and Washington, D.C. Other published sources included numerous newspaper and magazine articles. Additional information came from still classified police intelligence files and interviews with gang members, victims, public officials, and police officers in Canada, the United States, and Hong Kong.

Agnew, Derek. *Undercover Agent — Narcotics*. London: Souvenir Press, 1959.

Anslinger, Harry J. and Will Oursler. *The Murderers: The Shocking Story of the Narcotics Gang*. London: Arthur Barker, 1961.

_____ . and J. Dennis Gregory. *The Protectors: Our Battle Against Crime Gangs*. New York: Farrar, Strauss and Giroux, 1964.

Appleton, Peter, with Doug Clark. *Billion $$$ High*. Toronto: McGraw-Hill Ryerson, 1990.

Asbury, Herbert. *The Barbary Coast: An Informal History of the San Francisco Underworld*. New York: Knopf, 1933.

_____ . *The Gangs of New York: An Informal History of the Underworld*. New York: Knopf, 1928.

Badey, James R. *Dragons and Tigers*. Loomis, California: Palmer Enterprises, 1988.

Beeching, Jack. *The Chinese Opium Wars*. New York: Harcourt, Brace, Jovanovich, 1975.

Beer, J.B. *Coleridge The Visionary*. New York: Collier Books, 1962.

Bennett, Georgette. *Crime-Warps: The Future of Crime in America*. New York: Doubleday, 1987.

Berridge, Virginia and Griffith Edwards. *Opium and the People: Opiate Use in Nineteenth-century England*. London: Allen Lane/St Martin's Press, 1981.

Bloodsworth, Dennis. *An Eye for the Dragon: Southeast Asia Observed: 1954–1970*. New York: Farrar, Strauss and Giroux, 1970.

_____ . *Chinese Looking Glass*. New York: Farrar, Strauss and Giroux, 1966.

Blythe, Wilfrid. *The Impact of Chinese Secret Societies in Malaya*. London: Oxford University Press, 1969.

Booth, Martin. *The Triads: The Chinese Criminal Fraternity*. London: Grafton Books, 1990.

Bowering, Marilyn. *To All Appearances a Lady*. Toronto: Random House of Canada, 1989.

Bready, J. Wesley. *Lord Shaftesbury and Social-Industrial Progress*. London: George Allen & Unwin Ltd, Ruskin House, 1926.

Bressler, Fenton. *The Trail of the Triad* [also called *The Chinese Mafia* in its U.S. edition, New York: Stein & Day, 1981.] London: Weidenfeld and Nicolson, 1980.

Calado, Maria, Maria Clara Mendes and Michel Toussaint. *Macao: Memorial City on the Estuary of the River of Pearls*. Government of Macao, 1985.

Cannon, Margaret. *China Tide: The Revealing Story of the Hong Kong Exodus to Canada*. Toronto: Harper Collins, 1989.

Chan, Anthony B. *Gold Mountain: The Chinese in the New World*. Vancouver: New Star Books, 1983.

Chatwin, Bruce. *What Am I Doing Here!* New York: Viking/Penguin, 1989.

Chen, Jack. *The Chinese of America: From the Beginnings to the Present*. San Francisco: Harper & Row, 1981.

Chesneaux, Jean. Editor. *Popular Movements and Secret Societies in China, 1840–1950*. Berkeley, California: Stanford University Press, 1972.

Clavell, James. *Tai-Pan: A Novel of Hong Kong*. New York: Atheneum, 1966.

_____ . *Noble House*. New York: Delacorte Press, 1981.

Con, Harry, Ronald J. Con, Graham Johnson, Edgar Wickberg, William E. Willmott. *From China to Canada: A History of the Chinese Commu-*

nities in Canada. Toronto: McClelland and Stewart Ltd., 1982.

Daly, Robert. *The Year of the Dragon.* New York: Simon and Schuster, 1981.

Deacon, Richard. *The Chinese Secret Service.* New York: Taplinger Publisher, 1974.

De Mont, John and Thomas Fennell. *Hong Kong Money: How Chinese Families and Fortunes are Changing Canada.* Toronto: Key Porter, 1989.

De Quincey, Thomas. *Confessions of an English Opium-Eater.* (originally published in 1822); London: The Folio Society, 1948.

Dubro, James. *Mob Mistress.* Toronto: Macmillan of Canada, 1988.

_____ . *Mob Rule: Inside the Canadian Mafia.* Toronto: Macmillan of Canada, 1985.

_____ . and Robin Rowland. *King of the Mob: Rocco Perri and the Women Who Ran His Rackets.* Toronto: Penguin, 1987.

_____ . *Undercover: The Cases of the RCMP's Most Secret Operative.* Toronto: Octopus Publishing Group, 1991.

Elliott, Elsie (Elsie Tu). *Crusade For Justice — An Autobiography.* Hong Kong: Heinemann Asia, 1981.

Endacott, G.B. *A History of Hong Kong.* Hong Kong: Oxford University Press, 1958; revised edition, 1988.

Fay, Peter Ward. *The Opium War: 1840–1842.* New York: Norton, 1976.

Ferguson, Ted. *Kit Coleman, Queen of Hearts: Canada's Pioneer Woman Journalist.* Toronto: Doubleday, 1978.

Fox, Stephen. *Blood and Power: Organized Crime in Twentieth-Century America.* New York: William Morrow and Company, Inc., 1989.

Fraser, John. *The Chinese: Portrait of a People.* Toronto: Collins, 1980.

Freemantle, Brian. *The Fix: The Inside Story of the World Drugs Trade.* London: Michael Joseph, 1985.

Geddes, Philip. *In the Mouth of the Dragon: Hong Kong — Past, Present, Future.* London, Century Press, 1982.

Gong, Eng Ying and Bruce Grant. *Tong War: The First Complete History of the Tongs in America; details of the tong wars and their causes; lives of famous hatchetmen and gunmen; and inside information as to the workings of the Tongs, their aims and achievements.* New York: Nicholas L. Brown, 1930.

Gray, James H. *Booze.* Toronto: Macmillan, 1972.

_____ . *Red Lights on the Prairie.* Toronto: Macmillan, 1971.

Hahn, Emily. *The Soong Sisters*. New York: Doubleday, 1942.

Harvison, C.W. *The Horsemen*. Toronto: McClelland and Stewart, 1967.

Hinsch, Bert. *Passions of the Cut Sleeve: The Male Homosexual Tradition in China*. Los Angeles: University of California Press, 1990.

Hutchison, Don. *It's Raining Corpses in Chinatown*. Seattle, Washington. Starmount House, 1991.

Kaplan, David E. and Alec Dubro. *Yakuza: The Explosive Account of Japan's Criminal Underworld*. Reading, Massachusetts: Addison-Wesley Publishing Company, 1986.

Kingston, Maxine Hong. *Chinamen*. New York: Alfred E. Knopf, 1980.

Ko-Lin Chin. *Chinese Subculture and Criminality: Non-Traditional Crime Groups in America*. New York: Greenwood Press, 1990.

Konkel, K.G.E. *The Glorious East Wind*. Toronto: Random House of Canada, 1987.

Kwitny, Jonathan. *The Crimes of Patriots: A True Tale of Dope, Dirty Money, and the CIA*. New York: W.W. Norton & Company, 1987.

Kwong, Peter. *The New Chinatown*. New York: The Noonday Press, 1987.

Lacey, Robert. *Little Man: Meyer Lansky and the Gangster Life*. Boston: Little, Brown, 1991.

Lai, David Chuenyan. *Chinatowns: Towns Within Cities in Canada*. Vancouver: University of British Columbia, 1988.

Lambert, Derek. *Triad*. London: Hamish Hamilton, 1987.

Lavigne, Yves. *Good Guy, Bad Guy: Drugs and the Changing Face of Organized Crime*. Toronto: Random House of Canada, 1991.

Lethbridge, H.J. *Hard Graft in Hong Kong: Scandal, Corruption, The ICAC*. Hong Kong: Oxford University Press, 1985.

Li, Peter S. *The Chinese in Canada*. Toronto: Oxford University Press, 1988.

Lindop, Grevel. *The Opium Eater: A Life of Thomas De Quincey*. London: J.M. Dent & Sons Ltd., 1981.

Longstreth, T. Morris and Henry Vernon. *Murder at Belly Butte and Other Stories from the Mounted Police*. Toronto: Maclean Publishing, 1931.

McCoy, Alfred W. *The Politics of Heroin in Southeast Asia*. New York: Harper & Row, 1972.

MacKenzie, Norman. Editor. *Secret Societies*. New York: Holt, Rinehart and Winston, 1967.

Malarek, Victor. *Haven's Gate: Canada's Immigration Fiasco*. Toronto: Macmillan of Canada, 1987.

_____ . *Merchants of Misery: Inside Canada's Illegal Drug Scene.* Toronto: Macmillan of Canada, 1989.

Messick, Hank and Burt Goldblatt. *Gangs and Gangsters: The Illustrated History of Gangs from Jesse James to Murph the Surf.* New York: Ballantine Books, 1974.

Mills, James. *The Underground Empire: Where Crime and Governments Embrace.* New York: Doubleday & Co., 1986.

Mo, Timothy. *An Insular Possession.* London: Chatto & Windus, 1986.

_____ . *Sour Sweet.* London: Sphere Books, 1983.

Morgan, W.P. *The Triad Societies in Hong Kong.* Hong Kong: Government Press, 1960. (1989 edition)

Morton, James. *In the Sea of Sterile Mountains: The Chinese in British Columbia.* Vancouver: J.J. Douglas Ltd., 1973.

Moscow, Alvin. *Merchants of Heroin.* London: Arthur Barker Ltd., 1968.

Murphy, Emily. *The Black Candle.* Toronto: Thomas Allen, 1922.

Naylor, R.T. *Hot Money: and the Politics of Debt.* Toronto: McClelland and Stewart, 1987.

Nelli, Humbert S. *The Business of Crime: Italians and Syndicated Crime in the United States.* Chicago: University of Chicago Press, 1976.

O'Brien, Joseph F. and Andris Kurings. *Boss of Bosses: The Fall of the Godfather: The FBI and Paul Castellano.* New York: Simon and Schuster, 1991.

O'Callaghan, Sean. *The Triads.* London: W.H. Allen & Co., 1978.

Owen, David E. *British Opium Policy in China and India.* New Haven: Yale University Press, 1934.

Pan, Lynn. *Sons of the Yellow Emperor: The Story of the Overseas Chinese.* London: Secker & Warburg, 1990.

Patrikeeff, Felix. *Mouldering Pearl: Hong Kong at the Crossroads.* London: Hodder and Stoughton, 1989.

Perlmen, Samuel K. and Mark Kai-Chi Chan. *The Chinese Game of Mahjong.* Hong Kong: Book Marketing Ltd, 1979.

Phillips, Alan. *The Living Legend: The Story of the Royal Canadian Mounted Police.* Boston: Little, Brown and Company, 1954.

Phillips, Vic. *The Heroin Merchants.* London: Methuen, 1986.

Posner, Gerald L. *Warlords of Crime: Chinese Secret Societies — The New Mafia.* New York: McGraw Hill, 1988.

President's Commission on Organized Crime. *Organized Crime of Asian*

Origin. Washington, D.C., U.S. Government Printing Office, 1985.

Rafferty, Kevin. *City on the Rocks: Hong Kong's Uncertain Future*. Vancouver: Douglas & McIntyre, 1989.

Robertson, Frank. *Triangle of Death : The Inside Story of the Triads — The Chinese Mafia*. Toronto: General Publishing Company, 1977.

Rohmer, Sax. [Arthur S. Ward]. *Collected Novels: The Hand of Fu Manchu, The Return of Dr. Fu Manchu, The Yellow Claw, Dope*. Secaucus, New Jersey: Castle, 1983.

Rowland, Wade. *Making Connections*. Toronto: Gage, 1979.

Roy, Patricia. *White Man's Province: British Columbia Politicians and the Chinese and Japanese Immigrants, 1858–1914*. Vancouver: University of British Columbia Press, 1989.

Sabljak, Mark and Martin H. Greenberg. *Most Wanted: A History of the FBI's Ten Most Wanted List*. New York: Bonanza Books, 1990.

Seagrave, Sterling. *The Soong Dynasty*. New York: Harper & Row, 1985.

Siragusa, Charles. *The Trail of the Poppy: Behind the Mask of the Mafia*. New York: Prentice-Hall, 1966.

Staunton, William. *The Triad Society or Heaven and Earth Association*. Hong Kong: Kelly and Walsh Ltd., 1900.

Starkins, Edward. *Who Killed Janet Smith?* Toronto: Macmillan, 1984.

Sterling, Claire. *Octopus: The Long Reach of the International Sicilian Mafia*. New York: W.W. Norton & Company, 1990.

Tully, Andrew. *C.I.A.: The Inside Story*. New York: William Morrow & Co., 1962

_____. *The Secret War Against Dope*. New York: William Morrow, 1973.

_____. *Treasury Agent: The Inside Story*. New York: Simon and Schuster, 1958.

Wacks, Raymond. Editor. *The Law in Hong Kong, 1969–1989*. Hong Kong: Oxford University Press, 1989.

Ward, J.S.M. and W.G. Stirling. *The Hung Society*. London: Baskerville Press, 1925.

Whitaker, Ben. *The Global Connection: The Crisis of Drug Addiction*. London: Jonathan Cape, 1987.

Wilson, R.S.S. *Undercover for the R.C.M.P.*, Victoria, British Columbia: Sono Nis Press, 1986.

Yee, Paul. *Saltwater City: An Illustrated History of the Chinese in Canada*. Vancouver: Douglas & McIntyre, 1988.

INDEX